SOCIAL ENTREPRENEURSHIP FOR DEVELOPMENT

This book presents a fresh approach to poverty alleviation by bridging the fields of international development and social entrepreneurship. The authors present a six-step model for developing an intellectual property business positioning strategy that allows developing country producers to position themselves better as owners of retail brands in foreign market countries. Readers will learn how producers can control the supply chain, including distribution to retail stores.

Focusing on Africa and least developed countries (LDCs), the authors demonstrate methods of utilizing intellectual property tools, producer ownership, market positioning, and branding for lucrative outcomes. Extensive research provides readers with a thorough understanding of what it means to work smarter in a developing business, while a rich set of international cases offers insight into the practical applications of brand positioning, trademarks, and licenses.

With a dozen online workbooks that outline methodology, skills, tools, and case studies, *Social Entrepreneurship for Development* is a valuable resource for any student of social entrepreneurship or international development.

Margaret Brindle is Vice President and Director of Education at Light Years IP, USA, and Adjunct Professor at George Washington University, USA.

Ron Layton is Founder and CEO of Light Years IP, USA. He has 40 years' experience working in intellectual property and international development.

SOCIAL ENTREPRENEURSHIP FOR DEVELOPMENT

A Business Model

Margaret Brindle and Ron Layton

Routledge
Taylor & Francis Group

NEW YORK AND LONDON

First published 2017
by Routledge
711 Third Avenue, New York, NY 10017

and by Routledge
2 Park Square, Milton Park, Abingdon, Oxon OX14 4RN

Routledge is an imprint of the Taylor & Francis Group, an informa business

© 2017 Taylor & Francis

Library of Congress Cataloging in Publication Data
Names: Brindle, Margaret, author. | Layton, Ron, author.
Title: Social entrepreneurship for development : a business model / Margaret Brindle & Ron Layton.
Description: New York, NY : Routledge, 2016.
Identifiers: LCCN 2016031861| ISBN 9781138181779 (hbk) | ISBN 9781138181786 (pbk) | ISBN 9781315646763 (ebk) | ISBN 9781317295976 (mobi/kindle)
Subjects: LCSH: Social entrepreneurship. | Social entrepreneurship–Africa. | Intellectual property. | New products–Marketing.
Classification: LCC HD60 .B745 2016 | DDC 658.4/08–dc23
LC record available at https://lccn.loc.gov/2016031861

ISBN: 978-1-138-18177-9 (hbk)
ISBN: 978-1-138-18178-6 (pbk)
ISBN: 978-1-315-64676-3 (ebk)

Typeset in Bembo
by Taylor & Francis Books

CONTENTS

LIST OF ILLUSTRATIONS

Figures

Table

FOREWORD

Lord Paul Boateng

CHAIRMAN OF THE AFRICAN ENTERPRISE CHALLENGE FUND AND CO-CHAIR OF THE AFRICAN IP TRUST

I was first made aware of Ron and Meg's groundbreaking work when I launched a DfID funded publication that the their team had authored on Intellectual Property at the World Economic Forum Africa Summit in 2008. This demonstrated how the 2 billion people globally who live in countries where there are distinctive products such as, for example, vanilla in Uganda; Shea butter in the South Sudan; and Black Soap in West Africa, might see $100 million more generated per product per annum. They explained how use of IP strategies, positioning and marketing alongside heightened ownership of import companies, in the way they outline in this book could transform Africa.

All too much of the development assistance expended in Africa over many decades has demonstrably failed. There are various reasons for this bad governance and misplaced policy prescriptions emanating from foreign capitals. Africa remains largely impoverished even with the above average GDP growth of recent times. Combined with growing inequality, poverty deepening through faltering global demand represents a real threat to the security of the continent. This combination condemns still more of its burgeoning youthful population to unemployment or underemployment that in turn, threatens even the modest gains that have been made. This also fuels the forced migration of many youths from the continent in the search for opportunity and represents a loss of some of the most resourceful and entrepreneurial to the continent, contributing to what has become known as the "migrant crisis" in Europe and increasingly a security threat to a wider world.

One thing is clear. Africa stands to gain from a growth in trade and private sector led development. This holds out the best prospect of sustainable employment for its population. There have been some marked successes in this area from which we can learn. One example is the UKs Africa Free Trade Initiative, taken forward by the UK government and its African development partners since 2010. This has supported and advanced some key African priorities, reduced trade costs, and delivered some real gains for the continent, its businesses and its trading partners. We have seen tariffs cut and red tape reduced for traders in Africa. Border crossings have benefited from enhanced investment and custom procedures have been streamlined. There have been some real improvements in key gateway ports with a crackdown on the graft that still bedevils some. The concept of cross border transport corridors has been widely accepted and in some noteworthy cases, implemented with very positive results in terms of trade facilitation. There has been increased private sector investment in agribusiness, logistics and the infrastructure of trade. The opening of the Addis Djibouti rail link is one such landmark achievement.

There remains however a huge and unacceptably wide investment and infra-structure gap. Still more remains to be done to create an enabling environment for private sector investment in agribusiness, research and transport infrastructure on the continent. This is critical not least in the promotion of inter African trade building on the success of the East African Economic Community, in particular. All the above are necessary together with a better utilization of internally gener-ated finance for development if there is to be more inclusive growth in the continent. We need however to do more. It will continue to be important to build up the participation of African nations and enterprises including SMEs and smallholder agricultural entrepreneurs in both global and regional value chains. Africa and its development partners must move on from the continents over-reliance on the export of primary products to greater engagement in enterprises which result in higher value added products.

There is, however, an important missing piece from the edifice of develop-ment. This is a keystone without which there is little or no hope of securing a better future for the millions of the impoverished. The The Africa Free Trade Initiative Inquiry Report[1] in 2016 promotes the method outlined by Margaret Brindle and Ron Layton in this timely book. It represents a practical guide to utilize techniques to the benefit of the impoverished that have long been avail-able to the private sector. There is no reason why African farmers and producers of distinctive products should continue to fail to secure a fair level of return on their products marketed in higher level markets.

I have since seen for myself as Co-Chair of the Africa Intellectual Property Trust how the authors of this book have worked on the ground to train women and men amongst the Maasai to organize and to better utilize and capture the value of their own distinctive brand in a way that reflects and respects the Maasai culture and traditions.

This book argues that one of the root causes of poverty can be illustrated by the following chart, showing the combined producers and exporters share of retail prices generated by distinctive African products, averaged across 20 dis-tinctive products averages about 3%, whereas 97% was captured by importers and retailers in foreign markets.

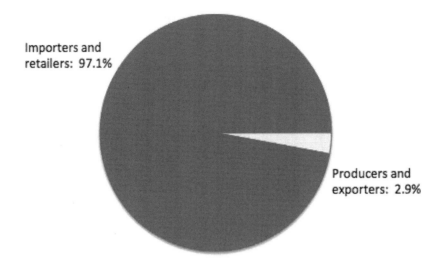

Importers and
retailers: 97.1%

Producers and
exporters: 2.9%

FIGURE 0.1 Percentage of retail price (20 distinctive African products)
Source: Light Years IP.

Simply put, if 97% of the retail value is taken by others, it is difficult for developing country producers to sustain production, improve, or, in some cases, even survive. This means productive, hard working farmers and producers continue to require aid. This situation exists throughout Africa and developing countries wherein farmers and producers of distinctive products receive this meager level of return from their products marketed on higher-end markets.

In recent years, USAID and DfID alone, as the two largest aid donors, offered collectively over $50 billion to international development solutions. While laudatory, the world still holds nearly 2 billion people living at poverty levels. Many of these 2 billion reside in countries where there are distinctive products, able to generate $100 million more per product per annum. But, we must address a root causes - trade isolation and lack of positioning and ownership.

However, what if there was a solution that enables the 3% to move to 30% share via using methods similar to corporate enterprise? That is what this book presents and details:

- A proven method to return higher income
- Intellectual Property tools to produce ownership of intangible assets combined with
- Business positioning and
- Case study examples involving millions of farmer/producers.

Two billion people in poverty must compel us to act – a solution is at hand. The solution is not merely theoretical, but one that has been tried and proven hundreds of times by corporations. It is called IP business positioning. It is a method that has enabled corporations from Coca cola to Sunkist oranges to earn billions.

Why is Coca Cola, for example earning billions in IP assets? (Coca-Cola reached the value of $83.84 billion U.S. dollars in 2015). Sunkist oranges, built by struggling California orange growers, earned over a billion from proper IP positioning propelling this stream of revenue beyond the actual orange, itself. Is there something corporations do that can be modeled by developing countries? This book demonstrates exactly how to do so.

By correct, we mean the IP tool alone is not the key, but rather the right IP tool as part of a full positioning strategy. The income from Coca Cola's intangible value and IP tool as part of a positioning strategy exceeds the revenue from the actual product. This is the case for many successful companies, and it is time for African and developing country farmers and producers to receive income from their distinctive products, cultural brands, and well-honed processes creating distinctive artisan products.

If the fact that 2 billion people remain at poverty levels in our modern, 21st century world were the end of the story, and there was little we could do to change this, besides pontificate and create temporary solutions addressing symptoms, I would advise putting this book down.

However, that is not the end of the story. We can. We must do better and the method presented here offers a solution for developing countries. It is not mysterious. It is based on 100+ years of tried and true method and practice. It is time to change our mindsets. This method of IP positioning is possible for developing country producers and it is time to apply aid and international development toward long term, sustainable solutions.

As Chairman of the African Enterprise Challenge Fund (AECF), we look for sustainable enterprises. This book contributes to enterprise with a sustainable, replicable method.

I have seen as Chief Secretary to the Treasury in the UK, as Head of the UKs Mission to South Africa and now as Chairman of the Africa Enterprise Challenge Fund in Nairobi, how the key to unlocking the potential of nations lies in an enabling state and a thriving entrepreneurial class. Africa has the largest remaining stocks of under-utilized arable land, vast stocks of untapped mineral wealth, the fastest growing middle class and the youngest population in the world. It is imperative if we are to make the most of the opportunity that all of this represents that Africa. All who seek to hold out the hand of friendship and development cooperation towards it move away from the failed prescriptions of the past. We need to wake up to the need for the sort of practical strategies that are illustrated in these pages and a policy and legislative context that supports their implementation. This requires a developmental state and entrepreneurial class that is willing to embrace opportunities and a dispensation that empowers grass roots producers to participate in the economy in a way that truly reflects the value that they bring to the market place. Dr Aggrey, the renowned activist and educator in the early part of the last century, called on Africa to wake up and take to the sky's as an eagle soars. This book outlines a key flight path by which it may do just that.

I wish its authors and all who read it the very best in this exciting endeavour.

Lord Paul Boateng
Westminster and Nairobi

Note

1 Published by the All Party Parliamentary Group for Trade Out of Poverty, London, UK, 2016.

INTRODUCTION

The power of method

What you can expect to learn in this book

This is a book about a specific business model called Intellectual Property business positioning. It demonstrates how developed countries use Intellectual Property with correct market positioning as a successful business strategy. It presents the full method for African and other least developed country (LDC) producers to achieve dramatically higher income.[1]

And, it is a book that is for the twenty-first-century entrepreneur aspiring to create sustainable change by establishing successful businesses, and adopting a proven method. It is a book about transformation and change, not by theory, not by aid, but by and through smart business. It demonstrates Intellectual Property tools, producer ownership, market positioning, and branding for successful outcomes.

There have been many efforts in the field of international development to advance agri-business. However, it has been a challenge to sustainably improve developing country income. This is a book about how developing countries can use similar IP business strategies to achieve dramatically improved income.

If the improved income were marginal, incremental or using the same failing methods as in the twentieth century, we would advise closing this book, now. But, it is not. The method demonstrates sustainable and dramatic income of $100 million more per year, per product. In Africa alone, assuming 45 countries in which the IP business method can be implemented, there is potential to improve income by $250 billion at full scale. As farmer and producer ownership of supply chains is built into the model, the additional income goes into the hands of farmer/producers, rather than being lost to importers.

Why an entrepreneurial business model for Africa matters

Theory does not feed people. Large-scale, transformational change and theories of empowerment must never become more important than the people to be advanced out of poverty, the nearly 2 billion women, men, and children working harder every day but in many cases, not gaining ground. Consider one such individual, a young Zambian honey merchant eager to succeed and located far from developed country retail markets.

The young Zambian attends our workshop on Intellectual Property business in Lusaka, Zambia. On the second day, he invites us out to his car and filling the trunk are jars of honey, fine honey – not the type of honey found on generic supermarket shelves, but thick, fine, artisan honey.

"I am only getting $1.00/lb at the export. Can you help me?" he asks.

We taste the honey. It is quite simply, delicious. We know that Manuka honey, from New Zealand, branded and positioned as artisan, distinctive honey is earning more than 25 times the amount paid to this energetic young merchant. Shall we say, "Sorry, young friend – you are just positioned in the wrong part of the planet? Work harder. Produce more." Or, provide a temporary (note, very temporary) moment and buy a case of honey to be kind and charitable, building false hopes.

Consider another similar scenario. This one in Nairobi, Kenya – a Maasai woman brings us a dress she has crafted for the Masai [sic] market, hoping to sell for $10.00 equivalent in Kenyan shillings. She is bright. She has seen that a famous US visitor, Hillary Clinton, had been gifted with a similar item. We know. According to the news reports, it was not genuine Maasai, but carried the name. Also, we have seen Louis Vuitton Moet Hennessey's (LVMH) spring fashion line of Maasai items and dresses selling for $1,200 at his Paris fashion show.

However, LVMH adds great value to the brand because he is, after all, Louis Vuitton. The LVMH spring Paris line of Maasai apparel includes Maasai scarves at 395EU; Maasai sandals at 650EU; and Maasai items made with higher end materials for thousands of Euros. However, the woman will sell her dress for less than the wishful 10.00 (Kenyan shilling equivalent) because there are hundreds like it in the Masai market and tourists, advised by some strange logic, will bargain her down further to $4.00–$5.00, Kenyan equivalent.

What is the difference between the Zambian boy selling honey in East Africa for $1.00/jar and the New Zealand honey of $25.00–35.00? What makes the Maasai dress sold locally for $5.00 different from the Maasai dress sold more dramatically under Louis Vuitton's French line in Paris at $1,900?

As any business or international development student knows, it is foolish to compare distant markets, to change this norm or to effectively rally against it. Buy Fair Trade – at least you will feel better, may be some comfort. These are popular arguments: Markets differ; positioning in lucrative markets is not possible from Zambia, Nairobi, Kenya, or 100 other remote places. When we add the fact that many developing country producers are 250 miles or more from ports and the costs to bring products to export ports does not equal the amount paid at those ports, the problem is compounded. It is a problem that contributes to cyclic poverty despite hard work and improvements in quality and production.

If this were the end of the story, we would advise that you close this book. But, it is not the end of the story. There *is* good news. There *is* a way to change the story and the outcome CAN be better and brighter – far brighter for millions of low-income farmers and producers.

What is different about this book is that it is not a book that theorizes or pontificates about Africa's problems. Those books have been written. Though serving a purpose to focus attention on the bottom billion and additional billion at the margins, these books tend to ignore the role of trade isolation and the fact that every one of the current 54 countries in Africa has been colonized, and thus trade exploited, with the exception of Ethiopia. Some books highlight and underscore problems with negative discourse eliciting pity or anger over empowerment. Neither approach serves the African future well. That future can be brighter than doomsday tomes sometimes assert.

This is a book for social entrepreneurs wanting to bring change, and willing to learn a systematic, proven method for how to do so. Tomorrow's entrepreneurs will not change Africa or LDCs by doing what yesterday's efforts failed to do, however sincere the effort or grandiose the funding. That is, the majority of aid and development projects go towards addressing symptoms rather than underlying causation. We applaud some important results. Where trade and business efforts for developing farmers and producers are engaged, they tend to focus on increasing the supply of products or focusing on products in commodity markets at the low end. Even with costly improvements in quality, the resultant overproduction has not produced and most likely will not produce dramatic income improvement. Tomorrow's developing businesses must be smarter. It involves people working smarter, not harder.

What does it mean to work smarter?

Lest we engage a ubiquitous, faddish phrase without meaning, "working smarter" involves using methods and tools that have proven to be successful and have proven to be the essential factor propelling developed countries to higher levels of success.[2] These tools and methods are the future, not the past. These tools involve Intellectual Property that derives from the intangible value of products.

Intangible value has overtaken physical properties as holding the largest share of value, according to Standard & Poor's 500 analysis. Consider, for example, the Sunkist oranges – an agricultural product owned by a cooperative that has achieved its fifth straight year of $1 billion revenue. It is licensed on 77 products, many without a trace of orange![3] The Sunkist orange case study is presented along with numerous other western cases to show how Intellectual Property business is a business strategy. It is a strategy with a method that can be learned and replicated for distinctive agricultural and cultural products. It is not haphazard.

To move from theory to practical application, 12 workbooks are included that delve into the specifics of the methodology, skills, tools, and case studies. Every successful discipline has a methodology, learning from trial and error, but not continually experimenting as entrepreneurship has sometimes done, despite sincere, individual effort and many successes. A six-step method is presented including case studies involving over 20 million people.

Overall the book is about power because real change doesn't happen without changing power. For the millions of developing country farmers, producers, and artisans of Africa, this power is deeply entrenched, taking the form of exporters, often driven to offer the lower limits of prices due to exploitive importers. In this book, we describe how to effect this entrenched power via the power of intangible value; the power of supply chain ownership; the power of scale and opportunity; the power of IP tools, and the power of advocacy and education. It also describes women's empowerment, not theoretically, but regarding changing power and dramatically improving income. We showcase a women's owned business created in northern Uganda and South Sudan involving 700 women, former abductees and marginalized, using IP tools; alongside supply chain ownership and high end brand positioning to receive a dramatic income increase.

More specifically, some key questions and issues are addressed such as:

- What is IP business and how does it change power and produce sustainable income?
- Business the world over understands that how you position your products in the marketplace is key to success. This is not magic, nor is it random. Positioning winter coats in the tropics is unlikely to yield effective results. While that example is obvious, positioning distinctive products on commodity markets is a ubiquitous practice with poor results. There is a method to learning business positioning. We describe this method as a six-step method that can be transformative to the already fine products grown and made in Africa and other LDCs.
- How did Africa become "out powered" and can the power be realistically changed? The core problem with most African aid solutions is they do not change the power balance. Well-intended strategies such as Fair Trade, and value-added strategies, or Corporate Social Responsibility (CSR) do not affect power. We explore how Intellectual Property business and positioning changes power. Based on a power/dependency model, the ways to change power are described as well as diagrammed.
- The six-step method: Business is not really about random success though surprises do happen. For one hundred years, business has followed tried and true methods with variations. Yet, when it comes to international development, there is a mindset that random, creative attempts oftentimes replace solid business methods. It is time to change this mentality as it is borderline unethical to learn on the backs of the poor, whereas methods that have worked for 20 million people *can* be replicated and learned.
- We present replicable steps and an IP business method that walk the student through six elements to first determine if a product is a viable candidate for

dramatic income improvement. We begin with the end in mind. We then describe a six-step method involving thinking like a business with IP tools; ownership of supply chains and import companies; creation of import companies and positioning.

- Do brands work for African producers? Brands are all the rage in the twenty-first century, and branding strategies have been promoted by international development experts as well. The problem of brands is multifaceted for LDCs: 1) Branding is often done without a full brand ownership and supply chain ownership strategy; 2) Brands are not positioned appropriately; and 3) Importers outside of the country generally assume the brand value is created by the work of their own brands outside of Africa. When importers do receive country branded products, they often rebrand the products to achieve best market position. Branding without commensurate brand ownership is futile. We describe the power of branding, alongside brand ownership and Intellectual Property strategies to achieve dramatic income results.

- The power of advocacy and support organizations: A new business model requires advocacy, education, and support. We describe the way education for LDCs in IP business has been designed and a delivery model. We also discuss the emergence of new forms of support and advocacy, such as the African IP Trust – a support and advocacy organization fashioned to support African farmers and producers.

- The power of Intellectual Property tools: IP is an essential part of a business strategy rather than merely a legal strategy. We discuss the elements of IP such as trademarks, licenses, geographical indications, and certifications, and how the various tools become part of changing the power for the producer in the marketplace.

- The state of the field: We will describe the history and priorities of the two largest international aid organizations – USAID and British Aid (DFID). Fundamentally, aid agencies are not about creating new African or developing country businesses, though many agri-businesses are supported, and progressive looking aid seeks new business solutions. The overwhelming majority of funds go toward the symptoms of poverty, such as health and vaccinations rather than root cause. While not an exhaustive history of aid, we will set the stage for why a new business model is needed. The aim is not to critique international aid that serves well in its focus on maternal and child health, disaster relief, and disease eradication, along with meeting deep poverty relief. The goal is to show why a business method has not been the focus of billions of dollars in aid and why a new business approach is needed.

- WWCD? What would a corporation do? Corporations in western countries own and control intangible value translated into Intellectual Property worth billions of dollars. Indeed the brands are worth more than the physical, tangible part of the products. As just a few examples, the Coca-Cola brand alone is worth $179 billion according to Forbes brand valuation.[4] Summaries of how IP business has worked for companies such as Coca-Cola; Apple; and Sunkist oranges are included to show how developing countries such as Ghana, Uganda, Tanzania, Kenya, Mozambique, Ethiopia, along with Caribbean and Asian countries can adopt *and benefit* from similar methods.

- What do corporations do? Corporations own and control their Intellectual Property, invest in understanding their markets, brand appropriately, and control their supply chains through to retail. They do not give away their products or their IP. While corporations have ethical challenges, the purpose is to analyze and learn what has worked to create and sustain multi-billion dollar enterprises and model the effective method for millions who struggle with less developed business methods. If it works for fizzy water, IP business can work for distinctive African products.

Chapter outline

Chapter 1: The power of positioning and scale

There is a potential to bring an additional $100 million per year per product in income to the African continent. This is based on just four–five Intellectual Property business opportunities per each of the 45 countries in Sub-Saharan Africa alone where it is possible to engage transformative business.[5] With an estimated improved trade income of $100 million per year/per product, this translates into over $25 billion per year. That is the potential of income at stake for African farmers, producers, and owners of cultural brands with IP business positioning.

This chapter describes the scale of the opportunity based on real, in-country analysis with thousands of stakeholders, and feasibility study analysis over 10 years. The feasibility study and business plans upon which the analysis is based were constructed by Ashoka award-winning social entrepreneurs; a range of academics from Carnegie Mellon, Columbia, and Oxford University, with advice from well-reputed global brand managers, such as Marc Mathieu, former global brand manager, Coca-Cola and Unilever.

The scale and opportunity is also based on proof of concept IP business positioning involving over 20 million people to date, and products in the pipeline for IP business strategies.

The chapter also describes the fundamental root problem – trade isolation and how traditional aid and development solutions need to be changed with IP business solutions to overcome trade isolation that contributes to low returns. We also outline global economics and show the urgency of the problem for the bottom 2–3 billion in developing countries, i.e. an income disparity that cannot be solved by increasing production, further philanthropic aid, or palliative strategies of Fair Trade.

Topics in this chapter include:

- The challenge of trade isolation
- The challenge of weak negotiating positions
- The reality of 3–5 percent return from retail for distinctive products
- The scale of opportunity across Sub-Saharan Africa
- Specific examples of IP business strategies
- East and West African opportunities and summaries
- The Ethiopian Coffee Case returning $100 million as an example of IP business positioning

Intellectual Property business positioning is a business strategy rather than merely a legal one, as described above. One core obstacle to why IP tools are not used more effectively by LDC farmers and producers, and those who endeavor to help them, is that IP is considered to be the exclusive domain of lawyers. In Africa, IP is delegated to and controlled by the IPO (IP Offices), which is quite rational under this assumption. However, IPOs do not typically understand nor are they trained in business. The case study illustrates how an IPO was trained in IP business positioning and assisted in this large-scale change, resulting in over $100 million in additional income to Ethiopia.

In this chapter, we provide the details of how the Ethiopian Fine Coffee Trademark and Licensing Initiative progressed, from start to finish. This case study also includes a workbook. The purpose of the EFC case study is to offer a real example of how an IP method worked for 1 million coffee farmers. It can be studied, learned, applied more widely, and used to create transformational impact for other distinctive products.

Chapter 2: Changing the power

Empowerment has become a very popular word in the twenty-first century, and that is underscored when it comes to empowerment for African farmers and producers, and in many cases, for women. While empowerment is simultaneously used as a noun, concept, and outcome that one cannot be "against," our view is that it is used ubiquitously, without really changing the power for farmers, producers, and women in sustainable ways. It may empower a woman to sell a product in the marketplace in Nairobi, Kenya such as the Masai Mara market, or in the Ugandan city of Kampala. Empowerment is relative – the woman or man *may* be more empowered by selling any product, even if the returns are quite low, than by not being in the local marketplace, at all. However, in our view, true empowerment changes the economic power. We intend to provide a method demonstrating true, sustainable empowerment that changes the power of:

- Scale with real income improvements
- Supply chain ownership
- Product ownership via IP tools for ongoing ownership, income improvement, and sustainability
- Stakeholder organizations

Topics in this chapter demonstrate:

- Why empowerment requires more than rhetoric
- The goals and challenges of strategies such as Fair Trade, and branding
- The challenges of Corporate Social Responsibility (CSR) and value-added strategies
- How increasing production does not change power
- Why power is about reaching final markets with ownership
- A power model that diagrams challenges and opportunities
- Four major ways of changing power more sustainably

In order to understand how to change power more permanently or sustainably, it is important to dig deeper into root causes of the powerless situation. It is also important to understand what has not worked well such as Fair Trade, Corporate Social Responsibility, or branding and value-added programs, despite sincere intentions. A great many people have placed their hopes on Fair Trade, and consumers, predominantly in western markets, have come to believe that Fair Trade holds the answer for developing country producers. This chapter applauds the Fair Trade efforts, but shows how and why this strategy keeps farmers, producers, and cultural brand owners locked in patterns blocking real income advancement.

The key take-away in this chapter also enables the student to understand power and dependency, to diagram entrenched patterns, and develop skills for reaching across the barriers. A power model showing dependency, power, and alternatives is provided. This is a key training and learning tool used in the classroom for business students to assist the reader to better understand how to carefully strategize and how to overcome barriers; explore alternatives; and select best options.

Chapter 3: The power of the method: a six-step method for Intellectual Property business positioning

Dramatic income improvement is about a method rather than wishful or haphazard thinking. The business method involves six steps beginning with the end in mind of placement in higher end retail markets.

While IP utilizes or uses legal tools, IP business rests on the same foundation as business. An understanding of relevant retail markets, and positioning toward those markets as well as supply chain ownership, is fundamental. It also involves effective stakeholder organization. The best way to make these points is to study US and global corporate business models that are based on intangible value such as these success cases that most people are familiar with as building blocks.

Topics in this chapter include:

- Determination of distinctiveness
- Supply chain analysis
- Four-point models of farmer/producer–export–import–retail prices
- Determining the correct IP tool
- Building a stakeholder organization
- Producer ownership of import companies
- Branding and positioning
- Social impact investment

While these steps are not easy, they are similar to steps and methodology successful companies would take to build brand reputation and income on Intellectual Property, from Coca-Cola to Nike and Sunkist oranges, or African companies such as Safaricom.

The chapter highlights numerous developed country IP business case studies to show how relatively simple products, including agricultural products, have traversed the historical trajectory from low income, poor producers to multi-billion dollar brand success.

Chapter 4: The power of distinctive products and the Ugandan vanilla case study

This chapter shows how to differentiate mediocre or good products from truly distinctive products that hold intangible value capable of translating to IP assets. Rather than haphazard guessing, the chapter describes a method for differentiating distinctive products – a critical aspect of a successful IP business repositioning strategy. A full chapter is devoted to this aspect of the IP business method because it is – simply put – vitally important and too frequently overlooked.

A dominant reason why Intellectual Property strategies have sometimes been attempted but failed in LDCs is the incorrect assumption that Intellectual Property is in the form of branding alone, or geographical indications (GIs). The assumption is that brands and GIs can be transformative and should work for all manner of products. While everything *can* be branded, brands will not always be successful. Branding alone is not IP business. Branding is part of an overall IP positioning strategy that should also include stakeholder ownership, positioning, marketing, and beginning with the end in mind.

Further, branding commodity products that are mediocre or even good but not truly distinctive are more likely to fail, as the intangible value assets cannot be readily accrued when the underlying product lacks distinctive qualities. For example, Belizean mangoes are good, but unlikely to become successful with an IP strategy. Similarly, Ugandan cotton is good, but not distinctive. While it may be branded, the brand is unlikely to achieve significant retail price differentiation.

Why does this matter? Millions of dollars have been spent, and are being spent on branding and attempts to enable lower income producers to do better at selling their products. These vary from beads to soaps, and larger-scale products like cotton, nuts, coffee, and flowers that are farmed and produced by millions of farmers in Africa and LDCs. However, just as IP strategies fail if they are not done holistically with supply chain ownership and import company ownership, positioning and enforcement, choosing the wrong products initially can also lead to failure or diminish intended results.

Topics in this chapter include:

- Why distinctiveness matters in product evaluation
- How to determine if a product is distinctive from mediocre or commodity-based products
- How to perform market analyses using a variety of sources
- A case study example of Ugandan vanilla – a most distinctive product with the six-step methodology for improved income.

Also, to engage a full IP strategy is not easy or inexpensive. It is important to begin with distinctive products to create a ratio of investment in the strategy to outcomes that are worth the necessary expenditures and investment and most importantly, to achieve success. While some define success as an increase in low wage jobs, which is a reasonable goal, we define success for an IP business strategy as improved income rather than an increase in low wage jobs.

Chapter 5: The power of Intellectual Property tools

This chapter will teach students about specific Intellectual Property tools for business. We assume no legal background and present the basics of trademarks, licensing, and certification marks. The goal is to increase understanding of how IP tools can be used effectively for businesses.

Topics in this chapter include:

- Trademark and the business history of the "Trade Mark"
- Why trademarks are valuable for poor producers, and trademark limits
- What is a license and why is it valuable for income generation?
- The value and limits of certification marks
- The IP tool of geographical indications (GIs)

- Successes and limits of IP tools relative to a full IP business strategy.
- Interview with David Cardwell, licensing agent overseeing Star Wars and other most lucrative licensing strategies of the twentieth–twenty-first century.

Along the lines of learning IP business from successful implementation, the chapter provides an interview with Mr. David Cardwell who received the UK lifetime achievement award for licensing strategies. His achievements include the Star Wars licensing strategy, wherein the films achieved revenue of approximately $7 billion, whereas the product licensing achieved $27 billion.[6] Mr. Cardwell provides insight into the capacity and methodology for LDC producers, such as the Maasai of Kenya and Tanzania, to model some key aspects of licensing for their cultural brand.

Chapter 6: The power of education and enforcement

Most successful western businesses advance their IP power through lawyers. For example, Nike is a brand worth $26 billion and achieved the title of most valuable sports brand in 2016.[7] Their capacity to achieve and retain this success is due in large part to the reality of employing over 100 lawyers, in addition to successful business positioning and other business elements. Microsoft, a longer-standing successful company, engages nearly 1,000 lawyers.

Lower income groups cannot hire myriads of lawyers. IP offices in LDCs such as Tanzania and Uganda are much smaller affairs, staffed by an IP lawyer and small number of staff, compared to the US and its office of Patents and Trademarks – the USPTO – which employ thousands of lawyers and specialists. However, for IP business to be successful, advocacy, support, education, and enforcement of IP rights is needed just the same, albeit on much less grandiose budgets.

This chapter highlights the means and methods of advocacy and support for farmers and producers advancing their ownership of IP and supply chains against powerful interests. It addresses important questions such as, is it realistic to assume IP advocacy, protection, and support on a fraction of developed country budgets? If Microsoft employs 1,000 attorneys, and the entire Zanzibar IP office may involve 10 people, it is, to be sure, harder to see the desired outcomes of IP ownership and protection.

The chapter describes the African IP Trust, a support and advocacy organization that was funded by the Obama Administration. Chaired by Lord Paul Boateng and Congresswoman Diane Watson (ret.), it involves high profile leaders from business and politicians and human rights activists designed to support Africans in their IP business opportunities and challenges.

As developing country farmers and producers and women's owned businesses assume greater power and control over their distinctive brands and product distribution and Intellectual Property, a backlash from existing businesses sometimes occurs.

An interview with Dick Wilder, Associate General Counsel of the Bill and Melinda Gates Foundation, previous Associate General Counsel for Intellectual Property Policy at Microsoft Corporation, and former Director of the Global Intellectual Property Issues Division of the World Intellectual Property Organization, provides commentary on the criticality of support and enforcement.

Topics in this chapter include:

- The challenges faced by LDCs seeking enforcement of IP and advocacy
- Historical precedents and the role of advocacy, education, and enforcement of IP
- The African IP Trust
- Education specific to LDC stakeholders to achieve stakeholder constitutions
- An interview with Mr. Dick Wilder, Associate General Counsel, Bill and Melinda Gates Foundation on the criticality of enforcement and the African IP Trust.

Chapter 7: The power of the brand: the Maasai Intellectual Property case study

This chapter explains what effective branding is with the inclusion of modern experts such as the firm Innate Motion who have recently reconfigured hundreds of Unilever brands. Although branding has been taught in business schools and has been a major focus of consultants for nearly twenty years, and has more recently been embraced by international development experts, branding requires a fuller business positioning strategy.

As this book is intent not to critique failure as much as to pivot it based on heightened knowledge and case study examples, we demonstrate the vitality of brands for developed country producers when coupled with full supply chain ownership and correct positioning. As the twenty-first century features increasing emphasis on intangible value, we demonstrate how brand values achieved multibillion-dollar range for products otherwise considered ordinary, such as Sunkist oranges which is in its fifth straight year of billion-dollar revenue growth and payments to growers of $1.1 billion in 2014.[8]

This chapter explores the essential question: Are brand and lucrative licensing strategies the domain of developed countries *or* can African businesses achieve similar scale, following comparable strategies? Our point of view is no secret. Of course they can.

Case Study: This chapter also describes the Maasai Intellectual Property Initiative. Over 1,000 companies use the Maasai brand with projected value of over $200 million per year. This case study involves the specifics of how the

Maasai will soon benefit from achieving more ownership and control over their iconic brand. The Maasai have built a stakeholder organization across Kenya and Tanzania and are poised to receive sustainable revenue.

The case study of this iconic tribe is explained in depth due to its implications for other indigenous peoples, who comprise 6 percent of the world's population. For example, the Cherokee, Guyaki, Tuareg, Apache, and Navajo tribal people, whose name, images, and cultural attributes are also used by firms and corporations for the benefit of the latter without acknowledgment or benefit to the indigenous people.

Topics include:

- Modern branding concepts
- Creating brands and case study examples of highest ranked popular brands in developed countries
- The Maasai Intellectual Property Initiative case study with:
  a The creation of a viable stakeholder organization
  b A seven-point plan for achieving more control and income for cultural brands
  c The use of IP strategies such as trademarks and licensing
  d The implications for income return to other well-known, highly visible indigenous people.
  e Examples of IP misuse and strategies for indigenous peoples comprising 6 percent of the world's population including the Cherokee, Navajo, Guyaki, and others.

Chapter 8: The power of women's owned IP businesses

Women and girls' initiatives are a current and pressing agenda of many aid organizations and groups such as Acumen, The Thomson Reuters Foundation, The Clinton Global Initiative, USAID and DFID, among others. While it is well known that girls and women comprise half of the world's population and half of the world's farmers are women, women also are a large part of the artisan workers and creative producers.

What is less well understood is how to advance women's income in these endeavors.

This chapter presents the challenges, showing how international development and social entrepreneurship together with a new model of IP business can address the pressing issue of poverty and lack of advancement for millions of women and girls. We provide the case study of Bead for Life, a 10-year-old initiative in East Africa and the Ugandan and South Sudanese case study for Ugandan shea butter as a replicable model.

Topics in this chapter include:

- The scale of poverty for women and girls across Africa
- A summary of recent international development focus on women
- The case study of WONS: Women's Owned Nilotica Shea
- How former child soldiers have learned Intellectual Property business strategies to create their own import company in London, trading at higher end for more sustainable income
- Women's IP business opportunities across Africa: four short case studies of success and failure
- Lessons learned for a replicable model

Chapter 9: The power of the historical record: Intellectual Property business is not new!

Businesses built on Intellectual Property methods are not entirely new. Legions of farmers ranging from French grape and cheese producers to producers of products such as Scotch whisky have struggled and achieved victories for many centuries using variations of IP business strategies. This chapter describes some key historical cases involving millions of poor farmers and producers, beginning with Roquefort cheese as long ago as 47 AD.

The goal of demonstrating historical precedent and years of effort, challenge, victory, and defeat is to determine what can be learned from the historical record. For example, people often cite French champagne as the poster child case of IP. Yet, it is important to look at what worked and why and whether or not the model can be appropriated for LDC producers, or whether other factors in history and context were more pivotal than the use of the IP tool.

Using the historical record enables a comparison of: the product; the context and degree of government support or antipathy; the IP tool and its effectiveness; the positioning and markets as a variable; and the critical role of stakeholder organization, enforcement, and advocacy. The question to be addressed here is: Where have IP business strategies been effective and where and why have they failed?

Topics in this chapter include:

- The historical record including successes over several centuries
- The case study of Roquefort cheese, first noted in 47 AD
- The case study of Scotch whisky - the sixth largest export in the UK with historical roots from the fifteenth century
- The case study of French champagne
- The failed case of Ceylon tea involving 2 million farmers
- Lessons learned from early IP success stories.

While it is relatively easy to assert that history teaches lessons, it is important to fully understand historical cases. For one, the misuse of analogy often occurs when history is misstated or understood peripherally. Innumerable policy mistakes are the result of taking bits and pieces of the historical record, applied wholesale to very different contexts. This chapter explores four case studies in depth as the history of poor producers using IP takes place over centuries, and lessons are to be learned about which factors, contexts, and elements were effective and which were not to draw lessons for today's IP business strategies.

Chapter 10: The power of international development: historical trends and challenges

This chapter details how USAID began in the US after World War II, and was followed soon afterward by large-scale UK aid programs in Europe, Japan, Canada, Australia, New Zealand, and other countries. It discusses how large-scale aid programs have not been historically or dominantly about business creation. While this may seem obvious, historical roots create the foundations of policy that continue to shape the present, in both thinking, decision making, staffing and in allocation of funds. Often, the choice of projects, focus, and funding is more a product of historical roots, and the culture of the aid and development agencies, than about the merit of individual proposals.

The chapter will provide a brief history of USAID and a summary history of approaches at DFID; CIDA; AFD (France); and Danish and German aid programs. It will not delve into these agencies' deep history, but will provide an overview of the general mission and intentions of aid as it was first construed, and has developed over the past half century.

Another goal of this chapter is to illustrate how some of our efforts to date have not worked – we are not solving global poverty, and why increasing production has been ineffective. This chapter is not to levy unfair criticism, but to set the distinction for why a different strategy is needed that is not based on producing more goods or twentieth-century manufacturing models.

We end with this chapter because the goal of the book is to present a *new* method, not to criticize old methods. Yet, a fundamental question is addressed – if the method of IP business has the potential to transform Africa, why has it not been done before on a wide scale? In 2015, over $37 billion dollars were spent by USAID, about a quarter of this in Africa. A different approach is needed.

Topics in this chapter include:

- A brief history of USAID as founded by John F. Kennedy
- A brief history and focus areas of the British Aid organization, DFID
- Trends and transitions in the larger western international development agencies toward trade-based solutions

- Why USAID and DFID have not engaged more effectively in business strategies
- Why there is room for a new model focused on entrepreneurial business creation.

Supplemental materials

The book also includes supplemental learning tools. These include 10 colorful, interactive workbooks. The workbooks include fundamentals and case studies.

Fundamentals of IP business positioning include:

- Intellectual Property business fundamentals
- Intellectual Property business positioning: the six-step method
- Determining the value of distinctive products
- Intellectual Property tools: trademarks, licensing, certification marks, and geographical indications
- Market research fundamentals for IP business
- The African IP Trust: building partnership and support organizations
- Product specific workbooks/case studies of African and Caribbean opportunities:

    - The Ethiopian Fine Coffee trademark and licensing case study
    - The Ugandan women's shea butter project case study
    - The Zanzibar spices workbook
    - The Maasai of Kenya and Tanzania: IP case study and implications for indigenous people
    - The Tanzanian tea case study[9]

Learning from failure

We also believe in learning from failure. One of the authors published a book[10] comprising cases of real life business failures categorized into 10 themes reported by MBA students. This book on power emphasized how to diagnose power and provided a model for more effectively managing powerlessness. The point was to show how to turn around failure into success.

Drawing from this model, we describe historical cases of failure and success to demonstrate what went wrong, and what could have been done differently. For example, there is a trend in international development currently promoting branding. However, branding without a full business method and strategy sometimes fails. In a section on IP tools used successfully and failing, we analyze what went well and wrong, and also suggest how to pivot these situations for many millions of African and LDC producers.

One such case presented in this chapter is Mozambique cashews: This multi-million dollar USAID project created many low wage jobs for the Mozambique cashew industry by setting up primitive processing of branded cashews. Upon export, the cashew exporters were receiving less for the branded, processed cashews than prior to the processing, when they sold the cashews whole. The branding was done without a full IP business strategy, marketing or repositioning. We detail the Mozambique cashew case because over 1 million cashew farmers live largely in poverty in Mozambique and to better illustrate how to learn and pivot such IP failures.[11]

In Ethiopia, as one example, IP Business involved a Trademark and Licensing strategy to bring $100,000,000 to the Ethiopian coffee farmers of three fine coffees – Yirgacheffe, Sidamo, and Harar. This did not require more coffee yields via more production. This required working smarter, not harder. In these chapters, we will illustrate how we turned $2 million of investment into $100,000,000 for the Ethiopians. We will describe a detailed method and its steps and how this same model has been applied to other fine African products.

The urgency for change

Our urgency for writing this book is that Ethiopian coffee is not an isolated situation. Our analysis in Africa of feasibility study and business plans demonstrates four–five distinctive products per 45 African countries in which the intellectual property business method can produce $100 million per product or $25,000,000,000 – yes, that is $25 billion per year by conservative estimates at full implementation. These four–five products per country will not happen overnight, of course. But, the promising news is that the distinctive products are *there* and the method works to turn these approximately four–five products per country into a far higher income return for farmers and producers.

We want to get back to the Zambian honey merchant and tell him, "there is more than hope, or workshops promising 'empowerment.' There is a way, a method that will enable you to reach beyond your border." We have indeed returned to the Maasai mama and engaged her in a Maasai IP initiative that brings far more income via IP licensing than she could acquire through making thousands of dresses sold on local markets.

When we began our work in Ethiopia, birthplace of arguably the best coffee in the world, coffee farmers of the fine brew were turning their plots into the more lucrative legal narcotic, Xate. That is because the coffee export price was so low that despite having the finest coffee in the world, coupled with great demand by western markets, the farmers could barely make 0.05 per pound profit above their costs to farm; dry; wash; bag; and transport the coffee to cooperatives. No one can feed their family, let alone advance out of poverty on 0.05 return out of $20.00 retail. The Ethiopian coffee farmer deserves to earn a living, and not have his or her profits lost, simply from being in the wrong position in the world.

When Mary Robinson, former President of Ireland, headed the UN High Commission on Human Rights, she agreed to meet with Howard Schultz, CEO of Starbucks as support for the Ethiopian Fine Coffee Trademark and Licensing Initiative.

"This is a human rights issue," Mrs. Robinson asserted. We agree.

Howard Schultz is not the problem, nor is the problem other CEOs or corporate greed. When companies, such as Big Coffee, fail to pay fair prices for products such as coffee, it contributes to the problem. However, in our opinion, blaming corporate greed is easy, but solving trade isolation and a pattern of low prices paid to farmers from least developed countries (LDCs) requires a different approach.

We also know that a visit from Mrs. Mary Robinson, however valued her reputation or skilled and formidable she is as negotiator, is insufficient to reposition Ethiopian fine coffee correctly in the market to overcome trade isolation, and a poor negotiation position, or centuries of dominance by modern coffee. Some have suggested that it will "just take awhile for Africa and LDCs to 'catch up.'" It has been suggested to us by a highly placed US trade leader that it is merely "Africa's turn to make low commodity priced products."

But, we don't think that answer is the right one, either. With 1 billion people at poverty level, and another billion barely above those levels, continuing on a pathway of marginal or in some cases, "negative income," meaning earning less for products than the cost to bring them to market cannot be sustained. While certain advances in agricultural methods, production, and quality may be part of the solution, the faster advance will be about working smarter, not harder, and utilizing an asset already in place. The products with intangible value are there and positioning these correctly will not be easy, but the alternative is implausible.

In this book, we will demonstrate how success factors can be modeled and applied to numerous other distinctive products and entire sectors in Africa and LDCs. The solution is a business model that is not magic, but is definitely a model with steps, rigor, and results.

Consider one more story: In Addis Ababa, Ethiopia, young boys line up outside of a workshop. They want to show us their new shoes, acquired for their new and appropriate role as students in school. Their fathers, Ethiopian fine coffee farmers, are part of the 1 million Ethiopian coffee farmers who earned $US 100 million more income cumulatively.

The farmers did not increase production – fertilize, plant, tend, harvest, wash, dry, bag, weigh, transport or sell more coffee beans. In this book, we will show you the method that was effective and changed the situation for the Ethiopians and is applicable to entire sectors. We will show you how to replicate it with a rigorous six-step method with steps and stages that is applicable to over 250 million developing country farmers and producers of distinctive products. And, we will discuss how intellectual property business strategies make the world go round, and are a different and superior way of competing in the global market place. This pathway is "Open for Business."

If this sounds too good to be true, we freely admit that the method is not easy. It requires every bit of the rigor, planning, smarts, and skills that enabled western companies to be profitable. Coca-Cola, or more to the agricultural sector, Sunkist oranges, did not become profitable overnight. Indeed, Coca-Cola, emergent from an Atlanta pharmacist, expanded out of the US only during World War II; and Sunkist was founded by poor orange farmers, who now have the Sunkist name on over 77 products. Of course, we all know the story of Apple, now valued by *Forbes* with the highest brand value of 2016, as founded in the Jobs and Wozniak parents' garages.

Is Africa capable of achieving such success? That question may have been asked a few decades ago, as many African countries were emerging from western colonialism. Recall, nations such as Kenya were still under British colonialism as recently as the early 1960s. However, these nations have modern aspirations. There is an emergent young entrepreneurial sector that is nothing short of a collective tour de force and growing. The majority of the population in Uganda, for example, are under 30 years old, many of whom are determined to change their country for the better.

Returning to our young Zambian friend, the honey merchant with hopes and dreams. 'Friend – We have not forgotten your question. It burns in our hearts. It keeps us awake in the night.' For the honey merchant is not alone in his inquiry! We see a generation of bright, educated African, Caribbean, and South East Asians rising up. There is a groundswell of young people, far more determined and educated and aware of the world beyond their borders than anything ever seen in developing countries. They are determined to find answers. They are today's social entrepreneurs; businesswomen and men. They will lead and need methods that work.

In some cases, they are the ones who achieve fellowships to western universities, populating our business schools. Are we serving them well? Or, are we serving them yesterday's answers for tomorrow's problems? I hesitate to answer, as I have seen this group around the world, and in my own classrooms, and I feel that we can and must do better. This book is our offering to that quest and question – how can the beekeeper's honey sustain him, *and* grow an industry, as well?

The resources are there – distinctive, premium products growing prolifically throughout Africa at the hands of diligent men and women farmers and producers by the millions. The high end markets are there. The tools to do this are there and utilized every single day by western businesses. We can and must do this.

They say, "If you give a man a fish, you feed him for a day. If you teach a man to fish, you feed him forever." We say, African and LDC men and women already *do* know how to fish and they *do* know how to farm. So, let's teach the entrepreneurs how to own the fishing supply chain and create import companies. Let's teach them how to brand and position their many distinctive products and reach final, lucrative retail markets, while acquiring Trademarks and Licenses to achieve dramatically improved income. Then, they will prosper and own the prosperity for generations to come.

Let's get started.

Notes

1 The United Nations defines Least Developed Countries (LDCs) as those countries with less than $US $1.065/year income over three years and assesses LDCs every three years. According to the UN's most recent review, there were 34 countries in Africa in LDC status; nine in Asia; four in Oceania; and one in North America. Although other terms such as developing country are used interchangeably with LDC, for our purposes we will utilize the United Nations term and definition.
2 M. Brindle and P. Stearns, "Facing up to management faddism," New York: Quorum Press, 2002.
3 Sunkist website, "Sunkist announces 5th straight billion dollar revenue year." www.sunkist.com/press-room/annual-meeting-release-2015.
4 L. Munson, "The world's most valuable brands," *Forbes*, May 11, 2016.
5 The calculation of 25b is derived from 45 countries in Sub-Saharan Africa, each with approximately four–five opportunities to achieve $100 m more income annually, as per a DFID funded study by Light Years IP. There are IP business opportunities in the Caribbean, Asia, S. America, and Latin America, as well.
6 D. Cardwell, Interview, London, March 2016.
7 M. Ozanian, "Forbes Fab 40: The most valuable sports brands 2015," *Forbes*, October 22, 2015.
8 Sunkist website, "Sunkist announces 5th straight billion dollar revenue year." See more at: https://www.sunkist.com/press-room/annual-meeting-release-2015.
9 R. Layton and M. Brindle, "Improving export income in the Caribbean," published by OAS (Organization of American States), 2010.
10 M. Brindle and L. Mainiero, *Managing power through lateral networking*, New York: Quorum Press, 2000.
11 As this book goes to press, TechnoServe, consultants to USAID, have been pivoting the Mozambique cashews situation toward a more successful outcome.

1

THE POWER OF POSITIONING
AND SCALE

This book is fundamentally about changing Africa by changing the power of African farmers and producers. To demonstrate how to change the power, we describe how and why Africa is severely disempowered. This disempowerment takes place every day in a thousand ways, and no amount of rhetorical "empowerment" strategies short of changing the underlying root problem will work.

Millions of Africans are disempowered. Their finest quality, distinctive products receive very low prices at export for two main reasons: 1) They lack negotiating power; and 2) They face trade isolation. But, before delving into how to change the situation and truly empower Africans for the longer term, it is important to note the enormity of the opportunity and why Intellectual Property business solutions are the best strategies to overcome trade isolation and a poor negotiating position.

The method, tools, and cases described in this book lay out a replicable pathway to increase export income from distinctive products. The method is based on improving the business positioning of export sectors to substantially increase negotiating power. To change power there needs to be much more than rhetoric, however. Explicit business opportunities, case studies, and methods to improve income are presented in detail.

Why should we look toward transformational power for Africans and least developed countries?

- Most importantly, the scale of opportunity to enact relatively straightforward, but system-changing business practices is within the scope of African producers, now in the twenty-first century.
- There is nothing else that can be as impactful to African farmers and producers given trade isolation, competition, and cyclic poverty, even with ongoing

low wage agri-businesses. Several reasons for this are explored in this chapter, including low wage competition.

- Ten years of research indicates there are four–five highly distinctive products per African country where farmer/producers and artisans can earn $100 million more income per product per year.
- Intellectual Property business positioning is the way of the future. Low wage, commodity export priced agriculture is the way of the past.

In this chapter, we will discuss:

- The problem of weak negotiating positions, and trade isolation.
- How Intellectual Property business positioning strategies can overcome both.
- The scale of opportunity for IP business: There are an estimated 250 opportunities capable of each returning an additional $100 million export income per year.
- East and West African opportunities and summary case studies.
- The power of scale in earning intangible value.
- The benefits of building collaborations among businesses to grasp these opportunities across sectors.
- The dramatic results from the Ethiopian Fine Coffee case that brought $101 million to the Ethiopian exporters as proof of concept.

Problem – an imbalance of negotiating power for distinctive exports

Millions of farmers, producers, and artisans across Africa create highly distinctive products that are sold in wealthy foreign markets. The distinctive nature of these products is the result of unique geographic niches, hundreds or even thousands of years of heritage, and the hard work and expertise of the developing country producers. The intangible elements of distinctive products translate into high retail prices paid in the final foreign markets. However, very little of that value is returned to the poor producers who are often responsible for the distinctiveness in the first place. A study across 20 distinctive African exports found that on average, producers and exporters receive only 2.9 percent of the retail price.[1]

This low producer and exporter share of the retail price is due to a fundamental imbalance of power along the supply chain. Though these products attract high prices in final consumer markets, producers typically have little information about those markets or the supply chain. The producers do not operate beyond selling to traders or their cooperative, have little or no access to the end consumer, and do not use Intellectual Property as a source of leverage or control.

It is therefore easy for large importers and exporters to exploit producers through imposing commodity prices on the product exports. With such low prices, the quality incentives are also lacking, which further endangers the long-term viability of the high quality product.

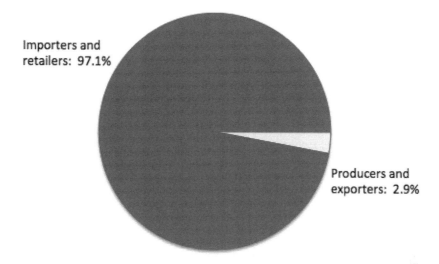

Importers and
retailers: 97.1%

Producers and
exporters: 2.9%

FIGURE 1.1 Percentage of retail price (20 distinctive African products)
Source: Light Years IP.

For example, if you are a farmer in Uganda producing vanilla pods on vines that grow well in the Ugandan climate, the vanilla export price is about $0.08 per 2 pods. This provides little quality incentive, even though the pods retail at $12.00 per 2 pods. Though Uganda has the highest quality vanilla in the world, as determined by vanillin content, and is laborious to grow and tend, few can afford to produce these *and* advance quality with such minimal returns. An export business model utilizing IP business strategies with dramatically different positioning would, however, improve the Ugandan vanilla farmer income significantly, and it creates an incentive for quality.

The power imbalance does not only manifest in low producer prices. Producers cannot capitalize on the distinctive nature of their products when they compete on commodity markets which center on non-distinctive products and lowest cost.

To continue the example of Ugandan vanilla, the finest vanilla is often crushed and sold to commodity markets that are available, rather than enabling Uganda to do what a developed country business might do by branding, marketing, and selling final consumer goods at higher prices outside of their borders. Once a vanilla pod has been properly dried, it is ready for the foreign consumer to use in cooking fine quality crème brûlée and other taste sensitive items.

Commodity prices generate cyclic poverty that reduces quality incentives, income, and in some cases turns the farmers toward growing commodity crops based on short-term price fluctuations, holding them in poverty. (The Ugandan vanilla power points illustrate this case study more fully as found on the website accompanying this text.) The commodity markets also subject poor farmers and producers to wild swings in prices, and make their future income impossible to predict. With an uncertain future, they are unable to make decisions about investing in their business, and they often forgo investments in quality of life issues such as schooling or medical care. Thus improving income stability is as important as increased income to reducing extreme poverty in extremely remote Africa.

The long-term solution to this imbalance is to empower large groups of producers, farmers, and artisans in Africa with business education to improve their positioning to take control of relevant intellectual property and to control the foreign supply chain. This is the core of the approach presented in this book. Throughout Africa, there are millions of farmers and producers of high end quality, distinctive products that can and need to benefit from the same IP business strategies long utilized by developed country business. In this book, we will walk through a systematic and proven method to enable the latent opportunity and transform business "as usual," into business "as transformative." First, we turn to a few of the principles underlying the method, such as intangible value and why it matters.

The problem of trade isolation

Millions of African producers of distinctive products suffer the severe economic consequences of extreme isolation from developed country final markets. There are 15 landlocked countries in Africa comprising 30 percent of the total population of Africa, with a population of over 300 million. These are the countries of Botswana, Burkina Faso, Burundi, Central African Republic, Chad, Ethiopia, Lesotho, Malawi, Mali, Niger, Rwanda, Swaziland, Uganda, Zambia, and Zimbabwe.

Thirty percent of the total population of what Paul Collier has identified as the population comprising "the bottom-billion," live in landlocked countries. It is also an overwhelmingly African problem, with approximately 30 percent of Africa's population living in landlocked, resource-poor countries. An additional challenge for Africa's landlocked countries is the landlocked countries are generally surrounded by poor countries, even those with maritime coasts. This differs, for example, from a European landlocked country such as Switzerland, which is landlocked, but surrounded by wealthier economies, with highly developed transport infrastructure and relatively small land mass.

In addition, there is a vast area of Africa that is more than 250 miles from the coastline and a vast area that is 500 miles or more from the coast. In developed countries, airfreight and high-speed international transport systems reduce or even negate the cost and challenges of distance from the port, but in Africa, trade isolation has enormous consequences. Extreme isolation elevates the transport cost of exporting. In the world's newest country, South Sudan, for example, there are only a little over 100 miles of paved roads even though it has a land mass equal to France.

Consider, for example, producer cooperatives harvesting Shea nuts near Lira in northern Uganda, paying for the nuts to be pressed for oil in a processing plant in Lira, and absorbing the cost to transport the product to the nearest international port of Mombasa, as there is little market demand in Kampala. It is likely that the cost of transport over at least 1,200 km by truck will mean that the income per cooperative member will be minimal. For producers situated more than 1,200 km away, i.e. north of Gulu, the income reduces indeed to a few shillings per kg (less than 40 cents/kg equivalent).

The real challenge is that remote producers cannot absorb the cost of transport to export if the export price is set at the low commodity price, keeping producers locked into poverty cycles despite hard work. You might think that distinctive export products would earn more than commodity price at export, given the ultimate high retail prices. Regrettably, the negotiating power of foreign importers keeps these exports at commodity pricing.

This situation is unfortunately true for millions of producers, and many hundreds of products particularly when harvested or produced in any extremely isolated part of Africa. Trade isolation and consequentially very low income returns from products is the situation for fine coffees across most of high elevation East Africa; it is true for cottons in Uganda; and teas, spices, flowers, oils produced in remote parts of Africa. Simply put, the combination of low commodity prices and cost of transport to export ports wipes away export revenues for producers 500 miles from the nearest port.

For example, when the author began work with Ethiopia in 2004, the retail price of the three most famous Ethiopian fine coffees averaged $20 per pound (across the US, Japan, and Europe), about $16 per pound above retail prices for commodity coffee, but the FOB (freight on board) export price the Ethiopians received was $1.10 per pound. The pattern of low prices at exports repeats throughout Africa, exacerbating the effect of trade isolation. Millions of African farmers are doubly challenged, as they receive low prices from export, and have disproportionately higher cost of transport.

A real challenge and opportunity in moving toward the end of extreme poverty is that producers of distinctive export products face extreme isolation from international trade.

In the map in Figure 1.2, the lightest colour represents African producers and farmers who are 500 miles or more from the coast. The next grey band out reflects Africans who are 250 miles or more from the coast – often trade is isolated due to transport challenges.

Why focus on international consumer markets?

Highly distinctive products offer Africa access to high retail prices, as large numbers of quality sensitive consumers pay premiums for the best goods under brands and labels confirming the superior nature of the products. Such consumers also

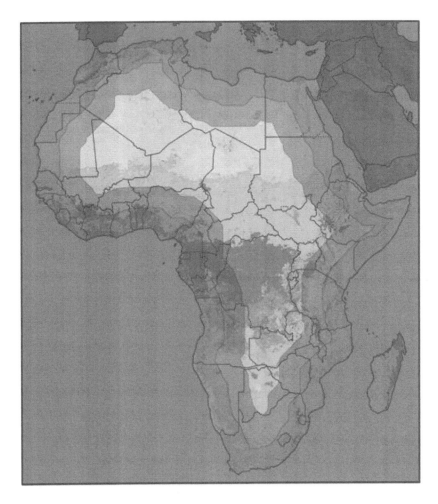

FIGURE 1.2 Map of Africa showing area within 250 miles of the coastline and within 500 miles of the coastline
Source: Light Years IP.

exist in Africa, particularly in cities like Nairobi. In the next 20–30 years, the number of people in Africa whose consumption is brand-intensive and sensitive to quality will increase dramatically. This is based not only on population growth, but education and a growing number of middle- and upper-class African consumers who are brand conscious. Advances in business curriculum and burgeoning social entrepreneurship institutes will open opportunities for African businesses.

The focus of regional integration has substantially been to invest in trade facilitation (e.g. Trademark East Africa and USAID Trade and Investment Hubs) that reduces barriers to trade between African countries. However, at this point in time, many African countries produce commodity products identical to their neighbors. Until price incentives for quality are enabled by widespread adoption of positioning, this weak situation will continue. The future lies in building skills in the methods to earn much higher income based on high-level consumption and prepare for the Africa of the future.

As impact investment genius, Arthur Wood, put it, "most existing development efforts and investment are focused on the 2% of the final retail price that reaches Africa; positioning focuses on the 98% that doesn't."[2]

The importance of intangible value

In recent decades, the intangible value of products in wealthy markets has overtaken the physical value as the main source of corporate income. In 1982, 62 percent of the value of Standard & Poor's 500 companies could be attributed to tangible assets and 38 percent to intangibles. By 1998, only 15 percent of the assets were tangible, while 85 percent were intangible. The shift in the value of assets reflects the ability of these intangible assets (such as brands) to generate income.[3] As discussed below, the non-physical element, the intangible value, is the largest component of global consumption expenditure and global income.

Intangible value is also reflected in the price of individual goods. Fifty years ago, 50 percent of the retail price of most goods was represented by their physical value (materials and production costs) and most of the rest went to the distribution margin. In contrast, today's physical and production costs typically make up only about 5 percent of the retail price, while 95 percent goes to rewards for the design or brand (intangible value) and the distribution margin. Note that the 5 percent of retail price allocated to physical and production costs mirrors the approximately 3–5 percent of retail price received by African producers and exporters of distinctive products.

For producers, artisans, and farmers in the developing world to capture a larger share of the final retail price, they must develop and control intangible value, rather than just the physical (commodity) value they receive now. Producers of exports distinctive enough to have significant intangible value can utilize business positioning with IP to escape the volatility and low prices of the commodity market, securing a higher and more stable income.

The scale of opportunity: 100 million plus producers

Our research indicates there are about 220 products and 100 million producers throughout Sub-Saharan Africa who can benefit from the IP business method, with the potential to deliver large-scale income growth opportunities. We will describe exactly how this can be done with the business method in this book. Unlike other approaches, the method focuses on a fundamental and permanent change to the supply chain power balance, through producer ownership of intellectual property and new producer-owned importing businesses in final market countries.

How an African business can assess opportunities

IP repositioning does not apply to every product out of Africa, but rather to those considered distinctive by quality sensitive consumers paying more for them in retail stores. This section addresses the issue of how to identify opportunities for an African business, whether a producing cooperative or a private sector company buying from producers.

Many African agricultural businesses work across many different products over time, as commodity prices fluctuate. As one example, when Madagascar suffered major damage to vanilla production, export prices shot up to $300/kg from the usual $20–30/kg. A number of Ugandan families revived their vanilla vines and export businesses increased buying vanilla. As usual with commodities, the new production in Uganda peaked at the same time as Madagascar production rebounded. Of course, prices then fell in Ugandan commodity markets. Naturally, many farmers turned their backs on vanilla due to this common outcome, but the opportunity to use positioning for sustained income was grasped by one Ugandan resident who formed a UK retail brand called Ndali.

Opportunities for improved IP Business positioning meet several criteria:

1. Products that are truly distinctive to consumers, with distinctiveness reflected in retail prices in wealthy countries being notably higher than for generic or non-distinctive equivalent products.
2. There is substantial potential income to be obtained by graduating from the existing commodity price to a new distinctive products price and there are enough stakeholders to justify the investment.
3. The farmers, producers, or artisans in the sector can become highly motivated to undergo training in quality control to the standards of the final consumer.
4. The supply chain structure indicates that the strategy cannot be blocked by entrenched interests or foreign ownership.

While the scale of potential IP business is great, it does not apply to every product. To differentiate products with an Intellectual Property component and thus capacity to generate the level of income commensurate with the effort of African stakeholders to engage in IP business positioning methods, it is critical to perform detailed analysis, and to be clear in ruling out products that are unlikely to achieve dramatic income improvement, scale, and promise. The subsequent IP business positioning method and distinctive products chapters delve further into these issues.

The producing business, whether private companies working together or cooperatives or any combination can learn this process from the workbooks associated with this book. The business needs to be willing and able to undergo:

1. Capacity building and training of the business leadership in the intellectual property strategy for the initiative.

2.   Creation of a subsidiary – a new import and marketing company in a key foreign market country. This company will need to be able to control distribution to retail stores. Although beginning an import company may sound complicated, it is actually straightforward, requiring limited space and staff. It is the ownership that is vitally important.

3.   Thorough business planning resulting in a robust, financeable business plan, detailed work plan, schedule, and budget for the pilot period, and profit and loss forecasts.

IP business scale and opportunity

In this book, we reference three large-scale IP business cases. These are Ethiopian fine coffee; Ugandan shea butter; and the Maasai IP because:

1.   The cases have involved in total almost 20 million stakeholders, considering the farmer/producers and their families combined.

2.   The Ethiopian coffee case demonstrates dramatic returns of $101 million that have implications for millions of African and LDC coffee growers.

3.   All three cases involve ownership and control of supply chain plus IP tools.

4.   The Maasai IP Initiative involves a cultural brand of indigenous people with implications for the indigenous people of the world, approximately 6 percent of the global population.

Case study: Ethiopian fine coffee initiative

In the 2006 film, *Black Gold*, Tadesse Meskela, General Manager of the Oromia Union of Cooperatives in Ethiopia, talked about the large gap between the export price paid to Ethiopia and the retail price for Ethiopian fine coffee in UK stores. Tadesse was a forlorn man when walking through UK supermarkets searching for his Ethiopian coffees, as he realized that the return to Ethiopia was as little as 5 percent of the retail price of the fine coffees that Ethiopia had brought to the world. By fine coffee, we mean the coffees prized for many centuries, and the three most notable brands emerged onto the world markets as follows:

•   *Harar* arrived in the Arab world after Harar city became Islamic in 1216 AD
•   *Sidama* is thought to have reached Amsterdam around 1630 AD
•   *Yirgacheffe*, a Sidama-type coffee that Ernesto Illy regarded as the finest in the world[4]

Ethiopian coffees have been in high demand for decades. Harar coffee, for example, secured retail prices in the range of $15.00–$25.00 per pound in Japan,

North America, and Europe in 2007; however the export price paid to Ethiopia was in the range of $1.00–$1.20/lb. This amounts to about 5 percent of retail.

Demand for the fine coffees from Ethiopia continually exceeded supply, which should have led to an increase in price for the Ethiopian producers to grow more coffee, but the export price tracked or followed the price of commodity coffee so that producer prices were too low to cause higher production. Economists regard this as a market failure, when retail price signals do not reach the producing sector. The causes of this market failure are still in place for most African producers and producing businesses exporting distinctive, superior or gourmet products. Very simply, this is because the negotiating power of foreign importers vastly exceeds that of export sectors.

Was Fair Trade helpful? In 2006, the Fair Trade premium was $0.10 more per pound than the commodity price. The importers paid a premium of about $0.10 for Harar and Yirgacheffe. Neither premium was enough to bring forth more production. Over 2006–2007, an initiative had been started that would involve Tadesse in much more than fair trade premiums – the Ethiopian Fine Coffee Trademarking and Licensing Initiative. The initiative directly sought to increase negotiating power for the Ethiopian fine coffee export sector.

The business strategy for the Ethiopian fine coffee sector was sophisticated but not complex and was executed in 2007. It included the following steps:

1. Ethiopia would take ownership of the three brands by registering trademarks for the three fine coffee names in important current and future market countries.
2. Using the power of trademarks to restrain trade, Ethiopia could then require distributors and retail stores globally to obtain licenses to sell any of the three branded coffees.
3. The Ethiopian export sector would gain negotiating power as Ethiopia began to issue licenses, which would make all distributors worldwide obliged to ask Ethiopia for a license.

In business language, the Ethiopian fine coffee sector was being *positioned* with power as the owner of the three popular brands and an Ethiopian-controlled network of licensees. Greater negotiating power resulted in doubled annual fine coffee export income from $100 million in 2007 to over $201 million in 2008.[5] In mid-2007, Tadesse Meskela negotiated export prices from $1.10/lb up to $1.85/lb, then raised prices to $2.75/lb before easing back to an average of about $2.20/lb.[6] Meskela and other export negotiators had effectively taken the three Ethiopian fine coffees out of the commodity market.

Impact on coffee farmer incomes

When the initiative was being designed in 2004, the farmer price was found to be 55 percent of the export price, drawing on detailed field research.[7] The many small rural traders and the exporters, together moving the coffee bags from washing stations to Djibouti FOB (Free on-board ship), together earned the balance of 45 percent of the export price. Rural income was estimated to be 80 percent of export income.

The rural multiplier effect

Poor producers living in rural areas tend to spend the majority of their income locally. This local spending produces an effect known as the rural economic multiplier effect. In Ethiopia, the rural multiplier effect is estimated by the World Bank to be 2.0–2.5 times. Therefore, increased coffee income in Ethiopia is estimated to have produced a total economic impact of 2.05–2.5 times the initial income increase.[8] This means that for every $10 million increase in rural income in Ethiopia, the impact would result in $20.5–25 million in increased economic activity.

For example, the rural multiplier effect for Ethiopia included:

- An increase in the number of older children going to school for the first time
- Renewed roofing for housing
- Upgrades in rural health services through cooperatives

The rural multiplier effect of the Ethiopian Fine Coffee Initiative based on the $101 million increased export income created about a $160–$200 million increase in rural economic activity.

The second phase of the initiative was designed to make coffee distributors exclusive and have them compete for licenses to sell the fine coffees. This phase is expected to further increase the negotiating power of the Ethiopian fine coffee sector and raise their annual export income by a further $300–500 million annually.

Positioning strategies

The Ethiopian fine coffee case demonstrates the application of integrated parts of a positioning strategy. These components are the key factors of correct positioning:

- Retail brands valued by wealthy consumers willing to pay substantial intangible value for fine products
- Ownership of these brands being held by the export sector and the producers
- The power of trademark owners to restrain trade being exerted for a specific result; increased negotiating power when dealing with foreign importers
- Increased negotiating power resulting in increased export prices and incomes.

Business best practice includes:

- The final retail product must be positioned well in the retail market with consumers asking for it under the brand. This was the pre-existing situation for Ethiopian fine coffee.
- The producing business gains most by owning the retail brand on the final retail product – this was achieved for the Ethiopian fine coffee sector, but not by producers of Mozambique cashews, as described in the subsequent chapter.
- The business should, if possible, control the importing and wholesale supply to retail stores in foreign markets.
- Wholesale exclusivity creates ability to control the entire supply chain.
- The process can then be managed to capture a growing share of retail value up to the share of retail value achieved by the most sophisticated competitor.

Positioning solves some tough problems as summarized here:

1. **Extreme remoteness.** Without positioning, remote producers face overwhelming costs of transporting export products that will be priced at global commodity prices at export, that is, when onboard ships at the export port. For commodity producers over 250 miles from a port, the transport cost means their income is at poverty levels.

   Moving Ethiopian fine coffee from Yirgacheffe and Sidama involves over 700 miles of shipment to port. Improved positioning was designed to overcome the transport cost by the export sector selling fine coffee to its own distribution chain – the network of licensed distributors.

2. **Positioning sets Africa on a more sustained pathway.** Many African export industries with distinctive exports are struggling to modernize due to weak negotiating positions. Through better positioning, much more income can be captured from supply chains, allowing investment in all parts of a vertically integrated chain. Sustained income is much more realistic in this structure than when exporting at commodity prices.

3. **Positioning reverses underfunded supply chain weaknesses.** Underfunding and low or non-existent price incentives for quality are holding back progress in many African export sectors, including Ethiopian Fine Leather discussed below.

4. **Counter proposition – incremental development.** Some donors hold the view that it is Africa's turn to manufacture the lowest value products, competing solely on lowest cost of labor, then gradually increase onshore processing.

This book aims to provide clarity on why positioning achieves power now and a direct guide to how to learn positioning.

Eight key learning components of positioning

1. Positioning works best with distinctive exports due to their higher retail value than commodities. Retail prices of such goods include substantial intangible value.
2. Some (importing) company is collecting most of the intangible value, so the African business can profit greatly from taking the position of the importing company.
3. Some African products are already known and valued by consumers, e.g. Ethiopian fine coffee, Ugandan vanilla. Promotion to consumers is not as expensive as in the past. Internet sales are not necessarily the only way for African business to capture consumers, but online promotion can send consumers into stores asking for the brand!
4. Once consumers ask for the brand, African business needs to focus on the company selling the branded product to the retail stores. Own the wholesaler/importer or control this role through exclusive licensing.
5. All processing needs to be controlled, but not necessarily owned – Divine outsourced final production to a European chocolate company, but did not give the chocolate company freedom to put their brand on the product. Almost all producing companies outsource something.
6. Building from highly profitable volume is much more effective than low margin growth which is almost impossible.
7. Brands build over time (Samsung!), so the time to start is now.
8. Accumulating 5–10 or more producing businesses is a more effective way to build the power to reach full positioning, which is the platform for a far more profitable business in 10 years' time.

During the colonial period, African businesses lost control of their options, becoming suppliers to importers who set prices. Post-colonial globalization led to corporations taking the role of setting prices, based almost entirely on the value of commodity products. It is possible to change this by the Intellectual Property business method of positioning described in this book.

Social entrepreneurship in combination

The combination of business entrepreneurship and social concerted action was notable in producing an extraordinary result. This involved business, social entrepreneurs from Light Years IP, and government working in concert:

1. The Ethiopian part of the initiative was the responsibility of the Ethiopian Intellectual Property Office, led by Getachew Mengistie, a highly competent Ethiopian IP lawyer and administrator. Getachew used his role in government to pursue the best interests of his country's fine coffee sector that included farmers, cooperative staff, small traders, and exporters.

2.   Tadesse Meskela acted on behalf of the members of the Oromia Union or Cooperatives and his country by negotiating higher export prices.
3.   The then Ethiopian Prime Minister, Meles Zenawi, decided the government needed to be strong against pressure from Big Coffee to dismantle the initiative during 2006–2007.

Lessons learned

- Trademark strategy alone did not change the bargaining and negotiating power for Ethiopia and did not return any income
- Cooperative unions alone did not return income
- Improving cooperation with Big Coffee did not return income
- It was a system change, enabled by changing the key power through positioning the Ethiopia sector with power. With 4 million coffee farmers and their families comprising 12–16 million people, the change was transformative. It is also a replicable method

IP business positioning: Women's Owned Nilotica Shea initiative (WONS)

The Ethiopian fine coffee sector was supported to use the same IP business tools that any western corporation would consider standard, indeed imperative. Another large group of producers who are being trained to use IP tools and positioning successfully are women producers of Nilotica (East African) shea butter. This particular group of women in northern Uganda and South Sudan are extraordinary. They have been through tremendous conflict alongside poverty. Yet, they produce the best shea butter in the world, as determined by olein content, moisture, and quality. They are, however, poorly positioned in terms of consumer markets.

The Nilotica Shea Initiative involved forming and training the first women's only cooperative in Uganda, with a standard Uganda cooperative constitution. The women have been trained in IP business repositioning, and via the train the trainers model, we have reached 700 women to form the WONS cooperative. Income for this Initiative will result from the sale of luxury skin care products under the producer-owned brand.

Brand experts in concert with a highly respected London-based cosmetics formulator have created packaging for superior product positioning. We will discuss this case study in detail in Chapter 10 as it at once demonstrates IP repositioning for the poorest producers who are extremely isolated from ports and has implications for millions of women farmers and producers of Africa and LDCs. There is no reason why the women, producing the finest shea butter in the world, should sell their butter at $5.00 per kilo to importers when they can reach retail themselves via IP positioning.

FIGURE 1.3 Initial retail logo for WONS shea butter
Source: Light Years IP.

IP business repositioning for cultural brands: The Maasai cultural brand

If the Ethiopian Fine Coffee Trademark and Licensing Initiative results seem spectacular, it is worth knowing that IP business positioning is also available to owners of cultural brands. Following the publication of Ethiopia's success in securing ownership of their famous brands, a group of Maasai elders and leaders asked if we could engage IP strategies for their cultural brand.

FIGURE 1.4 Logo of the Maasai Intellectual Property Initiative
Source: Maasai Intellectual Property Initiative.

Our research indicated strong demand for the cultural brand in the market-place, with over 1,000 companies using Maasai Intellectual Property to sell their products. In the past, a number of large corporate users have Maasai-related sales of over $100 million per year each. Maasai Barefoot Technology alone has sold over $1.5 billion in Maasai-branded shoes.[9] The Maasai receive nothing for the use of their cultural brand and have not been asked for permission. The initiative has created a Maasai representative body to consult with and issue licenses to use the brand. The capacity for income generation is sustainable and is under way.

The gross income over the first 10 years of licensing to the Maasai Intellectual Property Initiative (MIPI) is conservatively estimated at $36 million, based on industry standard royalty rates. This initiative is described in Chapter 5.

We have touched on three large-scale cases that demonstrate IP business positioning: Ethiopian coffee; the Maasai tribe; and Ugandan shea butter producers. While these are only three cases, consider that they represent:

- 4 million Ethiopian coffee farmers, who with an average family size of 4 = 16 million producer families;
- 2 million Maasai with implications for indigenous peoples as the most well-known indigenous peoples group of Africa; and
- Shea butter producers, representing 2 million women producers.

Other IP business opportunities involve large-scale opportunities. This is potentially transformational at scale. It is not complex but sophisticated. It does not require more rainfall or more production. It requires a smart producing and exporting business using a smart entrepreneurial method, and good quality business planning to secure investment.

A summary of IP business opportunities in West Africa

Following the success of the Ethiopian Fine Coffee Initiative, the UK Secretary of State for International Development (DFID) expressed great interest in this method, and asked Light Years IP to identify other African distinctive exports that could produce substantial increases in export income. There *are* many products for which farmers and producers *could* be earning considerably higher incomes. Here, we present several opportunities for West Africa: an analysis of dozens of distinctive African products via desk research; consultations with marketing and brand experts; and in-country African workshops resulted in feasibility studies and determined that distinctive products in West Africa were plentiful.

The opportunities involved:

- Local production size and capacity involving over 100,000 producers per opportunity
- Local capacity to build and sustain stakeholder groups
- An estimated income gain through IP business strategies that was dramatic
- Government climates conducive to success

From this, we determined the following exciting African products representing 4 million farmer/producers based on the above criteria. The four examples are from 14 feasibility studies representing about 30 million African producers who could achieve far higher income using IP business and are summarized below in more detail.

- **Bogolan mudcloth: 2.2 million producers:** A distinctive African textile involving 2.2 million African producers in Mali. Bogolan is also created in Burkina Faso, Guinea, and the Ivory Coast with a total estimated retail value of $800 million per year. Only 3 percent of the retail value from this distinctive product reaches Mali.
- **Ghanaian and Togo black soap:** A distinctive soap with roughly 500,000 producers in Togo. It is also produced in Ghana. An IP Business strategy has been designed to create a new brand to access high end natural beauty care markets that are growing at $1 billion/year.
- **Senegalese tuna:** A highly valued tuna with potential to be classified as "gourmet." There are over 600,000 fishermen in small sector fishing in Senegal. Gourmet tuna retails at approximately $40.00/kilo though Senegalese fishermen only receive $1.00/kilo. There is potential to create an IP strategy for this market and build on already developed institutions in the Senegalese fishing industry.

In addition to West Africa, there are four–five distinctive products per African country, according to our analyses over the past 10 years. In addition, distinctive products abound in the Caribbean, in Latin America, and Asia.[10] IP business positioning strategies are available to developing country producers throughout the world. As one other African opportunity, Madagascar Cocoa responds to the increasing demand for high quality chocolate.

- **Madagascar cocoa:** There is a growing demand for chocolate in developed countries, dubbed "chocolate fever." Developed country consumers are being equipped with new information about the dramatic benefits of dark chocolate and contributing to a surge in demand and price. At the same time, Madagascar cocoa farmers are receiving $0.10 to $0.16 per kg for their cocoa beans. The distinctive island allure could add to an IP marketing and business strategy and follow the success of Ghanaian-owned "Divine Chocolate." The UK company is thriving and the farmer's cooperative based in Ghana is the largest shareholder.

These four distinctive products represent IP Business opportunities that could follow successful models with potential impact on several million producers. This is based on the following rationale:

- The products are highly distinctive and often unique with potential to earn significantly higher IP income.
- Several million farmers and producers in countries with existing stakeholder institutions are capable of forming such institutions.
- Products that could readily succeed in growth sectors of developed country markets. The products include popular products with growing consumer demand such as unique textile products; natural skin care; artisan, gourmet fish products; and gourmet cocoa/chocolate markets represent growing markets.
- The opportunities could be developed with stakeholder formation and capacity building; development of brand and marketing plans; and ownership of import companies in foreign markets.
- The advantage of each of these four products is the capacity to create high end brands to last 100 years with sustainable income return, rather than remaining dependent on volatile commodity or local markets.

Malian mudcloth: 2.2 million producers in Mali

The Business Positioning with IP opportunity for Mali draws on a unique textile made with natural dyes, and instantly recognized as African. There are roughly 2.2 million producers of mudcloth in Mali alone, though it is also produced in Burkina Faso, Guinea, and the Ivory Coast. Our feasibility study has focused on Mali because this unique cloth is most associated with Mali, and with 2.2 million producers, the potential to earn higher income can be transformative.

At present, Bogolan cloth is turned into various forms of clothing for both women and men; furniture cushions; rugs and hangings. Our estimates show that the retail market for Bogolan mudcloth alone, not including the finished product, is about $800 million/year. At present, only about 3 percent of this retail value reaches Mali.

Preliminary recommendations include:

- Given the increased demand for unique products, particularly textile and clothing that has a special story of origin, the opportunity for Mali to earn much higher export income is ripe as their product is unique and instantly recognizable.

- The formation of a Bogolan authority (L'authorité Bogolan) to create a register of the unique patterns, certification marks to differentiate true Malian mudcloth from counterfeit and to establish market strategies.
- The formation of a stakeholder organization to educate and engage artisans.
- Wide-scale education of women about the IP value opportunities possible in the larger, international markets.

Togo black soap

This unique soap is produced in Togo, Niger, Ghana, and Benin. We estimate that a total of 500,000 women in Togo alone are involved in the production of black soap, producing an estimated 550 to 1,700 tons valued at approximately $6–8 million/year. The volume produced is high, but our estimates show that only about 1 percent is sold on international markets. This is largely due to a lack of knowledge by the Togan, Nigerian, Ghanaian, and Benin producers regarding the value of the natural skin and beauty care market at the international level. As described further in Chapter 9 on women's empowerment, the natural skin and beauty care market is estimated at over $350 billion in 2015 data, with upward trends for natural products. In addition, seventeen Asian, Russian, and New Zealand markets had a combined cosmetics and toiletries market worth $60 billion in 2015.[11]

FIGURE 1.5 Bars of black soap
Source: Shutterstock.

There is need for IP education to create a viable stakeholder group and distribution through to retail in foreign markets. The soap is all-natural with significant healing properties, with vitamins A and E and has been proven effective for eczema and psoriasis. The natural beauty market is growing at about $1 billion/year worldwide with an ongoing search for new, innovative, and effective products of high quality, natural ingredients and effectiveness, particularly against aging. This soap is relevant to the baby care segment as well, another growing avenue. An additional promising note is that consumer willingness to try new brands is particularly high in the skin and beauty care arena. Togo black soap is poised to create a viable IP business repositioning strategy to:

- Create a women's owned import company in a high end market such as Paris or London.
- Develop a high end brand platform, utilizing LYIP brand and marketing experts with a skilled formulator and attractive packaging.
- Engage in widespread IP training and quality control training in Togo and Ghana to form a women's stakeholder group to learn the full IP business positioning method.
- Current returns show that Togo black soap producers are receiving less than 1 percent of the potential of the income returns from their product, but have the capacity to have a competitive advantage.

Senegalese gourmet tuna

There are approximately 600,000 Senegalese fishermen, with the small-scale fishing sector generating 60 percent of fishing exports with overall fishing generating 70 percent of the government's reported annual revenue. Dakar, the capital city, is an important Atlantic tuna port with one cannery operating in Senegal, SNCDS, exporting the majority of its production to Europe. There is an opportunity for Senegal to gain more income from traditional fishing and improve the livelihoods of thousands of fishermen.

FIGURE 1.6 Tuna
Source: Shutterstock.

Currently, fishermen receive less than $1.00 per kilo of tuna. Exporters/canners are receiving around $4.95 per kilo; wholesalers are receiving about $20.00 and retailers in gourmet tuna markets, $40.00/kilo.[12]

The IP business positioning opportunity:

- Producing a gourmet tuna brand and capitalizing on the environmental and cultural aspects of traditional fishing methods is recommended. Senegal has the opportunity to develop a product that is distinct in the final retail market helping the fishing industry to earn more income.
- The Senegalese inter-professional artisan fishing sector organization, CONIPAS, is taking action to strengthen the small-scale fishing sector by improving facilities including quays, preservation, and processing plants to foreign hygiene and quality standards.
- These above strategies combined could result in total income gains in the order of $40–70 million per year, based on the burgeoning increase for gourmet, artisan tuna, and western countries' movement away from meat products toward fish.

Madagascar cocoa

Industry leaders are calling the current surge in demand for dark gold, "chocolate fever." The feasibility study report by Light Years IP analyzed the chocolate market by products, sales category, and geography, and studies the major market drivers, restraints, and opportunities for the chocolate market in North America, Europe, and Asia.[13] The global chocolate market is expected to grow from $83.2 billion in 2010 to $98.3 billion in 2016 at an estimated CAGR of 2.7 percent from 2011 to 2016.[14]

The consumer trend to dark, rich chocolate, high in cocoa content and with strong natural flavor has sent the chocolate industry off in search of high end, single origin cocoa sources from all parts of the world. Some varieties of cocoa have seen an 800 percent increase in price in recent years with traders paying 10 times the market price for specialty cocoa beans. Around 60 percent of growers in Madagascar produce cocoa on small family farms of about 2–3 hectares. Data suggests that these cocoa producers are receiving between $0.10 and $0.16 per kilogram for their cocoa beans.

Madagascar is in a favorable position to raise its export income from cocoa through applying a careful business strategy to optimize earnings on the total volume available. As the world chocolate market burgeons, Madagascar has two important IP components to capitalize upon: An allure as an exotic island (unknown to most consumers) for which a strong brand platform could be developed; and a well-developed quality of cocoa.

The IP business positioning strategy:

Divine Chocolate is a UK-based highly successful distribution and marketing company with a Ghanaian cooperative as the largest shareholder. The model will be described as a detailed case study in subsequent chapters. Similar strategies that advanced Ghanaian cocoa growers could be applied to Madagascar such as creation of a viable stakeholder group; advancement in training and education; and IP business strategies involving the creation of an import company in London. These combined to be very effective for Ghana. A similar, replicable model could be created by Madagascar closer to retail to create a valuable brand platform with substantial packaging and retail presence. How to do this is not a pipe dream, or rhetoric about empowerment, but the specifics of how to create such businesses, based on the combination of distinctive product + Intellectual Property business tool + positioning product towards retail consumers + ownership of an import company = higher income and sustainable livelihoods for millions.

Summary

African farmers and producers, including children, labor for a fraction of the potential retail value of their products. With over 1.8 billion women farmers in the world, producing about 40 percent of the world's food supply, enabling them to earn a living income is within our grasp. Our initiatives over the past 10 years have included millions of farmers and producers.

To change the landscape forever will involve training in the same business methods common to most corporations. Most business is indeed Intellectual Property business as examples ranging from the estimated $27 billion Nike brand to Apple Computers and closer to agriculture, Sunkist oranges, clearly demonstrate. Herein, the brand is worth more than the product. An analysis of Standard & Poor's 500 companies shows that the overwhelming majority of value (70–80 percent +) is accrued from intangible value, rather than raw materials. This translates into trillions of dollars in the world economy based in IP.

What does this mean for Africa?

In just 13 feasibility studies, we have found that Africans are losing about an estimated $25 billion per year in income from failing to take advantage of IP business for growth based on their distinctive products. It is within our capacity to change this. Widespread training in IP business coupled with project-related implementation is fundamental. We have spent the last 16 years perfecting and implementing the methodology called IP business positioning. It requires solid business thinking, and learning at a certain level of sophistication, which is what the following chapters will illustrate. In the next chapter, we turn from the scale of opportunity to efforts that have tried to change power for farmers and producers, such as Fair Trade, value-added, and branding.

While the opportunities are ripe, it is important to note that the products selected above as case examples are the result of a stringent process of analysis. The positioning method with resultant income does not work if applied without rigorous assessment of final markets; analysis of global trends and niche markets; awareness of the need for stakeholder formation and ownership capacity; and other factors. These methods will be described as we go forward with subsequent chapters. For now, the opportunities in the pipeline include the chart showing the fine, distinctive product, country, investment needed to implement a full positioning strategy; potential beneficiaries based on farmer/producer numbers; and income projections. These are a sample of opportunities available for an IP business positioning strategy.

Notes

1 R. Layton, P. Tiffen, D. Layton, M.R. Chu, A. Dressler, H. Sarkissian, B. Popovich, and J. Howkins, "Distinctive values in African exports," Light Years IP, London, 2008.
2 Arthur Wood, Partner, Total Impact Advisors (TIA), in conversation, London, 2015.
3 Layton et al., "Distinctive values in African exports," p. 5.
4 T. Meskela interviewed for the film *Black Gold*, 2007.
5 Reported by the Ethiopian Ministry of Trade and Industry, that credited the Initiative as the cause of the $101 million gain. There was an increase in commodity prices in FY2008 over FY2007, but this acted only as a floor to freely negotiated prices that averaged double the 2007 export price. DFID, the World Bank, and Ron Layton funded the design with a team including Pauline Tiffen.
6 Tadesse Meskela in conversation with Ron Layton, June–December 2007.
7 E.Gabre-Madhin, "Of markets and middlemen, transforming agricultural markets in Ethiopia," IPRI, 2001.
8 J. Majok, "The rural multiplier effect report," Light Years IP, 2010.
9 Reports by Continental Enterprises and Qwest Research Investigations, LLC.
10 M. Brindle and R. Layton, "Distinctive values in Caribbean exports," OAS and CIDA, 2011. The analysis of 16 Caribbean IP positioning strategies can be viewed at www.lightyearsip.net.
11 US Department of Commerce, Cosmetic and Toiletries Market Overview, 2015, http://trade.gov/industry/materials/ITA.FSC.Cosmoprof.2015_final2.pdf.
12 Layton et al., "Distinctive values in African exports."
13 Ibid.
14 Markets and Markets, "Global chocolate, cocoa beans, lecithin, sugar and vanilla market by market share, trade, prices, geography trend and forecast (2011–2016)," website: (www.marketsandmarkets.com/PressReleases/global-chocolate-market.asp), accessed March 2016.

2

CHANGING THE POWER

Begin with the end in mind

What do we mean by begin with the end in mind?

Unless we know where we are going, it is hard to get there. Yet, many trade strategies do not begin with the end in mind. They focus on increasing production. If a country produces something, and better still, produces a lot of something, the common wisdom is to focus on that product and produce more. This often results in over production and diminishing or volatile prices. Other strategies begin with the end in mind – a vision – but fail to provide a systematic method for achieving the improved end.

This chapter will address:

- Beginning with the end in mind – changing the power through correct positioning
- Several twentieth-century trade policies intended to change the relative powerlessness of developing countries, including:
    - Fair Trade and its benefits and challenges
    - Branding
    - Value-added practices
    - Corporate Social Responsibility (CSR)
- A case study for 1 million Mozambique cashew farmers
- A power model that illustrates power and dependency and ways to change the power available to LDC farmers and producers.

We have argued that a fundamental reason why millions of African farmers, producers, and exporters remain poor is that the bulk of the value from their distinctive products accrues to importers and retailers outside their borders. In their present trade-isolated and commodity-based product focus, they will remain poor, no matter how hard they work, how much they produce, or how much money is poured into production-based solutions. There is, in fact, little to no negotiation – farmers and producers receive commodity prices that are on average 3–5 percent of the prices their distinctive products are sold for in developed country higher end markets, outside of Africa.

As we have described, the situation looks like that shown in Figure 2.1.

The figure shows the average results from 13 feasibility studies performed on African distinctive products involving 100,000 farmer producers or more. The average income to African exporters was 2 percent of the retail and the average income back to farmer/producers was 3 percent of the retail income. These products were distinctive products such as fine coffees, teas, oils, flowers, cocoa, artisan cloth, artisan tuna, and cut flowers.[1]

Why does this situation of powerlessness continue, and what can be done about it? So far, we have described the situation of weak negotiating power. And, we have shown that the bulk of aid from developed western countries supports alleviation of the symptoms of poverty – maternal health, HIV/AIDS, disease, disaster, and food security.

There have been many advances made against poverty. The number of people living in poverty has been reduced. Millions have been vaccinated against deadly diseases, advances have been made against malaria, HIV/AIDS, and in education.

The last billion people in extreme poverty include some who produce high quality distinctive export products that generate hundreds of millions of dollars in wealthy retail global markets. To remove obstacles involves changing the business

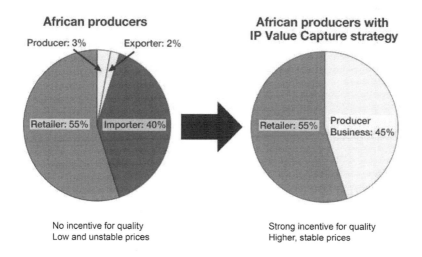

FIGURE 2.1 Transformational change
Source: Light Years IP.

positioning of these producers. Through rural multipliers, the direct impact of increased income for producers will spread to raise the economy of whole regions.

West Equatoria state in South Sudan is a very clear example – no sealed roads, 1,500 miles from the nearest port, a post-conflict region with continuing outbursts of civil war. There appears every reason to give up on West Equatoria until the conflict ends, *except* for the business reality that something can be done right now toward the ending of extreme poverty.

The power balance has not changed, and until that changes, hundreds of millions of Africans will remain in extreme poverty. Starting with that end in mind, the time is now.

The end in mind

This book sets out a business method that needs to be implemented with the end in mind at all times. It is not incremental growth with inadequate incentives to achieve substantially higher quality. It is directed growth based on a clear definition of the goal – African business correctly positioned through business best practice fully implemented.

Changing the relative power of African producers

The following section describes wide-scale initiatives aimed to change trade power and improve the negotiating ability of African farmers and producers. Have these worked? There have been and continue to be efforts to change the income power of LDC producers. Several of these are described below, including the positive effects and the limits of these interventions.

Fair Trade

Fair Trade is a social movement that began in the 1940s, when a few organizations in Europe and the United States began to reach out to poor communities to help them sell their products at better prices. Fair Trade has four major organizational arms, one of which began in 1989 and the others in the early 1990s to further advance fair trade: Fair Trade International, Fair Trade USA, World Fair Trade, and the Network of European Workshops.[2]

The movement has grown substantially in the UK where there are 500 "Fair Trade towns" as of 2010, 118 universities, over 6,000 churches, and over 4,000 UK schools registered in the Fair Trade Schools Scheme.[3] In 2011, over 1.2 million farmers and workers in more than 60 countries participated in Fair Trade, and $85 million in Fair Trade premiums was paid. According to Fair Trade International, nearly six out of 10 consumers have seen the Fair Trade mark and almost nine in 10 of them trust it.

Fair Trade has been an important strategy because Fair Trade has:

- Raised consumer consciousness about the origins of products and the supply chain conditions affecting the producers
- Helped African farmers and producers by raising awareness about the importance of final markets and consumer preferences
- Drawn attention to the incredible talent and effort of African farmers and producers
- Raised awareness about corporate profits made at the expense of poor farmers, artisans, and producers, prompting strategies such as Corporate Social Responsibility (CSR).

However, the unintended effects and limits of Fair Trade include:

- The concept of raising the producer price above the commodity level sounds good. However, according to basic economic theory, an increase in price will result in an increase in supply. Over-supply has always been a reality for Fair Trade participants.
- The cost of becoming Fair Trade certified is borne by low-income farmers and producers. It is often quite out of the reach of small plot farmers who are the majority of African farmers.
- Fair Trade membership cuts into already low profits for more isolated African farmers and producers. We cannot call them profit "margins" because there really is no margin, as the cost of transporting goods along with the additional certification cost reduces profits – usually to minuscule levels. In short, the question from the farmer/producer perspective is, is it worth it to become Fair Trade certified?
- In some cases, such as at Divine Chocolate, the distribution company and the branded product are correctly positioned and a large proportion of net profit passes to the Kuapo Kokoo farmers' union of cooperatives. Here, Fair Trade is part of the solution, whereas in most other situations, the farmer/producer may not benefit from Fair Trade except at the cost of other farmers.

Does Fair Trade work?

The goal of Fair Trade is to support small-scale producers and workers who are marginalized from the benefits of trade. The Fair Trade vision is a world in which all small producers and workers can enjoy secure and sustainable livelihoods, fulfill their potential and decide on their future.[4] And while outcomes and outputs such as reduced food insecurity; greater access to markets; better bargaining power; and overall fairer prices are important goals, the reality is more difficult.

According to a June 2014 report, commissioned by DFID and performed by SOAS of London, workers at Fair Trade farms in both Uganda and Ethiopia appeared to be worse off by wage and work environment criteria than those at non-Fair Trade sites.[5]

Further, "This research was unable to find any evidence that Fair Trade has made a positive difference to the wages and working conditions of those employed in the production of the commodities produced for Fair Trade certified export in the areas where the research has been conducted. This is the case for "smallholder" crops like coffee – where Fair Trade standards have been based on the erroneous assumption that the vast majority of production is based on family labor – and for "hired labor organization" commodities like the cut flowers produced in factory-style greenhouse conditions in Ethiopia.[6]

Fair Trade has raised consumer consciousness about product origins. Fair Trade has over 1 million farmer participants, and Fair Trade premiums of over $65 million have been paid out. The $65 million also represents the loss made by some producers due to over-supply.

Fair Trade has not changed the power balance. It keeps African and LDC farmers and producers locked into commodity markets, relatively powerless, dependent situations, all the while enabling richer country citizens to feel a bit better about their consumption patterns. Where Fair Trade *has* made some difference is in situations where it has been coupled with branding and repositioning strategies, alongside farmer and producer ownership.

For example, Divine Chocolate is an excellent example of a producer-owned cooperative and a smart branding, repositioning strategy. That Divine is also Fair Trade certified helped the growth of sales of Divine Chocolate during the boom in Fair Trade consumption, especially in the UK. Very good management at the company is also to be credited for successful brand launch and continued expansion since 1998.

Divine Chocolate is marketed in the US, the UK, and Europe, in 13 countries overall. The farmers own 45 percent of the Ghanaian-based cooperative. The chocolate is manufactured outside of Ghana, packaged, branded, and marketed in sophisticated, modern ways in higher end markets such as Whole Foods.

The revenue stream is sufficient to produce significantly higher income for the Ghanaian farmers. Since revenue streams are higher for Divine Chocolate, Fair Trade certification costs are worth the effort to the farmers.

Direct Trade

A number of social innovators have improved farmer income by eliminating intermediaries from trade supply chains in coffee and other products. Direct sales from farmer cooperative to foreign retailer make it possible for the cooperative to receive more income. Some developed country Fair Trade companies have moved to Direct Trade and promote the benefits, which can be substantial.

Achieving scale in direct trade has proven difficult. The Ethiopian fine coffee export volume in 2004 was around 100 million lbs (45 million kg), far too large to handle through direct trade arrangements, cooperative to retailer. A different solution with widespread scalable application is described in this book.

FIGURE 2.2 Divine Chocolate
Source: Divine Chocolate.

Branding

Branding is another trade strategy aimed at overcoming power imbalance. Brands are effective at signaling quality and intangible value, and brands have worked for modern developed country companies. For most well-known brands such as Coca-Cola, the brand is worth more than the physical aspects of the product.

The benefits of branding are that branding:

- Identifies products as distinctive
- Creates consumer awareness with the brand and
- Enables competitive advantage with consumers to the extent that they remain loyal to brands.

The failures of branding

- The benefit and price differential created by branding often stays in foreign market countries!

- Branding in isolation does not change the power balance that keeps developing country producers of distinctive products locked in a 3 percent share of retail value.
- Some African countries are now moving to "brand" their products by country brand such as Ugandan cotton or Kenyan tea or by the local name of a growing area (as geographical indications).
- However, country brands are often not preferred by consumers in foreign markets.
- Again, consider Divine Chocolate. It is from Ghana. Divine Chocolate's success in 13 countries is from a name that consumers recognize as fine, distinctive chocolate, but it is not branded, "Ghanaian chocolate."
- Consumers often do not recognize the brand value of a product from a country when those brands do not equate to an understanding by the consumer of a superior product. For example, Nike shoes have achieved brand recognition, but a tennis shoe branded American shoes may not. In short, the brand must have meaning to consumers first and foremost.
- Branding alone is not a full business strategy if the benefits of the brand such as improved income are not forthcoming.
- It is critical that African farmers and producers acquire greater control over the supply and distribution chain, and couple this with a variety of IP tools, which may include branding, but are not limited to branding.
- Branding is expensive and should be coupled with a fuller IP business strategy so that it returns income to the rightful owners of the brand – the farmers and producers.
- Branding does not change the power balance for developing country producers. A brand without control of the supply chain for that brand puts the burden of costs of the brand onto developing country producers, with the benefit of the brand still accrued to western importers!

The following case study of a brand applied to Mozambique cashews illustrates the point of a branding strategy that did not benefit Mozambique cashew growers. Their numbers exceed 1 million.

The case study of Mozambique: branding without positioning

Mozambique remains one of the world's poorest countries, with over half the population living below the poverty line. Mozambique is ranked 168th of 177 countries by the UNDP Human Development Index, and among the poorest citizens, half of all children are malnourished, and one in five dies before his or her fifth birthday.[7]

In Mozambique, a very fine cashew is gathered and it is known as one of the finest cashews in the world. Over 1 million farmers are involved in cashew farming in Mozambique. Cashews are important to the history of Mozambique, once the largest exporter in the world. For much of the twentieth century, Portuguese-run plantations made Mozambique the world's leading cashew producer. Into the 1960s, as much as half the world's cashews were produced in Mozambique.[8]

There is a natural desire to return to this state of former glory, although for the farmers who simply must grow the product that will provide enough returns, the aspirations are simply to receive reasonable income.

Currently, cashew nuts are not providing adequate income to encourage or convince farmers that investment will pay off. Indeed, the overwhelming majority of Mozambique cashew farmers are poor and processing workers put in hard work for modest pay in factories. What has happened here? It is an example of trade powerlessness coupled with efforts to execute a trade strategy, but without all of the critical pieces to do so effectively.

Much has been studied and written about the cashew industry in Mozambique.[9] Debates continue regarding the merits of one trade or tariff policy over another, the benefits of value addition, the need to increase production and reclaim past superlatives. Beneath the layers of debate and policy is the fact that farmers cannot earn enough income from growing cashew nuts to sustain even the most fundamental activities necessary to continue to produce and harvest the nuts. So they turn to other crops that, for the current harvest season, pay more.

Cashew exporters and processors fare little better, both earning small margins. Processors, though, incur significant capital costs and bear the risks associated with those costs.

To advance Mozambique, under USAID funding, TechnoServe, an international development consulting organization, designed a project to refurbish Mozambique processing factories, so Mozambique could sell processed nuts.[10] The rationale was that Mozambique produced great cashews and should follow the agro-industrial model of processing the nuts, selling them under a Mozambique brand and thus earn more profit. In Mozambique, there is a "triangle of production," and the majority of production and processing occurs in Nampula province with total processing capacity estimated at around 40–45,000 tonnes in 2008.[11]

In the first phase of the project, the "Zambique" brand was printed on international shipping boxes when the product was exported to the Netherlands and other countries. Regrettably, the importers were in complete control of the product on receipt and Zambique was not promoted as a retail brand. The importers threw away the boxes with the Zambique label as it was unrecognized by consumers.

The lesson learned here is that wholesale brands are almost always unwise. Without consumer demand for a retail brand owned by the export sector, a wholesale brand is worthless.

Value addition, shelling, peeling, and grading in the instance of Mozambique's cashews, ostensibly earns more revenue for Mozambique than exporting raw nuts. However, upon examining the costs of exporting raw nuts versus processing, one finds that the margins are effectively the same.[12]

What went wrong, despite best intentions?

Cashew farmers, exporters, and processors are trapped in an unequal trading structure based on the commodity market. Wholesalers and retailers together earn more than 95 percent of the total margins despite the fact that the quality of the nuts is directly linked to the cashew farmers and the growing conditions in Mozambique and is unrelated to any inputs or secondary processing that importers or wholesalers may perform. Sadly, however, the Mozambique cashew producers ended up getting less money for processed nuts than the unprocessed ones.

The lower income was due to two factors. First, import tariffs are applied at a higher rate to processed goods than unprocessed ones. More significantly, the larger share of the cashews' retail value was still taken by foreign importers outside of Mozambique. The strategy was an expensive disaster for farmers and the workers who were subject to very poor labor conditions inside of the processing factories. In addition, the profit margins were so low for the owners in exporting the cashews, they were unable to increase wages for the factory workers that remained low. The conditions were at near slave labor and once the factories were built and the expense incurred, these conditions were difficult to reverse.

During Phase Two, TechnoServe reports that it followed some age-old wisdom, as presented on the front side of their study, and discussed in their report:

> The place for the factory is by the side of the farm.
>
> *Manufacturers' Record, July 3, 1913*

In the case of Mozambique cashews, well-meaning development experts believed in a simple model that had worked for western exports for a century. This involves taking products that were grown or produced in a region, and enabling producers to process the products and augment them with value-added strategy. Experts believed this would help Mozambique employment, as well. The benefits, however, did not accrue to the Mozambique farmers or producers.

This is a particularly dramatic example of a value-added failure. It is dramatic given the scope of impact. Over 40 percent of Mozambican farmers, or as noted above, nearly 1 million households, grow cashew, which is one of the few reliable cash crops that farmers are able to grow in the country. In Nampula province, cashews account for nearly one-fifth of total household income.[13]

What *could* have worked here? Supported by DFID funding, we conducted a feasibility study to "pivot" the Phase One failure and most importantly, to address the situation affecting over 1 million farmers. It rests on the key distinctive element – Mozambique cashews ARE truly superior, in size, taste, and quality.

Pivoting the failure to success

We outlined a strategy whereby Mozambican cashew stakeholders could earn greatly improved margins for their nuts instead of exporter margins by establishing their own wholesale and marketing company, particularly if targeted at one–two importing countries rather than the world commodity market. If Mozambique sold last year's volume of cashew kernels to retail through a producer-owned import company, 2,000 metric tonnes would earn almost $25 million. By owning and controlling a distribution channel, Mozambique can earn significantly higher income on their cashews and more importantly, bypass the price fluctuations of the commodity market. Mozambique would negotiate prices from a more equitable position. Over time, prices will become predictable and farmers will be able to invest in their crops with good certainty of returns on their investment.

- Assess cashew markets around the world and determine the best positioning for Mozambique cashews and for the export sector in the supply chain
- Acquire top-level brand experts to create brand packaging, messaging, and product positioning
- Enable ownership of an import/distribution company owned by the Mozambique cashew farmers selling branded product direct to retail in one–two countries that currently purchase their processed cashews from middle men
- Enable stakeholder training to create and own a cooperative to receive the brand-generated revenue

Though this may sound simplistic, it is not. It is what a corporation would do to prevent importers and wholesalers from taking all of the profit.

Value-added

The Mozambique cashew project, overseen by TechnoServe, subcontractors to USAID, also engaged a Value-added, a popular trade-related strategy in International Development. This usually means helping least developed country (LDC) farmers and producers to do what they do better, i.e. if a country grows coffee, then supporting better irrigation and more efficient farming via tools and equipment would be a "value-added" strategy.

There are many examples in Africa, such as the Clinton Global Initiative (CGI) in Rwanda for coffee with supportive irrigation. Sometimes, value-added means simply more efficient processes or advancing awareness of marketing. We note this respectfully because value-added, like Fair Trade, can be an advance for developing country farmers and producers with improvements in farming and production. Our view is that it does not fundamentally change the power. The following section summarizes the benefits and challenges of the widely used "value-added" approach:

Value-added benefits:

- Attempt to support developing country farmers and producers in what they are already doing by way of farming and producing.
- Support local organizations to improve on methods ranging from better tools or advanced irrigation to organizational capacity building.
- Operate on a western model: industrialization with more efficient manufacturing and distribution helped elevate western nations out of poverty, and even more recently, S. Korea and China. The problem is that the manufacturing wave is over and African nations can hardly compete with the low costs of labor and manufacturing in countries such as India, as the case study of Mozambique cashews illustrates.

Value-added strategies often fail because:

- The value or higher price is still taken outside of the developing country in foreign markets because value-added is not coupled with producer ownership or correct positioning toward final, retail markets.
- Processed products are often more costly to export than raw products due to trade tariffs.
- Value-added by manufacturing is usually costly to implement, as in building factories with low price incentives to factory owners which sets up poor labor conditions (near slavery in some cases we have observed).
- Value-added strategies are non-sustainable because the country producers are still receiving low returns and there is no price incentive, creating dependency on more aid to support the output of value-added (failing factories) and other components of the value-added strategy.
- Competing in manufacturing is difficult against low-cost labor countries such as China and India.
- Sometimes the produces discouragement as another trade-based strategy fails.

Corporate Social Responsibility (CSR)

Corporate social responsibility came about as corporations were either pressured to provide something back to low-income farmers and producers, or arrived at the position from the realization that margins of 80 percent + from points of product origins created some ethical issues. In many cases, CSR operates as excellent PR as consumer consciousness has advanced over the past 15–20 years. And, we don't discount the reality that corporations are comprised of individuals, oftentimes with genuine conscience and goodwill toward low-income producers.

The value of Corporate Social Responsibility

- Similar to Fair Trade, CSR has advanced consumer awareness of product origins and conditions of manufacturing such as sweatshops.
- Some organizations have legitimate ethical concerns about low-income farmers and producers and have been public about this concern ranging from diamonds mined to environmental issues relevant to their businesses.
- CSR has put corporations into the position of stating issues and making public commitments to consumers.
- Nike, for example, with its sweatshop manufacturing has come to light in social media with some advances made.
- In some cases, CSR has been helpful in connecting like-minded, socially conscious individuals and networks who in turn support projects in social impact investment as in Acumen Fund initiatives and the Ashoka project in Hybrid Value Chains – projects linking corporations to low-income markets.

The failures of Corporate Social Responsibility

- The average CSR defined company gives under 1 percent of profit to support their CSR programs.
- In recent years, the Top Ten rated CSR programs including Citigroup, Bank of America, and Walmart gave 1–1.7 percent of their profits to CSR programs.
- It is debatable if CSR enables exploitive behavior by large corporations (80 percent profit margins from low-income producers) as the CSR model provides a means of justifying enormous margins from low-income producers under this ethical sounding rubric, Corporate Social Responsibility.
- CSR provides extraordinarily positive public image and marketing to corporations. It is hard to measure what it is worth to a consumer when, at point of purchase, they are reminded that their store is giving to build a well or dam or help children with school uniforms in a notoriously poor country. Very few consumers are likely to check facts to determine if a project actually exists, or consider the cost of a well, or school, if they are able to feel good about their purchase.

Making markets work/market development

Kenya Markets Trust, a Nairobi-based technical agency funded by the Gatsby Foundation and DFID, is doing extremely good work to raise standards of farm production and agro-processing plants. The work applies international standard best practice in technical fields aiming to increase farm income within the national borders. Quality improvements will help farmers in export markets, but at commodity pricing for exports, there is often little incentive to vigorously work on quality.

Trade facilitation

Similarly, trade facilitation aims to reduce the administrative, technical, and customs barriers to exporting among neighboring countries and to foreign export markets. Excellent projects are reducing the time delay for loaded trucks crossing the border from Uganda into Kenya.

However, the negotiating power between most African and LDC exporters and foreign importers remains unchanged at the border. Correct positioning means directly addressing the 95–97 percent of retail value that currently never reaches Africa.

The role of power in improving income from trade

In summary, many efforts have been under way to advance trade, beginning in the late twentieth century and into the twenty-first century. It is not surprising that trade-based solutions model elements of business that have worked in the developed world, such as branding and value-added, improved processing and quality control. The challenge is that "pieces" of trade strategies applied to lower income farmers are not wrong, and have some impact; however, they generally ignore the four critical components that most increase income.

1. Enabling intangible value in final consumer goods to be controlled by stakeholder-owned Intellectual Property.
2. Enabling stakeholder use of IP tools to generate income return to the producers.
3. Enabling ownership or control of the supply chain "to the door of the retail store."
4. Enabling sustained income gains when power is truly changed and placed into the hands of the export sector stakeholders including producers, producing businesses, and exporters.

IP business positioning has as its core objective altering the dependency position of African producers. Unless we change bargaining power, we cannot change income substantially. It can be modeled as follows:

One tool for considering the current dependency situation relative to income received, and how to address it, is in the form of a power model.

The following "power" model demonstrates a mapping of power-dependency situations.[14] The idea is if we can map out and draw the dependency, we can often see where to best intervene.

It begins with the following assumptions:

•   In any power-dependency situation, A is trying to accomplish something and A represents the Agent or Agents.

- B is the target. In the case of Africans, B represents a target market.
- The "X" is what is wanted and X1 is what is needed.
- C is the context, the history, laws, policy, norms, and rules that dictate the relationship.

The power and dependency relationship is more readily visualized when we diagram the four aspects of dependency. We can then see what the current power-dependency situation looks like, and where interventions may successfully alter power.

In the situation in Africa, the A are the African farmers and producers. They want a better price (X) but are largely dependent upon B or export markets, exporters that do not pay them a higher price.

In a power situation, it is incumbent upon B to keep A most dependent, such as being or appearing to be the sole buyer, or holding common price collusion with other Bs, by posturing, or engaging in tactics to keep A dependent.

The context, or policies, rules, history, and other elements of the trade situation, foster the dependency.

Figure 2.3 diagrams the relative dependency of African farmer/producers upon markets outside of their borders. In any relationship, power is the inverse of dependency.

For example, we consider a classic dependency situation and show its application to the powerless situation of millions of Africans. Consider for a moment an employment situation wherein the employer has thousands of real and potential

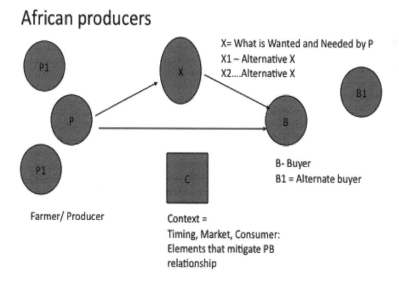

FIGURE 2.3 African producers and market dependency
Source: Light Years IP from Margaret Brindle and Lisa Mainiero, 2000. *Managing Power through Lateral Networking*, Quorum-Greenwood Press.

job applicants. When those who *want* something outnumber the opportunity, this creates or facilitates a powerless or dependent situation.

Such was the situation in the Americas during waves of immigration, wherein there were 10 people for every job in the steel mills. The steel mill owners were intolerant, gave few benefits, had control over labor. The term robber baron was born, to reflect the relative power of the steel giants who controlled entire cities as immigrants and low wage workers were dependent. This repeated in the UK and Europe during industrialization and throughout the nineteenth century with low wage workers at the mercy of bosses. The situation changed when employees organized into trade unions and exerted a situation of coalition, evening out the power balance. However, unions and organizations are limited if those unions remain dependent upon the same jobs, bosses, and factories that hold low wages. While workers can sometimes affect the power balance by organizing and reducing dependency, this has limits. It is based on the relative dependency of the workers and the resource desired, in this case, factory work and lack or abundance of options.

This situation repeats in many contexts. The essential point is that power is the inverse of dependency. If you are the only factory and there is demand, you have power, be it Walmart or steel mills. For African farmers dependent upon commodity markets and exporters at the port, such as the million Mozambique cashew farmer/producers, they are currently dependent upon limited importers who control prices – low, low prices.

But, there is a second important point. Power is not static. Power is a product also of construction – we enable others to have more power over us, relative to our own demand or dependency for the resource. Thus, if I decide that I can meet the need supplied by whatever or whoever has power over me, by myself or with others, or go around it to alternative others, be they buyers, jobs, or markets, the relative power changes.[15] In the terms of our model, if the As are able to go around B and gain knowledge, information, and alternative markets, power shifts greatly.

It is assumed that brands change power if they reflect distinctiveness. Branding of distinctive products is part of a business strategy to protect the intellectual property of distinctive products, as described above. However, if branding keeps producers locked into the same dependency on B – exporters and importers – the brand alone fails to change the power.

Examples include Coca-Cola which came from a pharmaceutical product used for indigestion, then fizzy water and additional coloring were added to create the Coca-Cola brand, first in Atlanta, Georgia, then in the second half of the twentieth century to expand internationally. The brand, Coca-Cola, is estimated to have a net worth value of 23 trillion dollars (US). This is calculated by measuring the market value of the total shareholding, less the tangible assets, i.e. buildings, manufacturing plant, vehicles, etc. The "brand" Coca-Cola is worth more than the tangible value of the product that is essentially carbonated water, flavorings

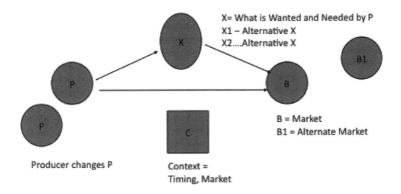

FIGURE 2.4 Power and dependency
Source: Light Years IP from Margaret Brindle and Lisa Mainiero, 2000. *Managing Power through Lateral Networking*, Quorum-Greenwood Press.

and a bit of "secret ingredient." Consider, however, how the "brand" name added to the product adds to and fundamentally changes the power relationship between P and M (producer and market) because Coca-Cola owns this brand and controls the brand, and controls supply chains. Coca-Cola does not allow the "B" in the situation to take power away.

A few things to keep in mind about branding:

1. In cases ranging from Marriott hotels to Sunkist oranges, Toyota cars to Apple computers, Nike shoes to Coach purses, the power of the brand is that it changes the market relationship and the power dependency of the producer. Rather than produce the goods, the owner of the brand has power to negotiate in the market. This power is different than that held by less distinctive, more generic products. There are several reasons for this power shift.

2. The first is that the owner of the brand can dictate who may and who may not profit from the brand. Consider the case of Nike shoes. I cannot independently make Nike "knock-offs" without consequences, legal and market.

3. The second is the difference in the commodity market v. more specialty market positions.

4. Consumers prefer brand for reliability. Consumers associate brand with certainty.

5. Intellectual Property tools, such as trademarks, were designed to protect the consumer, as much as the owner of the "Trade Mark," as per reliability, quality and power.

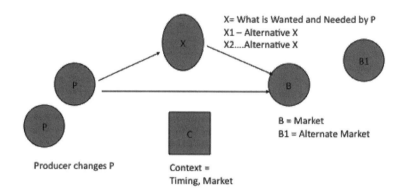

FIGURE 2.5 Changing the power
Source: Light Years IP from Margaret Brindle and Lisa Mainiero, 2000. *Managing Power through Lateral Networking*, Quorum-Greenwood Press.

Another way African farmers and producers can affect power is going to alternative markets, or alternative "B"s.

There are five options for changing the power balance and creating a better negotiating position via the use of IP business tools. One option deserving exploration is changing the target and exploring alternative markets. One reason why developing countries remain relatively powerless in the market is due to century-old construction of those markets by more powerful players and that those who control the more powerful markets have more power and control over those markets.

Consider these realities: Products from Africa and the Caribbean on the commodity markets are subject to continual price volatility and downward spirals. Many developing countries compete for the same markets and unfortunately, no matter how hard developing country producers work, there are those in other LDCs and more technologically advanced nations that have an easier time reaching and saturating the same markets in which they compete.

The age-old wisdom cited by the TechnoServe example for Mozambique cashews, from a 1913 trade journal, "Place the factories next to the farms," is incorrect today. It is more critical to position the product under a retail brand that is owned by Mozambique stakeholders and to position them in control of distribution to retail stores.

Figure 2.6 demonstrates this principle of the commodity-priced markets. It is based on data from the World Bank Economic Monitor. The problem with price volatility is it fosters an insecure economic situation. Farmers and producers work hard and prices go up for a season. This tends to create two situations: The first is that new entrants oftentimes enter markets as a result of price increases. Farmer/producers invest more in their farms and products – good things. However, when farmers and producers compete for the same markets, and demand fluctuates for a variety of external reasons and prices fall, farmers and producers are left with excess capacity.

The second problem with commodity market price fluctuation is that unstable demand and excess capacity generate frustration as planning becomes difficult and exploitation of the farmer/producer all the more likely.

Scenario 2, exploring alternative markets, serves to reduce the dependency of farmer/producers on one market strategy. As in all situations of dependency, power is at least partially socially constructed. That is, it is in part a product of choices and decisions by agents who accept certain power relationships.

In situations ranging from Africa to more developed countries, agents such as farmers and producers are not always able to act in their own best, rational interests. However, in the African case, market information and access can be severely limited. In addition to centuries of exploitation by powerful actors, current importers keep prices low.

As we described earlier, much of Africa is distant from ports. Considering the case of Ethiopian fine coffee growers, for example, the vast majority of the 1 million fine coffee growers live more than 500 miles from port with poor transportation, making them very dependent upon relatively few, powerful buyers. However, for those farmer/producers prepared to consider exploring, alternate markets is a critical option.

Another strategy that is part of an overall combination of strategic interventions is to consider changing the power balance via changing the distribution route of the product.

If we consider that in most situations where distinctive products are concerned, most of the value is captured outside of the borders via importer/wholesalers and

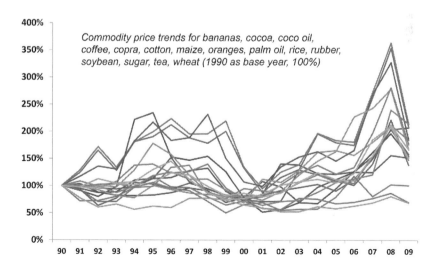

FIGURE 2.6 Commodity Markets – price volatility
Source: Light Years IP.

Alternate distribution routes

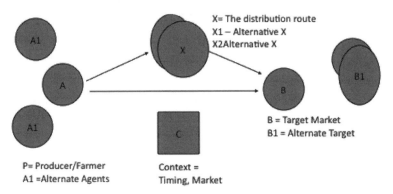

X= The distribution route
X1 – Alternative X
X2Alternative X

B = Target Market
B1 = Alternate Target

P= Producer/Farmer
A1 =Alternate Agents

Context =
Timing, Market

FIGURE 2.7 Change the power by changing x – the distribution route
Source: Light Years IP from Margaret Brindle and Lisa Mainiero, 2000. *Managing Power through Lateral Networking*, Quorum-Greenwood Press.

distributors who capture an average 75 percent of the price, consideration of how and where to affect the supply and distribution route is important.

Keeping in mind the reality that owners of a brand need not be dependent upon existing commodity markets, achieving a greater knowledge of where the price value is captured for distinctive products gives brand owners more options.

Consider, for a moment, modern companies such as Toyota. Toyota, the owner of its brand, has much to say about where and how Toyota cars are distributed and where the value of that brand will achieve best results. Toyota would not be much interested in distributing its cars through wholesaler markets, anymore than Nike or Coach brand purses would be willing to distribute their brand via street vendors. The selectivity of distribution and brand ownership facilitates where and how their profit margins are determined.

Distribution routes are an important part of strategic thinking to alter the fundamental power-dependency situation that keeps farmer/producers of LDCs stuck in commodity market thinking with low returns.

Changing the distribution route

What does it take to change the route of distribution? This option sometimes seems out of the reach of countries that have been in dependent positions throughout their modern history. This is certainly true of Africa, where trade routes have been dominated by colonialism, and then by globalization wherein African countries have not been in the power broker position, to say the least.

The worry and fear of disrupting existing distribution routes is genuine. Will the current buyer become angry with us? What if the buyer goes around us altogether? These are questions that come forth in our workshops and they are legitimate concerns.

They are also the concerns of anyone in a dependent situation. For example, consider the job applicant who is depending on one employer. If I look for other options, will the employer get angry with me?

The risk of altering an established relationship is genuine.

However, if we accept that change always involves a bit of fear of the unknown, plus the human tendency to count loss and be more mindful of what might be lost than what might be gained, we can also appreciate how power and dependency gets established and that the most difficult thing to change is our own belief system.

This applies to African producers and exporters seeking to change their deeply entrenched positions of dependency on foreign markets. At the same time, to establish a distribution company in a new market is entirely within the purview of African nations.

Consider Coca-Cola: This product that currently is the largest employer in Africa got started in Atlanta, Georgia by a pharmacist. The pharmacist started serving up coke syrup – a product known for its digestive assistance properties – at his pharmacy by adding some water to it. Soon, his recipe became popular locally.

Coca-Cola came to Africa in the 1940s and established a distribution company, but Coca-Cola continued to own the distribution and did not give it away.

Lower income producers and farmers remain in powerless positions. Oftentimes this is due to a lack of solid information about relevant retail markets. But, this is changing. It is hard to comprehend that products are sold for 500 x the price in retail markets on 5th Avenue in New York City that the price farmers in Uganda, or producers in Ethiopia may be receiving for those products.

Indeed, lack of knowledge reinforces poverty. We work very hard on IP business education for Africans and LDCs. The business education about strategies that change the power and change the position of African farmers and producers will change the future. The accompanying workbook on the power of distinctive products provides tools to put into the hands of African farmer/producers to advance their vision of what real prices are in distant markets (see workbook included on companion website).

In this scenario, the producer considers the buyer and negotiates a situation of heightened influence, utilizing tools of negotiation.

These would include consideration of what the buyer's needs are. For example, consider the changing consumer who is interested in worker conditions or situations of product origins. Nike, for example, wants to be perceived as having good working conditions and doing fair trade practices in Africa. They have a problem if perceived by their consumers as being unfair to African producers. In today's world of greater transparency, we can assume that African farmers and producers can use the powerful tool of information. However, the west has known for some time now about unfair labor conditions, sweatshops, and unfair

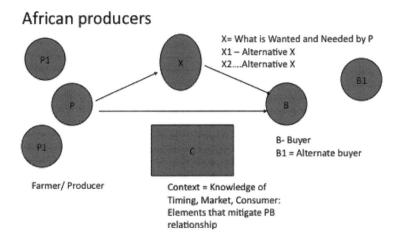

FIGURE 2.8 Context knowledge
Source: Light Years IP from Margaret Brindle and Lisa Mainiero, 2000. *Managing Power through Lateral Networking*, Quorum-Greenwood Press.

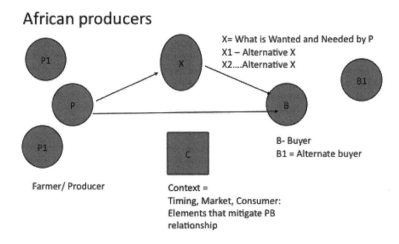

FIGURE 2.9 Change the negotiation position
Source: Light Years IP from Margaret Brindle and Lisa Mainiero, 2000. *Managing Power through Lateral Networking*, Quorum-Greenwood Press.

prices, but seems to have gotten used to this information. There is a great need for advocacy and support. No producer group has moved out of poverty without it.

This is the situation with Starbucks. They market themselves as using Fair Trade coffee and want their consumers to feel good coming into Starbucks to buy their $4.00 cup of Joe.

Let's take a look at how the power model can be used in a real-life scenario:

In a real case, in Ethiopia, the coffee farmers were dependent upon five German coffee companies who purchased the bulk of their coffee, and redistributed it. For many years, the Ethiopian coffee farmers were in a dependency situation that looked like this. Before the Ethiopian Fine Coffee Initiative, 4 million coffee farmers/1 million fine coffee growers sold to 450 export companies and four unions of cooperatives who tried to negotiate with five large, foreign distribution companies who controlled prices.

For the most part, the coffee farmers had no idea what happened to their coffee after they sold it to exporters, and little idea at what price the coffee was sold to consumers in foreign countries.

Due to the Ethiopian Fine Coffee Trademark and Licensing Initiative, the power shifted. The result looked like this. The Ethiopian coffee farmers acquired a trademark and were able to negotiate with the distribution companies on more even ground. The Ethiopians held greater negotiation power because the distributors in foreign markets were required to have a license. This changed the power.

In the terms of our model above, A, the Ethiopian fine coffee sector becomes less dependent upon the Bs, the bulk buying distribution companies and deals only and directly with the buyers and retailers that are licensed by Ethiopia.

Summary

For decades, Africa and LDCs have been out-powered. This will not change by increasing production. More volume does not change power. It actually may diminish power as over-production often causes prices to fall, and produced goods to be less valued.

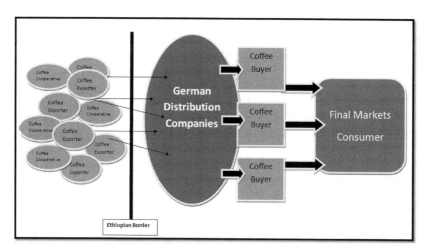

FIGURE 2.10 Ethiopian Fine Coffee and the power of German distribution companies
Source: Light Years IP.

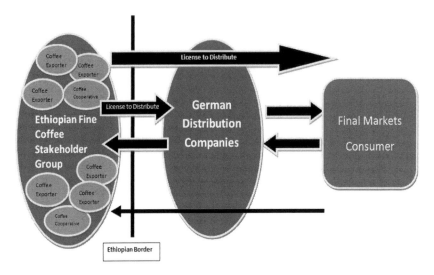

FIGURE 2.11 Ethiopian coffee exporters reaching final markets
Source: Light Years IP.

And, as we saw in the case of Mozambique cashews, increased processing and placing factories next to farms does not change power. Here, the increased processing led to lower prices, low wages, and very poor labor conditions. Adding a meaningless brand does not change power, if the brand is not equated with distinctiveness, and brand value accrued is not owned by the creators of that value.

There have been many strategies implemented to change the problems of trade isolation and African/LDC farmer and producer power. For one, Fair Trade has increased awareness of unfair trade, unfair prices, and sweatshop labor. While Fair Trade has advanced consumer consciousness, it has not fundamentally changed power. The cost of Fair Trade is borne by low-income farmers and producers and unless coupled with more ownership of supply chains, the income accrued by Fair Trade accrues to importers and retailers in foreign markets, and does not help low-income LDC farmers and producers significantly. It also runs the risk of being more of a marketing strategy for western brands, and a smoke screen at worst to hide tremendous trade inequity.

Brands alone do not change power. Aid and dependency do not change power, as we have seen through 60 years of pumping dollars into failing economies. And, saying we are and have "empowered" people, particularly does not mean power has changed. Women earning $1.00 in local markets for products that fetch $1,000 in higher end retail markets is not very empowering.

Power is changed when low-income farmers and producers think like corporations and gain knowledge and information about the real value of their distinctive products in final markets. Power is changed when they engage in Intellectual Property tools and methods – often worth many, many times the value of the physical product. Power is changed when farmers and producers can then reduce their dependency upon low-paying exporters, and reach final, higher end retail markets. This is possible. This is scalable in a large and sustainable manner. The remainder of this book is dedicated to showing you exactly how to do this.

In the following section, we introduce the power of the method, the power of the brand, the power of supply chain ownership, the relevant IP tools and strategies, and the power of advocacy and enforcement. Changing power is not easy. It cannot be done half way. To engage in a business strategy is comparable to brain surgery. We cannot do it half way, or it will be comparably disastrous. Yet, considering the advances of the past half century, and the potential of intellectual property ownership, the potential is formidable. Also, as Chapter 9 will describe, the historical record of poor farmers and producers achieving massive and sustainable income such as in the case of French champagne and Scotch whisky leads us to say: It is time for African farmers and producers to engage in the full method of IP business and change the power – forever.

Notes

1 Layton et al., "Distinctive values in African exports."
2 J. Bowes, ed., *The Fair Trade Revolution*, Chicago, Illinois: University of Chicago Press, 2011.
3 J. Pauli, "The Fairtrade movement: Six lessons for the organics sector," 3rd ISOFAR Scientific Conference at the 17th Organic World Congress, Gyeonggi Paldang, South Korea, 2011.
4 Taken from the Fair Trade International, monitoring and evaluation report, December 2013.
5 C. Cramer, D. Johnston, C. Oya, and J. Sender et al., "Fairtrade, employment and poverty reduction in Ethiopia and Uganda," Fair Trade Employment and Poverty Reduction report, April 2014 (http://ftepr.org/wp-content/uploads/FTEPR-Final-Report-19-May-2014-FINAL.pdf), accessed March 2016. This opinion represents the point of view of authors of the thorough FTEPR report of 143pp. The authors of this book believe Fair Trade *has* had some positive impact as discussed elsewhere in this book.
6 C. Cramer, D. Johnston et al., "Fairtrade, employment and poverty reduction in Ethiopia and Uganda," SOAS, April, 2014, pp. 15–16.
7 J. Hanlon, "Is poverty decreasing in Mozambique?" Paper presented at the Inaugural Conference of the Instituto de Estudos Socias e Economicos (IESE), Maputo, September 19, 2007.
8 Ibid.
9 M. McMillan, D. Rodrik, and K. Welch. "When economic reform goes wrong: Cashews in Mozambique," National Bureau of Economic Research, Brookings Trade Forum, 2003. http://www.nber.org/papers/w9117, accessed September 2016.
10 B. Paul, for TechnoServe, "Factories in the fields: Rural transformation and the organization of work in Mozambique's cashew triangle," July 2008, http://www.technoserve.org/files/downloads/factoriesinthefield.pdf.
11 M. Ru and P. Tiffen, "Mozambique feasibility study," Light Years IP, DFID, 2008.
12 R. Layton and M.R. Chin, Mozambique Feasibility Study, funded by DFID, Light Years IP, 2008.

13 TechnoServe, "New Mozacaju project to support Mozambique small scale farmers and cashew processors and fight poverty," September 2013 (www.technoserve.org/press-room/detail/new-mozacaju-project-to-support-mozambican-small-scale-farmers-and-cashew).

14 M. Brindle and L. Mainiero, *Managing power through lateral networking*, New York: Quorum Press, 2001.

15 Ibid.

3

THE POWER OF THE METHOD

A six-step method for Intellectual Property Business Positioning

Common wisdom applauds learning by doing. In today's world, there is renewed appreciation for learning from failures. However, when it comes to advancing people out of poverty, we believe there are methods that *do* work. There are a number of business methods that have been tried, refined, proven, advanced, and can be used successfully by African and other LDC businesses, and are scalable for major transformational change.

This chapter is about the six-step method called Intellectual Property business positioning. It is about the details of the six steps needed to create an IP business strategy. We also are frank that using Intellectual Property does not work for every product, and is far less likely to work for the generic commodity products. In the following chapter, we describe how to differentiate products and situations likely to be effective and ineffective.

In this chapter, you can expect to learn:

- Why a business method matters
- The methodology, including:
    - Selecting a distinctive product
    - The retail and export price gap analysis
    - Market research for an IP business strategy
    - Analysis of a four-part value chain
    - How to determine if and where there is leverage in the supply chain
    - The importance of stakeholder ownership
    - Determination of a financeable business plan

Why a method matters

In most fields, there are methods, such as business, finance, mathematics, science, medicine, engineering, and many others. The methods in these disciplines emerge over many years of proof with consequences and outcomes. Yet, oftentimes when it comes to the field of international development, the approach is more driven by the structure of the donor government organizations than by business practice.

Sometimes, it is simply poor quality project design. At a recent conference at a prestigious university, a senior professor was applauding a trial and error method in international development. Introducing a recent multi-million dollar failure by a large corporation whose customers did not fit the African product promoted, he asserted, "Well, they tried. We should applaud them for trying and for their honesty at admitting failure."

While we understand the challenges of bringing genuine change to LDCs and systemic poverty in international development, and surely appreciate transparency and learning from failure, we believe there is a better way. It is not always possible to build upon failure and the stakes are quite high for poor people. Oftentimes, failures challenge trust.

In Pittsburgh, Pennsylvania in the US, there was a bridge that couldn't be finished because the architect/builders could not gain permission to complete the access ramps on the other side. For nearly a decade, it stood and was simply defined as "The bridge to nowhere" – a quirky landmark in town. Though we grew accustomed to the bridge to nowhere, international development should aspire to adopt methods that actually work, and bring poor people to somewhere worth going. There are simply too many failures, half-done projects, meaning people in LDCs are often left distrustful of aid and of new business efforts

Business models and methods have a strong foundation of success. For example, the concept of vertical integration came into practice at the turn of the century – the last one! In the early 1900s, ownership or control of supply chains was an innovative idea from manufacturing gurus such as Andrew Carnegie and Frick who promoted a business method to which a considerable part of developed country growth and prosperity is attributed. Regrettably, control of African supply chains by developed country corporations has held back millions of Africans for decades. Intellectual Property ownership was added onto the developed country business model, building to considerable importance by the latter part of the nineteenth century.

In agriculture, a favorite example is Sunkist oranges, begun by poor California farmers. Achieving brand ownership, trademarks, and supply chain ownership, the corporation provides higher income to stakeholders than commodity prices for oranges. For corporations, much more income is generated from intangible value, controlled by Intellectual Property than from the physical value of commodity products.

The IP business positioning method foundation

The method described here is based on two important foundations:

1.   Thousands of successful, global businesses operate on the foundations of striving for optimum positioning with ownership of Intellectual Property, control or ownership of supply chains, especially the import company and correct positioning of the consumer product under the brand. These are not flukes or creative, variable rolls of the dice, but are sound business methods.
2.   IP business for Africa and LDCs is based on proof of concept cases affecting several million people. In Ethiopia, 1 million coffee farmers fared better, and if we consider their average family size of five people on average, the effect involved 5 million people. With 4 million coffee farmers in Ethiopia who could benefit from using the same strategy, the potential impact could be improved lives for 20 million people. In the Maasai case, there are 2 million Maasai benefitting from acquiring control over their cultural brand. In addition, as described in Chapter 1, there are approximately four–five distinctive products per African country wherein the method could be applied, improving lives for about 200 million producers.

The quest to demonstrate how to replicate the method involved the large question posed following the Ethiopian success with its return of $101 million. The Rt. Hon. Hilary Benn, UK Secretary of State for International Development, asked in 2007 if the positioning model is applicable to other agricultural, artisan, or manufactured products of Africa.

We set out to define the replicable method that could be widely applied and performed in-depth feasibility and business plan analyses on dozens of products. Granted $1.25 million by the USPTO for education, we refined the method, so that it could be easily understood and thus, replicated. It is business. It is not entirely new or unproven. It is based on tried and true business best practices with Intellectual Property.

What is the six-step method?

The following points summarize the six steps that determine whether or not a product is likely to be successful for an IP business strategy. Each step is then described more thoroughly.

1.   **The product holds genuine distinctiveness:** For example, while there are many honey products, some honey is distinctive by its rareness of flavor from particular trees, health-enhancing qualities, story of origin, reputation or is perceived by consumers to hold particular value. Manuka honey from New Zealand, for example, retails at up to $70.00 per 8-ounce (0.225 kg)

jar due to its healing properties. A similar differentiation or distinctiveness can be found in numerous African products.

Another example is coffee with variance between commodity pricing and distinctive coffees. Coffee that is not distinctive is suitable for the commodity markets that will move prices to clear the volume produced and give efficient signals to producers. While there are many coffees, some are distinctive by origin, growing conditions and reputation, such as Ethiopian Yirgacheffe. The step of product distinctiveness is so vital that we have devoted a full chapter to it following this one.

2.   **Retail market price, intangible value, and export price gap:** Generally fine products generate "distinctively" higher prices in consumer markets, so IP business positioning strategies are worth developing. In considering any export product for positioning, the first quantitative step is to measure the intangible value. Simply, the retail price of the most valued product shows the most intangible value, measured as the amount higher than commodity equivalent. Fine Ethiopian coffee retailing at $20/lb is $16 more than commodity coffee retailing at $4/lb. Hence, the intangible value is $16/lb, enough to justify working on a positioning strategy for producing businesses to capture a larger share.

In many examples, there is a dramatic gap between export prices and retail prices. We have found large price gaps for many African exports with the large majority of the retail price/value remaining outside the export country.

One example is Nilotica (East African) shea butter wherein the product achieves only $5.00/kg at export, but when positioned as a branded high end consumer product, generates retail value over $1,000/kg. This is obviously a substantial price gap and provides room for IP strategies to "capture" a much greater share of the retail value.

3.   **Intangible value chain analysis shows potential for better positioning in the supply chain:** The next step is to assess all aspects of the supply or value chain to determine how to create the best IP business opportunities. Some value chains are simple four-point models: The farmer/producer – the exporter – the importer – the retailer. Others are more complex involving farmer to processor to exporter and importer and additional processing to retail.

Value chain analysis then leads to an assessment of where in the value chain there is, or in some cases, is not potential for positioning to create increased income for the farmer/producers. This is coupled with use of IP tools ranging from trademarks to licensing and other IP tools, specific to the situation. In some situations, the supply or value chain is already controlled and this makes it hard to find a point to apply positioning.

4.   **Clear income impact for farmers and producing businesses:** A clear point of leverage. The use of IP business positioning so far has been to help

achieve higher and more secure income for stakeholders who most need it. Most African producers of distinctive products have little or no incentive to work on increasing quality due to the following factors:

- Continuing fluctuations of farm gate prices due to the volatility of the global commodity markets mean post-harvest prices are very difficult to predict
- A low export price level due to weak negotiating power means the entire supply chain from the farmer to export is unable to build in quality incentives
- Marginally profitable production of one product due to global over-supply means shifting to another (e.g. peanuts to vanilla for one–two years, then back to peanuts), eroding traditional special skills and preventing the sustained growth of new skills.

The fourth step to successful positioning is to determine if the distinctive product has potential to generate a significant income return for large collectives of low-income farmers and producing businesses. There are benefits of scale. A collaboration of larger numbers of farmers, producing, processing, and exporting businesses makes possible ownership of retail brands in foreign countries and control of supply chains beyond the country border. This combination secures higher, quality-based income sufficient to warrant the cost of investment. Together, these elements contribute to capturing the benefits of correct positioning for a sustainable business.

In one example, we worked on Jamaican honey from bees harvesting pollen on dogwood trees. This fine product could fetch significantly higher prices at retail, but there are too few honey producers, numbering in the hundreds, and dogwood trees are too spread out in mixed growth forests.

In some situations, vertically integrated modern companies owning retail brands have a strong grip on production, so there are limited opportunities for new entrants. One such example is Caribbean rum. Bacardi Rum and other commercial rum companies have used positioning to capture sufficient income and profits to build recognition for their retail brands over decades.

Where new producing businesses wish to secure the same profitability in the rum business, they would need sufficient capital to build competing brands to Bacardi, outsource processing to high quality factories, and manage the quality to secure a market share that gives a return on investment. This and other examples of correct positioning are most valuable to illustrate where the harder challenges lie and help identify easier challenges for positioning distinctive products with less intense competition.

The opportunities are prolific. It is important, however, to perform rigorous feasibility and business planning to ensure that engaging farmers and producers in an IP business positioning strategy is sufficiently promising to succeed.

Not all products or situations work equally well, and the six-step method of criteria and assessment helps in selecting the most promising opportunities.

5. **Local stakeholder interest and enthusiasm:** If farmers and their producing cooperatives together decide to have a stake in the new correctly positioned business, their full participation will take these business strategies forward to sustained high income. Producers with strong price incentives tend to become active stakeholders and act vigorously to support the business strategies. Given the value of building collaborations with scale to carry out business positioning, exporters need to engage with producing cooperatives and producers with price incentives for quality.

   Some products have a special history in a country. For example, cloves are reputed to play a role in elections of the governments of Zanzibar due to the past history of large-scale exporting. Such governments can help the special clove sector achieve correct positioning, provided these key concepts are applied. Farmers and producers in such situations will be unable to achieve control of retail brand in foreign countries and capture the value of IP without a highly commercial approach.

   Coffee is central to Ethiopian culture, with a deep history since it was discovered in the region of Kaffa. Ethiopia has 70 years' successful experience of owning a globally known airline that is commercially managed and very well positioned. As a result, the late Prime Minister, Hon. Meles Zenawi, approved the formation of a similar corporation to manage the Ethiopian Fine Coffee opportunity. A recent UNDP-financed study recommended implementing this component to drive Phase Two of the Ethiopian Fine Coffee Initiative.

6. **Investment-ready projects:** Businesses wanting to benefit from IP business positioning need to design initiatives that are ready for investment. Business positioning strategies in fully developed business plans can compete for capital from impact investors and other funders. This step is discussed further in a simplified form. Business planning teams knowledgeable in positioning are available from Light Years IP and Position Limited.

Intangible value

The following section explores each of these steps more thoroughly.

Step one: what is distinctiveness and how can distinctiveness translate into $100 million more income per product per year, as a conservative estimate?

That seems like a big claim. Here is how it works:

Distinctiveness usually translates into intangible value – the non-tangible aspect of a product that leads consumers to pay higher prices for the distinctive products due to perceived quality, superior effectiveness or reputation.

In recent decades, the intangible value of products in developed country retail markets has overtaken the physical value as we have described earlier. But, how to determine whether a product is truly distinctive is a critical task.

Consider the Cuban cigar as a simple product example. This product's distinctiveness earns the company that produces it far more money than the materials used to create it. Tangible aspects include the tobacco and the wrapping, with label; intangible aspects include its origin, flavor, and the refined image associated with smoking it. Consider the low apparent value of tangible aspects and the high price of the cigar. The intangible value of the cigar is measured by the difference between the price of the Cuban cigar and the price of a non-distinctive cigar.

As we have described, the importance of intangible value has grown steadily. In 1982, 62 percent of the market value of Standard & Poor's 500 companies (an index of the leading US companies) could be attributed to tangible assets and 38 percent to intangible assets. By 1998, only 15 percent of the assets of Standard & Poor 500 companies were tangible, while 85 percent were intangible. This shift in the value of assets reflects the ability of these intangible assets to generate income because consumers will pay much more for the intangible value in superior cosmetic oils, spices, teas, coffees, etc. The good news is this can be an advantage for producers of African distinctive products.

It is important to assess what products are truly distinctive and *can* readily be suitable for this method. The IP business method is not applicable to every product. In fact, it is not readily applicable to commodity market products such as maize, corn, ordinary cottons, wheat, and generally not applicable to ingredients. The IP business model does not work well with commodity, non-distinctive products. Therefore, we have included a full chapter on determining distinctiveness following this and a workbook to walk through additional exercises.

IP business is applicable to distinctive products. There are at least four–five products per African country that demonstrate measurable intangible value in wealthy retail markets. The challenge is to determine if a product is truly distinctive.

We cannot emphasize this enough, as many branding strategies, many agri-business strategies, many women's empowerment efforts, and a great deal of funding to LDCs for business creation have failed because they have tried to brand mediocre, commodity products and the investments have not yielded results. In recent years, Ugandan cotton was branded, for example, but this cotton is not distinctive and there were great challenges to achieving additional income to warrant investment.

The next step in the method is to determine if a product can utilize the IP business method concerns analyzing the retail and export price differences.

Step two: retail price analysis and difference

Intangible value is measured by higher prices in the retail marketplace. Determining the intangible value of a distinctive product requires price analysis.

Our research has also found there is often a very large difference between the retail price in foreign markets and what the farmer, producer or artisan is receiving, frequently translating into millions of dollars overall. This creates an opportunity for intellectual property business strategies for the farmers, producers or artisans to intervene and potentially receive much larger income.

The following describes a process for determining what the retail price and export prices are with the process to collect data following similar steps:

Stage 1: market exploration

First, collect basic information about what consumers value in a lucrative retail market; what the prices are, and how much value is being captured by other producers of other distinctive products. Learn about what makes the product distinctively valuable, and learn about the consumers in the final markets.

Stage 2: make decisions

As planning moves forward, pool information among collaborating producers, design the unifying producer organization, refine the market data from before, and choose the most likely target lucrative market. Also, gather more detail about competitors in the chosen market.

Stage 3: operational details

As the planning begins to turn into a proper business plan, collect specific data about costs, regulations, advertising, products standards, tariffs, and so on.

Ugandan vanilla is one example that illustrates the retail price and export price gap. Ugandan vanilla sells for up to $12.00 for two pods at Whole Foods Markets in the US. The exporters receive about $0.05 and the farmers about $0.03 per pod, depicted below. Turning this situation around for Uganda is described in detail in the following chapter, but here, Ugandan vanilla illustrates the retail and export price gap step of the IP business model.

How did we determine what Ugandan vanilla is selling for currently in western markets? We selected Whole Foods because they are a price leader – known as the large volume grocery store with the highest prices per square foot of space, so the prices set by Whole Foods are important to know. We added to this other higher end stores such as those in the UK – Sainsbury's and Waitrose, online markets, and gourmet food stores to determine the size of the price gap between export prices from Africa and high end retail.

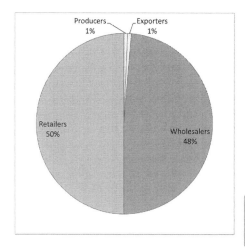

One Kg of Ugandan gourmet vanilla pods retail value is $1100 p.a., but the export price is only $20/Kg

FIGURE 3.1 Ugandan pie chart
Source: Light Years IP.

Farm Price	Retail Price
$0.40-$0.60	$11.95-26.00

FIGURE 3.2 Estimated farm and retail price (Sidama fine coffee prices over 2005–7, per lb)
Source: Light Years IP.

One can also gain solid comparative information on the retail price by asking the following questions. In this example, we would be looking for vanilla and seeking to develop information about the retail and export price gap.

What consumers buy your product (or products in the same classification as your product), and how much of it do they buy? This data is often provided by for-profit and non-profit market research companies, by development agencies, and by specialized industry groups. You can also use Google or another search engine to search for your product online.

Returning to our example of the Ethiopian coffee case study, a large amount of intangible value was being captured outside of Ethiopia before Light Years IP designed the Ethiopian Fine Coffee Trademarking and Licensing Initiative. The gap between the retail value and the export price is illustrated in Figure 3.2 for distinctive Sidama coffee.

The importance of analyzing the price gap, as we call it, meaning the price differential between the farm price and the retail price, is it demonstrates there is room to implement an IP business strategy to "capture" more of this value.

Many of the first questions asked in an IP business strategy are about the final consumers of the product. The target market is the place where you intend to sell your product, and the group of people who will buy the product. LDC producers, farmers, and artisans, often lack knowledge about the size of the target market or the needs and desires of the buyers in that market. It is a knowledge gap to overcome. Understanding the size of the target market will allow stakeholders to estimate the value of sales if they capture a share (or "percentage") of that market.

Example – Estimating the value of sales in a target market

If the target market buys $10 million of nutmeg each year, and our company captures 15 percent of that market, we will have sales of: $10 million x 0.15 = $1.5 million.

Understanding your market is critical to IP business strategy because it is all about returning income (value) from the final markets. Understanding who in the final markets is capturing the value you create and creating a strategy to bring this value back in the form of income is an IP business process.

It is not unlike the process any business strategist would engage: Envisioning the target market and understanding how your product fits in and where it does not fit in. The reason this may seem profound for poor producers is they are accustomed to experiencing business as focused on just one side of the goal line – the production side with quality control and processing as newer priorities. However, if you stay focused on the production side without understanding the higher end retail target, you will always stay stuck in a cyclic poverty mentality, in our opinion.

The types of questions posed to move the African farmers and producers toward developing knowledge of the retail markets and helping them to develop a vision coupled with practical knowledge of the final retail markets include:

The size of the market

- What countries or people already buy products like ours?
- How much of it do they buy?
- How much do they pay for it?
- Is the amount they buy increasing or decreasing (i.e. is the market growing or shrinking)?

Consumer (buyer) preferences

- Why do consumers buy the product? What qualities do they care about?
- Are there "cheap" and "expensive" versions of the product out there? The cheap ones are generally the commodity, non-distinctive versions. What makes them different?

Challenges to entering the market

- Are there special legal requirements to sell this product in certain markets?
- What competing products are sold in the market?
- Is the market dominated by a few large sellers, or are there many small sellers?

Now would be a good time to work through the market research workbook to develop additional knowledge about the focused market (see workbook included on companion website).[1]

Step three: supply chain leverage:

Where in the supply chain is it possible to obtain the maximum leverage for stakeholders?

Creating leverage for LDC producers and farmers differs by product, by market, and by context. It also differs by whether the product is a tangible product, such as a fine coffee, tea, spice, soap, butter or cocoa, or if the product is a cultural brand that is widely used to add value to top end retailers, such as the Maasai iconic brand. Leverage will also vary based on the current state of development of the farmers and producers, and the complexity of the supply chain.

For example, for Divine Chocolate, leverage was created for the cocoa farmers not by processing cocoa into chocolate in Ghana, but rather by processing the cocoa where cocoa processing was already well-engineered and developed outside Ghana. It would have been both extremely costly and unlikely to succeed if the farmers and leadership of Divine had decided to process the cocoa inside of Ghana. The power for the Ghanaian cocoa farmers was in creating a strong cooperative under ethical leadership and ownership and creating a brand that is not labeled Ghanaian cocoa, but rather Divine Chocolate. Divine resonates well with the final market consumer. The business positioning is critical. Divine sells well in final markets and manages distribution to retail stores. The Kuapa Kokoo farmers do well. The trademark and IP secures the higher retail value. Eventually, cocoa may be processed into chocolate in Ghana but better leverage was achieved by processing it outside of Ghana for the first years.

This is a common mistake made in international development. Oftentimes, business strategies begin with light processing and trying to bring local processing up to global standards. Though it is logical on one level, it often fails because the capital costs to develop competitive final processing are extraordinarily high. If the product is sold to importing companies, the brand and IP value is often taken outside of the country. Better leverage is generally created for low-income producers by beginning with the end in mind.

For the purposes of the method, it is important to ask: Where in the supply chain can the *best* leverage be acquired for the local farmer/producers to acquire power?

For Ethiopian coffee farmers, the leverage was in a trademark and licensing strategy. For the Maasai, the leverage is in creating a stakeholder group to own their iconic brand, and leverage is in this ownership coupled with a licensing strategy. The trademark alone will not produce leverage.

For the Ugandan WONS (women's owned Nilotica shea) the leverage will be in processing the shea butter into final retail cosmetic products outside of Uganda *and* by owning their own import company closer to higher end retail. This follows the Divine model. Leverage will be gained by designing a brand with higher end marketing. This differs dramatically from the many projects under way concerning shea butter in West Africa, wherein the shea is an ingredient for other brands.

In order to determine *where* in the value or supply chain the most advantage or leverage can be created, it is necessary to conduct a basic value chain analysis.

In IP business analysis, supply chains are simplified to four elements to help understand where value is assigned out of the total amount paid by a retail buyer. The supply chain will be different for each product or service.

The supply chain

1. We believe the most effective business planning begins with the end in mind. Though the term, "Begin with the End in Mind," was coined by the late Stephen Covey, and made famous in a series of business books, beginning with the end in mind is applicable here. So often, in international development and aid for trade, the focus is on the low prices farmers receive in the country. While important to note, we begin with the retail price – what is possible with the right IP tools, and the right business strategy to reposition the product and the producers? In terms of the model above, begin with the far right and include the retail price from at least 10 different retail outlets and online sales, high and lower end. Consider what is possible, rather than what has been commoditized. As described in distinctiveness, we can look at coffee such as commodity coffee like Folgers at $3.99/lb or Ethiopian distinctive coffee retailing at $20.00/lb. If we are assessing Zanzibar spices, these may be retailing at commodity prices, or at higher end stores with a large price differential.

2. Estimate the price paid by retailers buying from importers, to understand how much of the intangible value in the final market is going to importers or to the retailers.

3. Establish the price at which the product is being exported. An IP business strategy applied by the export sector will be aimed at increasing the export price to a higher percentage of retail prices, so it is valuable to examine the percentage currently earned by other exporting/producing businesses with comparable products.

4. Extend the value chain analysis to producer prices, by examining research papers or conducting primary research through farmer cooperatives.

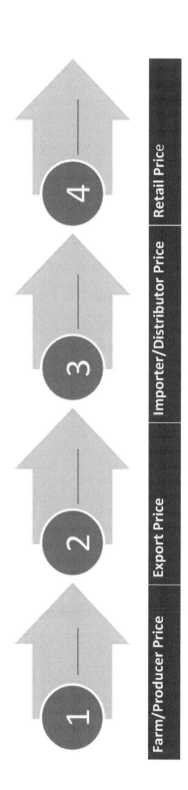

FIGURE 3.3 The power of the method

Source: Light Years IP.

From the above value chain analysis, it is possible to forecast the impact of IP business strategies in capturing the existing retail intangible value.

Where to achieve best leverage? One size does not fit all

It is vital to note that business planning is needed. It is also important to note that just as in any business, one size does not fit all. It is important to present the concept of where leverage can best be achieved very accurately to investors and leaders of stakeholders. Otherwise, LDC stakeholders come to believe that if only they owned the trademark, or if only they could improve in country processing, volume and export increase, will they achieve improved market incomes.

The goal is not to acquire an Intellectual Property tool but rather to understand that IP is a tool, and a means to an end. What is the end? It is to change the power of the farmer/producer and *increase income* that is sustained. Just as a hammer does not build a house, an IP tool such as a trademark does not build income.

A trademark alone does not improve income, nor does an owned brand.

Brands alone do not create leverage. There are plenty of brands across the developed world, as well as the developing world, that are not helping.

Have you ever heard of Zambique cashews? No? That is unfortunate, mostly for the Mozambique cashew growers. There are over 1 million Mozambique cashew farmers who grow the best cashews in the world. A large-scale USAID project conducted by TechnoServe decided to brand their cashews Zambique. They did not finish the job by creating a brand that consumers could identify with, demand, and thus improve the plight of extraordinarily hard working Zambian cashew farmers. Although over 1 million Mozambique cashew farmers aspire to higher income, they were capturing just 2 percent of the retail value of their cashews. Unfortunately, adding a brand name did not change the power one bit and ended up with Mozambique still capturing the small share of the retail value. The major share of the retail price was taken by importers and retailers.

Returning to the Walmart failure referenced at the beginning of this chapter, the project failure had much to do with assuming the Maasai could achieve leverage where they could not realistically. For example, the Walmart model was to encourage the Maasai mamas to create volumes of traditional handicrafts and to sell the handicrafts at Walmart stores. Generally speaking, the average consumer goes to Walmart for bargains, not highly distinctive products or cultural handicrafts. The handicrafts were priced and positioned in the wrong retail market, and despite continual discounts, did not sell. To an extent, the Maasai handicrafts competing with other low-end handicrafts were considered commodity goods, rather than distinctively unique products.

Our approach to the Maasai cultural brand is radically different from that of Walmart. We applied a version of the six-step method for the Maasai who now own their cultural brand. The leverage is for the Maasai to build a representative stakeholder organization that can manage the cultural brand with authentic

FIGURE 3.4 Kinkiri ole Tialolo (Isaac) Maasai Elder
Source: Light Years IP.

Maasai values. The Maasai name and image is currently used on a wide range of products. As the Maasai organization takes control and licenses all use, royalty revenue will be earned that will benefit the community.

In order to understand where low-income farmers and producers can acquire leverage, it's important to know where they are currently in the supply chain and to understand that well, so to see where in the value chain the best intervention can be made, as described below. From the above value chain analysis, it is possible to forecast the impact of IP Business strategies in capturing the existing retail intangible value.

Before continuing with the steps in an IP business strategy, let's consider the way these first three steps are applicable in a real case study analysis. This also concerns coffee, but a less well-known brand than Ethiopian coffee. Consider as you read: Does Tanzanian coffee pass the first three steps for an IP business strategy?

- Is it truly distinctive with a large enough intangible value to justify a positioning strategy?
- Is the price on retail markets significantly higher than the farmer/producer and export level to create space for investment in increasing income?
- Consider the value chain analysis and whether or not it is worth creating an IP business strategy for the Tanzanians.

Executive summary

For the purpose of this analysis, the international coffee market can be broadly simplified into two segments: commodity coffee and high quality, gourmet or

FIGURE 3.5 Fine coffee beans
Source: Light Years IP.

"fine" coffee.[2] Commodity-grade coffee retails in the US for about $4 per pound, while fine coffees – distinctive high quality single-origin beans with unique flavor profiles – fetch retail prices of $20 per pound and above.

Fine coffees with distinctive qualities hold brand value that reflects those qualities, so there are opportunities for Tanzania to use positioning. The best opportunities are in those retail markets where fine coffee is widely sold as a premium product, that is, in most developed countries other than France, Italy, and other countries where espresso blends dominate the form of delivery to consumers. Espresso markets offer opportunities for different strategies.

Tanzanian peaberry has an established position in the choices of fine coffee consumers in the US, UK, and Northern Europe (a peaberry bean is a natural aberration, with two beans joined). However, importers and distributors take almost all the retail premium for this coffee, as in the Ethiopian case up to June 2007. Averaging export prices from 2000 to 2010, Tanzanian producers and exporters together have been earning an export price that is only about 5 percent of the retail price.[3] In comparison, Jamaican Blue Mountain fine coffee producers receive export prices over 40 percent of the retail price.

There are limits on the value that can be captured from the unusual nature of Tanzanian peaberries because peaberries only occur as a small portion of Arabica beans.[4] However, consumer recognition of the Tanzanian peaberry brand is a valuable component in a combined strategy, discussed below.

Improved positioning means building the peaberry brand recognition to cover normal beans, successfully presenting both to retail consumers. Benefits to the Tanzanian coffee farmer come from capturing retail value in the form of higher export and farm gate prices. By forming a new distribution company to import and distribute peaberry and conventional beans of Tanzania coffee, Tanzania would be able to extract more value from its fine coffees. This distribution company, owned by Tanzanian producers and exporters of both types of coffee, would sell Tanzanian coffee to retail stores.

Opportunities

The specialty coffee segment is the most rapidly growing portion of the US coffee market, having increased from 1 percent to 20 percent in market share over the last 25 years.[5] Around 15 percent of American adults drink specialty coffee on a daily basis.[6] Even during the 2008 downturn, 84 percent of American coffee drinkers did not move away from their consumption habits of choosing specialty coffee.[7] Specialty coffee is much more than a passing trend.

A number of Tanzanian Arabica coffees have penetrated the US specialty coffee market and are being sold at premium prices by well-established coffee companies.

With its multiple coffee-growing regions and unique geo-climatic niches, Tanzania has the potential to sell even more of its coffee in higher-value specialty markets. Though opportunities may exist for many of Tanzania's coffees, the next

Company	Name of Coffee	Price per kilo (Roasted beans)
Green Mountain Coffee	Tanzanian Gombe Reserve	$30.00
Peet's Coffee & Tea	Tanzania Kilimanjaro	$28.50
Intelligentsia Coffee & Tea	Tanzania, Edelweiss	$44.00

FIGURE 3.6 A sampling of Tanzanian coffees sold in the US specialty market
Source: Light Years IP.

FIGURE 3.7 Tanzanian arabica berries
Source: Light Years IP.

sections delve into the opportunities for better positioning of the Arabica peaberry export sector.

Arabica Peaberry

In addition to the coffees mentioned in Figure 1, there is a solid US market for Tanzanian Arabica peaberry coffee. Tanzanian peaberry is well known amongst American gourmet coffee drinkers, and is probably the dominant peaberry coffee sold in the US,[8] where it retails for the premium price of about $15 per lb.[9]

Peaberry coffee is regarded highly for several reasons. Coffee connoisseurs note that peaberry coffee is often sweeter and more acidic, having subtly different flavor notes than the rest of the crop. Coffee experts believe that because peaberries must be picked out from the rest of the crop, more care is taken to secure only the best beans for further processing and sale. Though these experts remark that peaberries are really only as good as the crop they come from, peaberries are often marketed as having more flavor than regular coffee because they consist of two beans fused together rather than just one bean.

Marketing campaigns capitalize on the rarity, unique appearance and formation process for peaberries, calling them "special," "mystical," or even "magical."[10] In a description of a Brazilian peaberry coffee in their lineup of special reserve coffees, Starbucks compares peaberries to precious jewels:

> A peaberry is a rare, single, rounded bean that resembles a freshwater pearl – and to coffee lovers it's just as valuable. While not fit to be strung on a necklace or mounted in platinum earrings, its unwavering flavor is just as elegant.[11]

As the above paragraphs indicate, peaberry is already recognized in the retail market as a special coffee with unique properties, worthy of premium prices. Among the many single-origin peaberry coffees on the market, Tanzania probably has the most name recognition as an origin for this distinctive product. Tanzania could capitalize on this situation by employing IP-based business strategies to capture more of the final retail value for its peaberry coffee.

Conclusion

Moving more of its coffees into high-value specialty markets will not necessarily mean increased income for Tanzania. The IP business repositioning is necessary to be sure of some portion of this income from high-value speciality markets returns to Tanzania. The key elements to positioning success are:

1. Expanding existing recognition of Tanzanian peaberry into an umbrella brand covering all fine coffees from Tanzania.
2. Intervening in the supply chain by setting up an exclusive distributor of these fine coffees in North America and one in northern Europe.
3. Ensuring the producing and export sector have significant shareholding in the exclusive distributors, sufficient to ensure the purpose of these companies is "hard-wired" and the majority of net profits accrue to the Tanzania part of the supply chain.

Potential to return income to large numbers of farmers/stakeholders

Why is it important to determine if there is potential to enable low-income farmers and producers to benefit from the IP business strategies? It would seem obvious that work that benefits farmers and producers also benefits their neighbors and regions. The first reason is that creating a full business positioning strategy is not easy. It involves financial investment and commitment for the longer term. Realistically, to launch a new brand that is well positioned coupled with a successful import company in a foreign country and sustainable farmer/ producer organization will involve investment in the range of $1,000,000–$5,000,000. Second, the results are not overnight, but generally involve a five-year forecast before appreciable returns are created and distributed. For this, we anticipate sustainable revenue for the long term that is remarkably higher than anything the farmer/producers will acquire on continually fluctuating commodity markets. However, it does take five years to see these results. Most international development grants have a shorter time horizon of three years, but investors have a longer time frame so it is often appropriate to get grant help to develop the business plan and investment to complete the strategy.

For the IP business to be successful, we generally look for a scale of 200,000 producers at minimum. This is not difficult as many products emerging from Africa and other low-income countries easily involve 200,000 producers. In fact, many of our feasibility studies involve upwards of 1,000,000 producers.

There are two important questions to ask:

- Approximately how many farmers, producers or artisans work in this sector?
- Is the supply chain constructed in such a manner that income gains achieved through IP Business are likely to be returned to the farmer/producer artisans?

In some situations, large numbers of people could be impacted with an IP business strategy, but the supply chain may be constructed in such a way that income gain is not likely to be returned to the farmer, producer or artisan.

For example, one industry that utilized the skill and hard labor of hundreds of thousands of low-income people is rum making. When we did an analysis of 16 potential products for IP business in the Caribbean, we found, upon a closer examination of Caribbean rum's supply and distribution channels, that it is largely owned and controlled by several very large corporations.

This corporation is unlikely to enable low-income sugar cane producers to earn substantially more income, even if higher prices are achieved outside of the Caribbean borders. This is not a commentary on a particular company, as much as it is a commentary on the importance of understanding the supply and distribution channels, because they may determine whether or not a particular intervention will, or will not actually return improved income to the producers. The road to market in international development is littered with situations like this one: well meaning interventions, that either did not earn sufficient additional income for distribution, or the additional income was absorbed by large corporations or organizations.

Sadly, this has been the case for some recent private sector development (PSD) strategies. The rationale was that if large importing businesses were involved, via their interest in developing African markets, with an undisguised mutual benefit for the businesses, this could be helpful to African business. Importers can and should advise lower income producers. However, the same importers are often owners of some of the most lucrative brands on the planet so that it is natural for them to channel the resulting product through their own brands.

We consider, then, an analysis of the supply chain critical to determine whether a product qualifies as a good IP business repositioning candidate. It is not the goal of Light Years IP, the NGO, to earn more money for the large corporations of the world, but we determine success in a very simple matrix: Does the IP business repositioning strategy return real income in a sustainable way for the farmer/producers?

Stakeholder organization

The formation of a stakeholder organization to own and sustain the initiative is a critical component of a successful and sustainable IP repositioning opportunity.

We have worked in African countries such as Kenya, Tanzania, Ethiopia, Uganda, Mali, Zambia, and Mozambique and the formation of stakeholder groups varies of course. In some situations the stakeholder groups emerge from cooperatives or form cooperatives. USAID has worked in all LDCs. Sometimes there are stakeholder groups that have been formed as cooperatives or agri-businesses under other projects.

FIGURE 3.8 WONS Cooperative trainers preparing to train women producers
Source: Light Years IP.

As in each part of the business strategy, we are dissecting the steps and stages to better inform and illustrate lessons learned. As in IP tools, or branding, or marketing alone, the stakeholder organization alone does not necessarily spell success. This may seem obvious, but we do note that there is such emphasis on creating cooperatives or state trading companies, or strategies that enable collective cooperation. These do not always change the power balance, improve negotiating capacity or return more income to the producers. Nevertheless, a stakeholder organization is a key element of an overall business repositioning strategy.

In the first example, the Maasai, we spent five years helping to build the Maasai into an IP rights owning entity. That is because the Maasai live in two countries, and are currently organized on a clan and sub-clan basis. It was vital to reach all of the recognized leaders and elders, to provide legal and business training to assist these leaders and elders in building the unifying Maasai IP Initiative Trust Ltd. The goal is to support stakeholder organizations that can both own and manage the IP business strategies going forward.

Step six: Social impact investing

The scale of opportunity is enormous as indicated by the broad estimates of potential gains in Chapter 1. Considerable increases in cash flow can also make it possible to upgrade on-shore processing, adding further to the total return.

The world of social impact investing has grown precipitously and the ROI (return on investment) for this type of investment is large. IP business strategies require sophisticated management and investment. The $2 million spent on the Ethiopian Fine Coffee Initiative translated into a $101 million return within 12 months, a sound and wise investment and rate of return much higher than most. However, if the price differential was determined to be very small, as in the case of, for example, African wheat v. American grown wheat, a commodity product, it would not be wise to engage in an IP business strategy.

To summarize, a product has *potential* to return significantly more income to farmers, producers, and artisans IF it passes these tests or criteria:

1. The product holds a distinctiveness that differentiates it from other products in the final retail market place. That is because consumers are willing to pay more for products that are truly distinctive and this creates a potential opportunity. We are looking at products that have a genuine distinctiveness in the marketplace, so there is income to be "captured" back to the owners – farmers and producers.
2. There is a substantial price gap between the retail price and what the farmer/producers are earning at export.
3. The supply-distribution chain has been evaluated with the four-point intangible value analysis and there is a point of genuine leverage. Leverage is determined based on whether or not there is an opportunity for the

stakeholders to intervene, change the power and earn significantly higher, sustainable income. Caribbean rum is an example of a supply chain where the stakeholders do not have leverage. Ethiopian fine coffee is an example of a situation where they do have leverage.

4.   The income from correct positioning will accrue to the LDC farmers and producers in significant numbers. All interventions and business creations do not necessarily bring higher income to the LDC farmer and producers. Often the case with CSR, or Fair Trade or supplying ingredient brands to lofty brands may be excellent PR, but it may not change the income balance for the LDC producers. It is obviously important to ask this question with open transparency.

The producers must be able to form a serious stakeholder organization.

5.   The product and project should be investment-ready. That is because funding for IP business is not fully on the radar screen of aid organizations that currently are thinking of processing and production or on products for

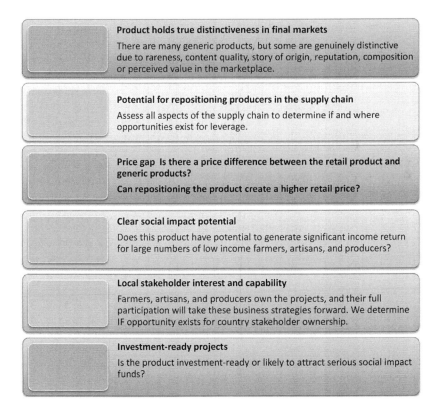

Product holds true distinctiveness in final markets

There are many generic products, but some are genuinely distinctive due to rareness, content quality, story of origin, reputation, composition or perceived value in the marketplace.

Potential for repositioning producers in the supply chain

Assess all aspects of the supply chain to determine if and where opportunities exist for leverage.

Price gap Is there a price difference between the retail product and generic products?

Can repositioning the product create a higher retail price?

Clear social impact potential

Does this product have potential to generate significant income return for large numbers of low income farmers, artisans, and producers?

Local stakeholder interest and capability

Farmers, artisans, and producers own the projects, and their full participation will take these business strategies forward. We determine IF opportunity exists for country stakeholder ownership.

Investment-ready projects

Is the product investment-ready or likely to attract serious social impact funds?

FIGURE 3.9 Criterion for successful IP business ventures by low-income producers
Source: Light Years IP.

the base of the pyramid. Social impact investors need transparency and clarity and trust. Products in countries with bad governments tend not to pass the trust test for social impact investors.

All of these questions and criteria must be affirmative for a genuine IP business strategy to return real income to the degree that makes an IP business strategy worthwhile. It is not easy to change existing patterns – the stakeholder change, investment, and implementation necessary for improving income over time require tremendous effort. This means every effort must be taken to be sure beforehand that the product qualifies – via careful scoping, feasibility studies, and business planning.

And, while scoping, feasibility, and business planning are beyond the scope of this book, it is worth noting that it is our habit to spend a year or more doing the type of analysis that culminates in a business plan of 60 pages or more to explore the various challenges. How to change the world does not mean haphazard thinking. While "learning by doing" may well be applicable to baking a cake or a myriad of technologies, we do not think it should apply to engaging business strategies involving poor people. *Learn first. Then do* is our motto.

Notes

1 C. McCormick, *Market Research Workbook*, Light Years IP, London, 2012.
2 Specialty coffee is an unfortunate designation, because it includes commodity coffee flavored with vanilla. Such coffees will not be included in fine coffee in this chapter. Most fine coffees are Arabica. Some fine Robusta coffees, notably Malabar, are being developed but are tiny in volume as of 2016.
3 International Coffee Organization historical data for coffee prices.
4 Tanzania's annual Arabica peaberry production is about 2,592 MT (from Tanzania Coffee Association statistics).
5 T.R. Lingle, *The state of the specialty coffee industry. Tea & Coffee Trade Journal*, July 2007.
6 Specialty Coffee Association of America.
7 National Coffee Association of U.S.A., Inc., 2010 National Coffee Drinking Trends Study.
8 See "The Tanzanian Peaberry Mystery" by Kenneth Davids: http://www.virtualcoffee.com/articles/spring04/article2.html.
9 Based on the prices in three retail shops in the Washington DC metro area.
10 Specialty-Coffee-Advisor.com, "Magical Peaberries" http://www.specialty-coffee-advisor.com/peaberries.html.
11 www.starbucks.com/coffee/starbucks-reserve-coffee/brazil-sul-de-minas-peaberry.

4

THE POWER OF DISTINCTIVE PRODUCTS AND THE UGANDAN VANILLA CASE STUDY

African and LDC farmers and producers can earn dramatically higher income with Intellectual Property Positioning strategies. However, Intellectual Property strategies do not work for *every* product – far from it. It would be unwise, for example, to engage in the positioning needed for higher income for products that do not hold a retail price far higher than commodity or export price. For example, exports such as bananas, mangoes, passion fruit, or rope would be unlikely to benefit from an IP positioning strategy. The price differential in foreign markets is insufficient to make the cost of marketing, branding, supply chain ownership, and holistic positioning worthwhile for country producers. Although clever branding and higher-level supermarkets do sometimes capture higher prices for specialty products, it is important to begin with distinctive products.

The first and most critical step in IP business positioning is to determine whether a product has sufficient distinctiveness to translate into intangible value. This is true whether the product is agricultural, artisan, cultural or produced. Intellectual Property business tools and strategies work best for distinctive products, rather than more generic, commodity-based products.

Serious projects are under way in many developing countries to achieve branding and trademarks, or other IP ownership such as geographical indications. Many of these initiatives are based on non-distinctive products and this is arguably where IP strategies often go wrong. That is because the greater value for products derives from intangible value – a product of distinctiveness. This chapter digs deeper into distinctiveness and how to correctly differentiate commodity and distinctive products. It is the foundation upon which success or failure often pivots.

Although distinctiveness was introduced as the first step of the IP business method, the overuse of branding and the infusion of multi-million investments into the wrong products with subsequent failure suggests the need to underscore the importance of selecting the RIGHT product. Some people argue that anything can be branded. While anything CAN be branded, branding is only aspect of a successful IP positioning strategy. Branding non- distinctive products coupled with inadequate positioning is the cause of many failed business strategies.

Products that work well for IP positioning need not be a haphazard guess, but should be based on careful analytics. We spend six months to a year to determine whether a product has sufficient distinctiveness by industry and market research standards to warrant investment in a full IP business positioning strategy. The Ugandan vanilla case study will show how distinctiveness translates into an effective IP business to increase income by 10 times for the Ugandan farmers.

In this chapter, we will:

- Highlight why intangible value derives from distinctive products
- Dig deeper into how to determine distinctive over commodity products
- Explore the ways products can be distinctive
- Describe available tools for determining distinctiveness
- Provide examples of IP business failure with multi-million dollar projects when the product was not distinctive and this stage was done poorly or ignored
- Delve deeply into the Ugandan vanilla case study as an example of a distinctive v. non-distinctive product and the six-step method to return higher income to the Ugandan farmers.

What is distinctiveness?

- Distinctive by definition means different or unique.
- If something is distinct it is different in some important way from commodity or generic products.
- Ways in which something can be distinctive: Quality or flavor; concentration; taste; history; origin or story of origin; quality important to a consumer *or* by trade industry standards; or reputation and perceived value.
- Sometimes product location contributes to distinctiveness such as Bordeaux wine; Virginia tobacco; Maine lobster; Ethiopian coffee; and Ugandan vanilla.

Why should we take time to determine distinctiveness?

- To understand why some products have intangible value. Typically, when conducting workshops in a country, we are approached with the common request that we consider particular products for an IP business strategy. People believe their product(s) possesses uniqueness and are better than other similar products on the market and that their hard work has created something valuable and unique. We respect that products are farmed and produced with diligence and care.

- *However,* not all producers or all farmers produce a unique product. IP business strategy is based on products that are distinctive to retail consumers who pay higher retail prices for them.
- If a product is considered distinct, consumers are often more willing to pay a higher price for it as consumers seek products that have meaning.

To demonstrate the difference between an IP business positioning strategy based on distinctive and non-distinctive products, the example of Ugandan cotton is highlighted, as it involves about 500,000 growers of cotton. Ugandan cotton is a good product, but it is not distinctive. The Intellectual Property business strategy did not work well in terms of advancing income for the Ugandan cotton farmers. The cotton is exported and the returns are low to the hard-working Ugandan cotton farmers and producers.

How do we determine if the cotton is indeed distinctive? The following would be good questions for a researcher to ask toward determining whether or not the product is *distinctive* or merely a good product:

- A process of comparison: What other cotton is on the market from other countries?
- Is Ugandan cotton different from the other cottons?
- What are the general distinguishing characteristics of cotton as determined by industry standards? In this case, cotton quality is determined by fiber count. There are industry standards for most products, sometimes by color, size, region and it is important to consider these standards, as others have already done the hard work to determine quality standards.
- Why do the Ugandans believe their cotton is unique?
- What do experts say about the product?

The process of comparison

Determining uniqueness is asking if the product is different and, if so, different in what way? Recall that uniqueness and distinctiveness are indicators of comparative advantage and consumer attribution. Meaning, we cannot tell if one product is distinctively superior without understanding the product within both a comparative and consumer framework.

Consider Ethiopian fine coffee, a product that we know is unique and distinctive. How do we know that it isn't our wishful thinking that defines the product as distinctive? We can search Ethiopian fine coffee. We can find dozens of articles about it. We can ask experts and access reports. But, when we can find higher prices in the retail market for Ethiopian fine coffee compared to commodity coffee, that is how we know it is distinct to consumers.

In today's Internet world, desk research and volumes of information are ready to be explored. However, desk research has limits.

There is no substitute for going shopping! It is important to go to the marketplace, to retail outlets in western markets. It is important to talk to buyers,
consumers, and to gain understanding of consumer market trends. We also look
at prices and product positioning. You can find us shopping and snapping photos
throughout retail outlets!

For example:

- Where is the product positioned in the store?
- What are the special features?
- How does the price compare to other similar products?
- What does the shopkeeper say about the product? This is particularly helpful
  if it is a specialty shop.

Stakeholders

It is important to listen to farmers, producers, and artisans. It is the stakeholders
who frequently educate us about what makes their product distinct such as stories
of origin and history. This has been the case with the Maasai and with Malian
mudcloth, and Ugandan shea butter. We spend many hours under trees listening
to cashew gatherers, vanilla farmers, and the women who gather shea nuts and
produce shea butter. The process of creating champagne, for example, is not
about the grape but the unique process that adds distinctive value and is the basis
of the reputation. Oftentimes, it is the process of creating the product and the soil
quality that makes a product more distinctive such as Ugandan vanilla. While
stakeholder point of view must be balanced with Internet research, retail and
import study and desk research, it should never be ignored.

Internet and desk research

The Internet is a valuable resource to help better understand a product and the
marketplace as a whole. Below are some suggestions of items to research to
increase awareness about your product as well as other products on the market.

General properties of the product

Simple Internet research today allows us to search product attributes. In cotton, for
example, quality is measured by length of the fiber. In vanilla, quality is a product of
the degree of concentration. In honey, quality is measured by the type of flower the
bee consumes. Other properties include vitamins, such as in shea butter. For cotton,
we have one industry standard – length of fiber. What is the length of the fiber in
Ugandan cotton compared to other reputable cotton? Is Ugandan cotton unique or
distinctive on this comparative variable? As an ingredient product mostly purchased
by manufacturers of clothing, the technical qualities are dominant.

International development agency reports

Oftentimes, there are development agencies working in an industry sector because the sector has been known historically as a large producer. For example, in Grenada spice was once about 80 percent of all agricultural exports. USAID has done far-reaching and well-reported projects throughout Africa. Background information is available for many industry and agricultural sectors, made public to enable others to build on groundwork.

However, just because a large amount is exported does not mean it is a distinctive product. In the case of Ugandan cotton, the International Development Association has put millions of dollars into a project to boost production of Ugandan cotton. Their underlying assumption is this: If a country is able to grow or to make a large amount of a product, advancing quality and production should enable higher exports, along with more employment. Often, this supports the goal of improving economic progress by boosting a product to create jobs and engage in a strategy of "value-added." While a reasonable strategy, a challenge is that if the products are not distinctive products wherein an IP positioning strategy will work in the long term, there is a risk of over-production for a commodity market.

Research that has already been conducted and made public on a product, such as Ugandan cotton, is important because it can be a starting point. However, keep in mind, products that are made public and reported upon are often more about large volume than distinctiveness.

Why is volume of production not a good measure of distinctiveness?

Remember, distinctiveness is about unique properties, so that value can be increased via Intellectual Property business tools. Volume of production often represents a commodity product – these products are marketed by commodity pricing schemes that are volatile. Value-added often does not return higher income to farmers and producers, as value is taken outside the country of origin.

Nevertheless, in doing research to better understand a product, it is worth reviewing international development agency reports that are normally made public. Since millions of dollars are spent producing the reports, it is a reasonable place to learn more information, as long as it is a beginning point. The researcher should check sites and use site-specific search engines such as:

- Department for International Development (DFID), www.dfid.gov.uk
- The World Bank, http://www.worldbank.org
- USAID, http://www.usaid.gov
- Natural Resources Institute (NRI), http://www.nri.org
- Please see the Workbook on IP Value Capture for a full discussion (see workbook included on companion website).

Product organizations

Sometimes, industries arrange themselves into different product organizations or cooperatives. Information about the organization's position relative to its competitors can be gathered from website information. As a researcher, one must use care to note that what a sector organization reports about itself is going to be biased, because its reports are used to market its product. However, one can get a sense of price, volume, and trends.

Consider the following sector organization websites to illustrate this point:

- Ugandan cotton, http://cdouga.org
- African cashews, http://www.africancashewalliance.com

Retail websites and price points

A review of retail websites will give a picture of how and why consumers may view a product, and therefore why they decide to pay for it and how much. If we move from cotton to finished products, we might try to search Ugandan cotton shirts, to see if consumers have picked up anything particularly unique about the intangible attributes of cotton by way of paying higher prices for the sense of reputation or story of origin, or other qualities we have discussed that underscore the uniqueness of the brand. This is true for West Indian Sea Island cotton shirts for example.[1]

In the case of Ethiopian fine coffee, one can find many different retail websites and coffee shops where the coffee is fetching a large price differential based on quality. In the case of cotton, we might consider sites and stores that sell high quality product shirts. For example, West Indian Sea Island cotton shirts sell at retail for $400.00–$600.00. Using a combination of industry reports, retail price points pointing toward higher end brands, and Caribbean export reports, one finds copious research explaining why the cotton is superior. That the Caribbean producers are receiving low export prices for their cotton suggests an IP business positioning strategy could be plausible for this product. Other factors of the six-step method need to be analyzed, but the Sea Island cotton is truly distinctive, as a starting point.

Retail price variation

The goal of assessing retail and Internet price points is to ascertain potential intangible value and IP positioning strategy feasibility. An assessment on price at retail should include at minimum 20–30 price points, alongside desk research on market trends. For example, Figure 4.1 shows the wide variation for cosmetic products made with up to 20 percent shea butter from West Africa. The chart also depicts great variance in price, deriving from the value of branding at the top of the chart. The wide range of prices from the same product in this sector suggests that intangible value is particularly high. This suggests an opportunity for African producers of cosmetic products to enter that market, provided they position correctly.

From the chart, the price positioning of the Mo' Yaa, a cosmetic product with East African Shea, has been set as a goal for the Womens Owned Nilotica Shea (WONS) business.

Figure 4.1 shows prices of Shea butter at retail (2013).

Another example can be seen with the Maasai cultural brand. Retail website searches reveal hundreds of sites that market and "sell" the Maasai brand, such as www.mbt.com, Maasai Barefoot Technology. Here, we can see shoes that use the Maasai image selling for about $200–$300 on the website. A simple Google search of *Maasai* illustrates many such examples of the Maasai brand being used

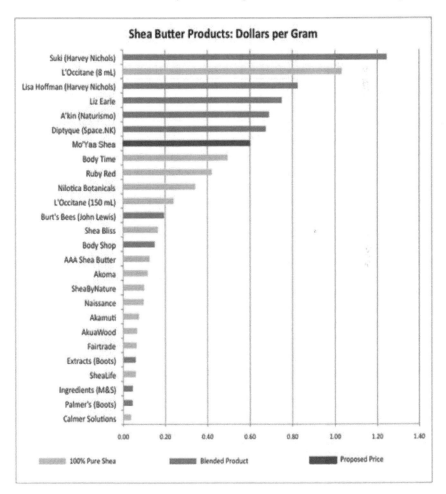

FIGURE 4.1 Retail value in UK for products based on shea butter
Source: Light Years IP.

inappropriately. Company-specific research is in a later section; however, the researcher should look at what aspects of the brand are appealing to consumers.

Understanding the brand

Reviewing the Maasai cultural brand in the marketplace, important questions to ask are:

- Why are consumers willing to spend money on brands associated with the Maasai?
- What aspects of the Maasai image are appealing?
- What is it that consumers associate with the Maasai that they want to imitate?

These questions will lead to a better understanding of why a brand is worth so much in the marketplace.

- **Comparative website search:** To provide a reasonable assessment, we must compare various websites to begin to acquire a picture of product distinctiveness.
- **REMEMBER:** Qualities the consumer associates with a product are important to understand. This can be good news for an IP business strategy!
- **Internet research for market value:** In today's world, with so much information available on the Internet, you can learn a great deal more about the potential of your product to achieve an IP business strategy than ever before.

What are we looking for by Internet research?

- Public perception: What does the product mean to consumers?
- Consumer attitudes: Why are consumers attracted to the product?
- Retail prices: What price range does the product fetch?
- Concentration of markets: Where is the product being exported to and to what markets is it imported?
- Comparative products: What are the comparative products?
- Comparative prices: This is where we begin to move from the product's distinctiveness as a physical property, to its uniqueness as a product of consumer perception.
- Examples:

  - Shea butter sells on Internet sites in a commodity way, undifferentiated for low prices, but it also sells for very high prices, up to $65.00 for 150 ml. We are obviously looking to ask: *Why*? This is where experts in branding and marketing enable advances – the topic of further modules in our series.
  - You can review Internet sites as a base for asking: What is the difference between those commodity prices and distinctive priced items?

FIGURE 4.2A Massai bag for $2,280
Source: Louis Vuitton.

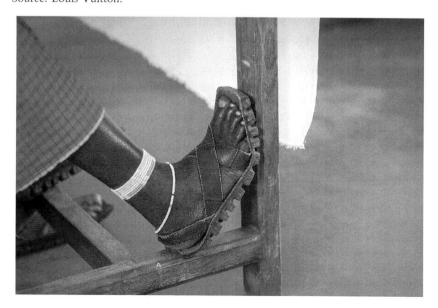

FIGURE 4.2B Massai Barefoot technology ($235)
Source: Maasai Barefoot Technology.

Google or other search engine research

Simple search engines allow you to do general research, but there are ways to optimize your research.

1. **Google.com/trends**

    This Google website enables you to review products and see trends in popularity over time. For example, one can type in *sweet wine* and view historical trends, cities, and countries that produce sweet wine, and whether a product is trending upward or downward. Figure 4.3 shows an example of a Google trend for *Ethiopian coffee*.

2. **Power searches**

    Power searches optimize returns by narrowing the search field. Just typing in a keyword into Google, such as *coffee*, returns millions of pages. However, if one types in *Ethiopian fine coffee*, the returns are fewer and more manageable, of course.

    To limit your search further, one can do a phrase matched search.[2] Typing in "Ethiopian distinctive coffee" within quotes, narrows results to four pages which all have the words "Ethiopian distinctive coffee" written in sequence. Here, we can review these pages and gain more focused information in order to review the most relevant sites for our needs.

    From this simple Google search, we can extrapolate that Ethiopian fine coffee has a serious web presence and learn a great deal about its distinctiveness. However, the same is not true when trying a Google search of Ugandan distinctive cotton shirts. No website pages emerge. These simple search engine tools enable a great deal of information to be accrued quite simply and are available to entrepreneurs in developing countries for the purpose of assessing market value, and potential IP positioning feasibility for a wide variety of products.

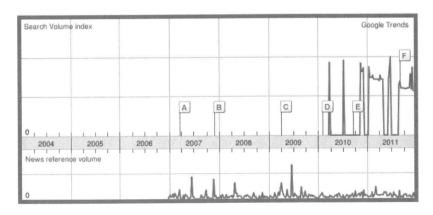

FIGURE 4.3 Google trend search

In summary, IP business pivots on product distinctiveness. Distinctiveness means unique. Uniqueness can derive from the product itself, or the story of origin or reputation of the product. Most products are not distinctive.

Our analysis is that Africa, alone, holds four–five truly distinctive exports per country on average, with some countries higher and lower.[3] LDC countries have distinctive products throughout. The challenge is that attempting to brand, trademark or acquire other IP tools for less than distinctive products often hits early barriers. That is because retail value and price is often not elastic. Prices for non-distinctive products are usually lower. This often means that despite a great deal of work to engage IP strategies, and branding, the products are not able to return higher income to the in-country farmers and producers.

Distinctiveness matters because it translates into intangible value and price differentials in the final markets. Distinctiveness determines what IP tools that are needed for the IP business strategy. Product distinctiveness can be initially assessed by sector organizations, reports, and web research, as well as listening to farmers, producers, and artisans, but it is best confirmed by analysis of price differentials.

Because intangible value is the aspect of a product that generates higher prices in retail markets, understanding what attributes of the product have intangible value is critical. Remember: Distinctiveness can be in the *process* as well as the *product*.

The following case study demonstrates a distinctive product of Uganda. It is a simple product, Ugandan vanilla, but involves about 300,000 farmers and producers growing and processing a product that has the highest vanillin content of any vanilla product in the world – a truly unique, distinctive export. The case study shows the process of determining distinctiveness, and intangible value. It also describes in detail how a product should be analyzed when considering an IP business strategy, as the product sells for $12.00 for two pods at Whole Foods and other higher end markets, but returns to Ugandan farmers just $0.08 for two pods. The essential question is to determine if Uganda could fare better, as defined by receiving appreciably higher income with an IP business positioning strategy.

Ugandan Vanilla Case Study: The power of a distinctive product

The following analysis of Ugandan vanilla, a superior, distinctive product shows how the IP business repositioning model can be used to generate significant export income for Uganda. The case study goes through each step of an IP business strategy to illustrate the business planning in detail.

First, we consider how to determine if Ugandan vanilla is truly distinctive, and then where the opportunities lie on the world markets. We analyze the supply chain, and the wholesale opportunity through to best opportunities to position the Ugandan import company. Though detailed, this type of business case is necessary to create genuinely successful IP business strategies. As in any business, there is no magic, but there is a method.

Currently, Uganda grows vanillin that is of the highest quality, with higher vanillin content than any other vanilla in the world. It retails for two pods at $12.00 at higher end markets such as Whole Foods, but the Ugandan farmers receive about $0.04/pod.

Ugandan vanilla is distinctive. It sells for about $12.00 per two pods in Whole Foods while the Ugandan farmers receive about $.04 per pod.

FIGURE 4.4 Ugandan vanilla farmer
Source: Light Years IP.

How do we know this?

Using our Uganda vanilla example, we take a trip to Whole Foods market. We use Whole Foods because it is the fastest growing retail grocery store in the US and known for having one of the most expensive shelf space per square foot.[4] Whole Foods reflects trends in presenting products to consumers. On the shelves, there are various types of vanilla, such as Madagascan, Ugandan, and the generic brand. From the prices of these goods we can see one price point for what a certain group of consumers are willing to pay. This is just the initial step, and ascertaining price by reviewing 20–30 price points is needed. Nevertheless, at the high end, we see the potential for customers who are willing to pay $12.00 for Ugandan vanilla.

Consumer preference: analyzing the retail marketplace

The next question: Who would buy such expensive vanilla? Here, we assess consumer shopping patterns and where Whole Foods and Waitrose, or Marks and Spencer's in the UK are located to reach consumers with distinctive products. This takes us to some desk research. We note where in the store the expensive vanilla is located, and the percentage of the store devoted to high-priced distinctive products such as spices.

For example, when analyzing natural beauty products in one large Whole Foods (Columbus Circle, New York City, USA), we noted that about 15 percent of the retail floor space in the store was devoted to specialty (often high-priced) natural beauty products. One can look at what is dominating and how it is dominating consumer purchases.

One can observe where products are located. At Whole Foods, coffee dominates the center of the store, arranged by beans and countries, offering consumers testing stations. This is a marked change from 10 years ago when coffee was sold already bagged in heavy plastic and on long shelves. A few American brands dominated such as Maxwell House and Folgers. Now, it is the specialty brands that dominate the higher end markets reflective of consumer changes toward specialty brands, unique and distinctive products, and the intangible benefits.

Differentiating distinctive products from generic ones

An exercise that advances our knowledge of the retail markets is to look for comparative generic products. What does generic vanilla sell for at the stores, even the same stores as distinctive vanilla? One might note a generic brand vanilla selling for the equivalent of $1.50, whereas the distinctive vanilla sells for $12.00.

Questions we ask

- Why will consumers choose a product costing $12.00, whereas they could meet the same functional need with a product that costs $1.25? Why would someone pay 10 times more for the Ugandan vanilla?
- What need or perceived need does the higher priced product meet?
- Is the product that is selling for the higher price truly distinctive or is it higher priced because it is marketed in a certain way?

1 Is the product distinctive or merely good? Can the distinctiveness translate into higher value/higher prices at retail?

Uganda's vanilla stands out among the many vanilla-producing countries due to high content of vanillin, the compound that gives vanilla its signature flavor and aroma. As the world's largest producer, Madagascar and its vanilla industry are known the world over; but Ugandan vanilla contains higher vanillin levels. Whereas high quality Malagasy vanilla contains 1.4 to 1.8 percent vanillin by weight, Ugandan vanilla contains 1.6 to 2.1 percent and often higher.

Two factors are required to produce quality pods with high vanillin content: high quality green beans harvested when ripe and proper curing technique. The growing conditions in Uganda, the rich, loamy soil, plentiful rainfall, and tropical environment, allow the beans to flourish and are thought to contribute to its especially high vanillin content. Each plant requires hand pollination and picking the beans when fully ripe is critical to obtaining optimal flavor from the beans as vanillin develops in the last few weeks of maturation. The traditional method of curing by sunning and sweating allows the bean's complex flavors and aromas to develop fully. The qualities that make Ugandan vanilla unique are both inherent in the fertile land of its origin and a result of attentive care on the farm and in the processing.

Vanilla farming in Uganda began in the 1950s, but production levels remained low until the 1990s. Since the mid-1990s, production – growing, curing, and exporting – has increased steadily; now an estimated 200,000–300,000 small-holder farmers cultivate vanilla. In recent years, Uganda's vanilla has gained recognition for its exceptional quality, surpassing that of Madagascar. A number of public endorsements from food aficionados show that Ugandan vanilla's superior quality is achieving recognition amongst wholesalers, retailers, and consumers alike.

What do experts say about Ugandan vanilla? Do they suggest it is distinctive and more highly valued by consumers?

Ugandan vanilla has been called "Ugandan Gold" by a US-based online purveyor of vanilla. While obviously reflecting some self-interested marketing, the online retailer carries vanilla from both Uganda and Madagascar. "In fact, an independent testing laboratory has reported significantly higher vanillin content in the current crop of Uganda vanilla beans than any reading we have seen to date on Madagascar beans … Uganda is now the origin of choice for the most discriminating baker, pastry or dessert chef or gourmet food processor. Try our UGANDA GOLD™ beans and compare them to any Madagascar gourmet bean you've ever bought. We believe you will become a believer, as we have, that Uganda is now the origin of choice for the most discriminating baker, pastry or dessert chef or gourmet food processor."[5]

A well-known chef in the UK, Hugh Fearnley Whittingstall, has said of one particular brand of Ugandan vanilla, "some of the best I have ever tasted. The pods arrive beautifully supple and bursting with tiny little seeds. The scent is rich and intense and the flavour deep, long lasting and absolutely true."[6]

Other chefs, such as Delia Smith, a well-known British TV chef since the 1970s, have also endorsed Ugandan vanilla. While celebrities' endorsements on their own do not equate to distinctiveness, they are one more piece of the quest to ascertain distinctive v. ordinary products, reflecting popular consumer opinion.

What are the trends for distinctive vanilla?

Celebrity and expert endorsements aside, it is important to analyze larger consumer trends when determining whether a product holds sufficient distinctiveness in the marketplace such as consumer trends.

Across a number of European countries, demand for healthy and environmentally friendly products is increasing. Consumers are variably sensitive to price; in Germany and the UK, consumers are generally willing to pay large premiums for organic spices and herbs whereas consumers in France and the Netherlands are more price conscious. However, consumers are consistently more aware of and interested in quality. Consumers are also demanding greater product diversity. There is a wider acceptance of culinary and ethnic variety and more interest in exotic ingredients. Both of these trends bode well for the marketing of Uganda's vanilla.

2 What is the retail market outlook for Ugandan vanilla? Is there a price gap relative to generic/commodity vanilla?

Market image and penetration

It is known that many European consumers and chefs are very conscious of the quality and origins of the ingredients they choose. Increasingly, they are attracted to natural products and products which they feel confident about, whether for health, social or environmental reasons. Vanilla pods are and will probably continue to be a niche market product with perennial favorites. However, Ugandan vanilla has garnered accolades among a variety of end user groups. And a new brand that stands for quality, consistency, fair practices, and represents the Ugandan vanilla sector equally will appeal to this set of discriminating consumers.

Opportunities

There are two main grades of cured vanilla pods, gourmet and extract grade. Gourmet pods are retailed as pods; extract pods are made into vanilla extract and used in food manufacturing or retailed as extract. Ugandan vanilla is exported primarily to the US, Germany, Canada, France, UK and Japan. Exporters estimate that 70–90 percent of Uganda's vanilla is sold to the industrial market. Commodity vanilla is dominated by a few French importers who control a purely price-driven environment. The majority of exported vanilla will be extracted and used in food manufacturing such as ice cream and baked goods.

One of Uganda's crop seasons coincides with Madagascar's vanilla growing season, bringing large quantities of vanilla onto the market in January/February. This condition leaves little room for Ugandan vanilla exporters to negotiate their commodity prices in the face of Madagascar's enormous volumes (around 50–60% of world production).

Figure 4.5 reflects Uganda's relatively small market share and the opportunity to increase the share. The high quality and small market share are factors that present an opportunity for Uganda to market its best pods to targeted market segments and in so doing, significantly alter its position in the world vanilla sector. With secure buyers whose interest is quality rather than only price, Uganda can improve its negotiating position within the supply chain creating a more stable environment for both farmers and exporters alike.

The supply chain

Analysis of the supply chain, which has been simplified into four groups of participants: producer/farmers, exporter/curer, foreign importer/wholesaler, and foreign retailer, shows the wholesaler and retailer earning, by far, the largest share of income and the largest margins. In the case of cured vanilla pods, wholesalers

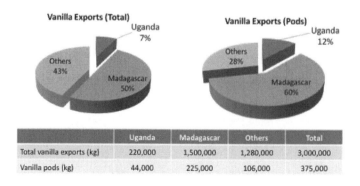

	Uganda	Madagascar	Others	Total
Total vanilla exports (kg)	220,000	1,500,000	1,280,000	3,000,000
Vanilla pods (kg)	44,000	225,000	106,000	375,000

FIGURE 4.5 Uganda's small share of world markets for vanilla
Source: Light Years IP Feasibility Study on Ugandan Fine Vanilla.

are performing no processing and incurring few other costs than packaging and distributing the pods. The pods are sold in exactly the same condition as when they left Uganda. In retail shops, Ugandan pods sell for $5.25 per pod or $1,155 per kg, and range from $1.60 to $3.30 per pod ($350–$730 per kg) from online outlets. In wholesale trade, cured unpackaged wholesale pods sell at $120 per kg and packaged pods sell for an estimated $450 per kg.

Currently one kilo of cured pods exports for $19 FOB (freight on board ship at Mombasa). Farmers receive 3,000 UGS per kg green beans (about $1.50) or $9 for the equivalent of 1 kg cured. In the existing system, farmers have no negotiating ability.

Comparing wholesale and retail prices with those of export, it becomes clear that the true beneficiaries of Uganda's superior quality vanilla are the wholesalers and retailers despite the fact that its quality derives from its origin. The gourmet pod, at retail, is sold in exactly the same form that it left Uganda. The sizable gap between exporter and wholesaler margins presents potential to utilize business strategies involving IP to capture value in the final markets.

It is evident that consumers are willing to pay premium prices for high quality vanilla pods. The perception that Madagascar's vanilla is the best is being challenged in the face of Ugandan vanilla's higher vanillin content. It is an opportune time for Uganda to assert control of its singular product. In the current situation, exporters receive 2 percent of the estimated total margin earned, wholesalers 30 percent and retailers 67 percent. By going beyond the border and reaching into foreign markets, Uganda can capture existing value in the final markets and increase income to its exporters and farmers. The following section will discuss specific business strategies including IP tools.

Begin with the end in mind: proposed strategy for branded Ugandan owned wholesaler

"Stop thinking like a commodity producer" is the motto behind the strategy.

Uganda's total export of vanilla is estimated at about 6 percent of total worldwide trade in vanilla. Given this relatively small portion, it is feasible to consider strategies that concentrate on specific market segments rather than trying to sell to all possible markets in all parts of the world. This would mean shifting from accepting commodity market prices that inevitably also mean very weak negotiating positions. A stronger position in the global market can be established by drawing together the finest vanilla into a single Ugandan-owned wholesale marketing channel that carefully targets selected market sectors in export countries. This new model would produce higher returns and justify abandoning "thinking like a commodity producer," that is, abandon the volatile prices shown in Figure 4.6.

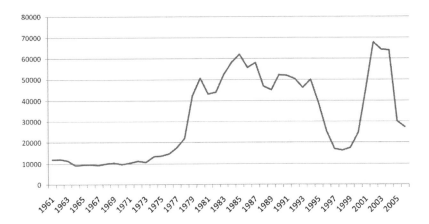

FIGURE 4.6 World commodity vanilla export price ($/ton)
Source: LYIP Feasibility Study on Ugandan Fine Vanilla.

3 Where is the point of leverage for stakeholders?

A Ugandan-owned marketing company in Europe

The large proportion of value currently captured by foreign wholesalers suggests a new Ugandan-owned wholesale company positioned in key foreign markets can realize significant gains. The wholesale company will establish unique marketing channels in countries such as Germany, Italy, and the UK where gourmet cooks will readily appreciate the world's best vanilla. The vanilla will be sold in the form of dark brown pods in brightly colored packaging along with the compelling story about Ugandan farmers working the most fertile land in Africa and curers sunning and sweating their vanilla beans in woolen blankets to bring out the most vanillin, flavor, and aromas.

Size of potential market and comparison to industry leaders

Consultation with exporters indicates that Madagascar exports an estimated 15 percent of their production for final use as gourmet pods, which amounts to an average of 225 tons per year. Including pods from Papua New Guinea and Indonesia who produce an alternate variety and use a different curing process, global retail consumption of gourmet pods is estimated at about 375 tons per year, see Figure 4.6.

Returns

In an average year, Uganda is estimated to export about 20 percent or 44 tons of vanilla that was retailed as gourmet pods, with export revenue valued at approximately $0.84

million. If Uganda owned a wholesale marketing company in Europe, this quantity of pods could have earned a gross income of $16.2 million (44,000 kilos at $368 per kilo). Allowing for the cost of packaging and labeling, shipping and handling, and marketing and operating costs, a very substantial increase of net returns to Uganda would result.

We often call the method of IP Business that acquires more value for low income farmers and producers Intellectual Property value capture, because the ultimate point is to return more value, meaning higher income, to the producers. Figure 4.7 depicts a situation wherein the Ugandan vanilla farmers would be organized, and own an import company, returning this income to Uganda, rather than the current situation.

In Figure 4.8, we see the commodity price paid to Ugandan farmers is $9.00 per kilo equivalent and $19.00 at export. Importers receive $121/kilo and considering the pods are sold in two-pod increments, the retailer receives $1,155. If the Ugandans owned an import company closer to retail, this is the point of best leverage. They would "capture" approximately $368/kilo.

The opportunity for Uganda is to own an import company closer to higher end retail markets. This is business positioning! The advantages for this strategy are that:

1. A large share of profit is taken by the import company, as can be observed in Figure 4.8. Note that $19.00 equivalent returns to the exporters, whereas $121 to the importer or wholesaler outside of Ugandan borders.
2. It is not difficult to open an importer in a foreign country, well positioned closer to retail markets. This may seem out of reach simply because it is not yet done routinely by African farmers. It is similar to the Divine Chocolate model of Ghana discussed earlier.

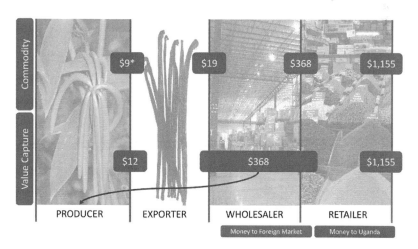

FIGURE 4.7 Gross share of retail value received by role in supply chain for Ugandan fine vanilla

Source: Light Years IP Feasibility Study on Ugandan Fine Vanilla.

To clarify the price analysis, an argument may be made that the import and retail prices do not reflect the costs incurred by importers or retailers. Real estate for convenient, well-positioned markets is expensive, such as the High Streets of London where consumers are willing to pay more for fine products, or Columbus Circle, New York, site of a busy Whole Foods market. It has been documented that Whole Foods pays the highest amount per square foot of shelf space of any large market. We emphasize that the financial figures here also do not take into account the farmer/producer costs. Highest quality vanillin does not fall from vines, but rather requires curing, tending, and care, intensive nightly labor to cure the beans and develop the coveted vanillin taste, and has been developed over many decades of knowledge transfer, alongside expensive transport costs to market. Hence, the actual price points are used in the comparative analysis for each of the price points in the four-point supply chain from farmer to exporter, importer and retailer.

Figure 4.8 depicts the commodity pricing of Ugandan vanilla compared to the upward trend for retail prices.

Security of income

A valuable consequence of stepping out of commodity exporting will be the stabilization of income for farmers and the sector as a whole. Unusual price fluctuations for commodity vanilla, either up or down, will have smaller impacts on the new Ugandan pathway to their special consumers than in the general market. With a wholesale company established in a EU country like Italy and consistent buyers and negotiated prices, the Ugandan supply chain will become predictable and stable instilling confidence in the industry's viability and future.

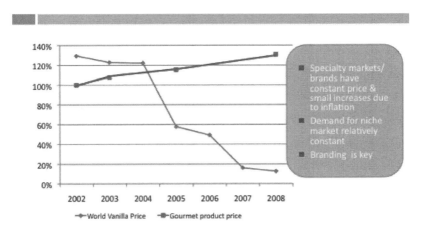

FIGURE 4.8 Difference in volatility in commodity pricing and gourmet product retail pricing, Ugandan fine vanilla
Source: Light Years IP Feasibility Study on Ugandan Fine Vanilla.

Over time, brand loyalty will improve further the security of the entire sector. Achieving higher prices for Ugandan vanilla farmers will help motivate them and ensure necessary continued supply. It will also provide much needed income to monitor and improve quality, all of which will add greater security to incomes.

4 Creating a viable stakeholder organization to position the Farmers

In creating a stakeholder organization to own the IP business through to retail, it is important to engage the farmers and representatives collectively, and to build on what has already been established. This venture is dependent equally upon farmers, the one exporting cooperative (Mukono) and the export sector. At present, farmers have little or no negotiating power as farm gate prices are set by exporters. They also must sell their green beans soon after they are harvested otherwise they can no longer be cured. This situation makes it easy for farmers to be taken advantage of by traders and exporters who are, themselves, squeezed by foreign buyers. It is essential that a new countrywide contract be established, to present a true picture to gourmet pod consumers that buying the product will directly and considerably benefit the farmers. The farmers should be shareholders in the marketing company.

Higher farm gate prices secured through the proposed value capture strategy should be structured to increase the Ugandan farmers' motivation to increase quality. This would reduce the temptation to turn away from vanilla farming, as historical instability of commodity prices is replaced with growing confidence and awareness of owning a stake in the outcome.

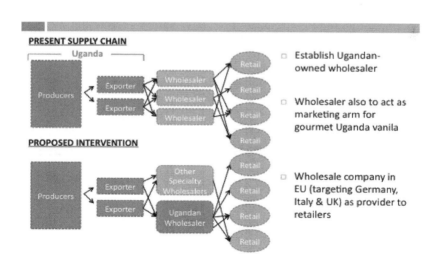

FIGURE 4.9 Proposed intervention
Source: Light Years IP Feasibility Study on Ugandan Fine Vanilla.

Stakeholder participation

The new marketing company will represent an opportunity for the whole sector. It will require investment capital and coordination of farmer and exporter efforts. The government can play a role in bringing the entity into existence and arranging resources, but it is wise not to put government in control of a business venture. A stakeholder grouping dominated by farmers and export business people would have the ability to hire high quality management for the new company.

Though it is beyond the scope of this case study to provide the full training programs for the sector, as they would be organized into a stakeholder organization, elements of forming a stakeholder organization and constitution are covered in subsequent chapters. Also, workbooks in IP business are included with this publication, and power points specific to a Ugandan vanillin sector are available upon request (see workbooks included on companion website).

5 Social impact investment

A branded Ugandan-owned wholesaling company as envisaged would ultimately return $48.5 million to Uganda per annum versus the current income of about $5–6 million. The wholesale company would earn a gross margin of $244 per kilo of cured gourmet pods. Rather than earning about $19 per kilo or even $40 per kilo for organic at export and contending with perpetual uncertainty, the wholesaling company would gross $368 per kilo, a radically improved income to exporters and farmers.

The critical additional value of the Ugandan-owned wholesaling company is to fundamentally alter the dependency of Ugandan farmers on foreign markets by taking control.

Further requirements for success in this strategy

Marketing

An IP business strategy featuring newly branded Ugandan vanilla pods will require concerted marketing efforts within identified segments. The intention is not to saturate all conceivable markets but rather to focus a deliberate promotion on a handful of screened markets that will be most receptive to the distinctive qualities of Uganda's vanilla. The promotion will highlight the story of Uganda and its gifted and fertile land and the vanilla farmers who labor on their small-scale farms, often employing sustainable and organic practices for very little gain. This promotion will also complement and augment Uganda's national branding strategy spearheaded by the Ministry of Tourism, Trade and Industry, Tourism Department.

Incentives

The problem of farmers harvesting too early because of an announced price or because they are in great need of immediate income must be addressed. It is important to sensitize farmers to the importance of quality. Producing a certain percentage of gourmet quality pods is directly related to and dependent upon crop management on their farms. Offering incentives to farmers for gourmet quality beans will begin to increase this percentage and set in motion a quality control process. Over time quality incentives can help to alleviate some of the capital input issues that farmers face so they are not under such intense pressure to harvest and sell their beans before they are ripe. Additionally, as farmers earn consistently higher incomes, more farmers will become motivated to increase production. From the exporter/curers' perspective, it is also in their interest to encourage farmers to wait until their beans are mature before harvesting them. Immature beans are smaller and will yield low vanillin contents that will not be suitable for gourmet grade. What is different in this strategy is that agri-business typically begins with production and quality control, whereas we argue that beginning with the end in mind and demonstrating higher prices creates incentives for quality control that are more realistic and sustainable.

The target value chain shows farmer prices increasing to $20 per kilo of processed pods, equivalent to around $3.20 per kilo of green pods, an increase of over 100 percent. It also shows exporters' gross margins moving up to $20 per kilo. These gains should be effective incentives, while both groups would also benefit from long-term profit proceeds from the new wholesaling company.

Summary

In this book, we have argued that African and LDC countries are poised to earn substantially improved income, via their many distinctive agricultural, artisan, and cultural exports. These products involve products that can be demonstrated to hold intangible value, as these products are selling for much higher prices at retail levels, outside of the countries.

However, distinctiveness is a somewhat loose concept, subject to interpretation, and sometimes wishful thinking. Some have advocated that "anything can be branded," and with the right amount of marketing, the underlying product is less critical. There are strong reasons to take time and effort to determine if a product is distinctive and build the IP positioning strategy from a truly distinctive product. This is true despite the fact that there are non-distinctive products that can become popular with sufficient marketing. The goal in creating an IP business positioning strategy with agricultural products is to look for the intangible value to differentiate the product from commodity pricing schemes. This is largely les likely with non-distinctive products such as, for example, ordinary teas, coffees, rope, fruits, and vegetables.

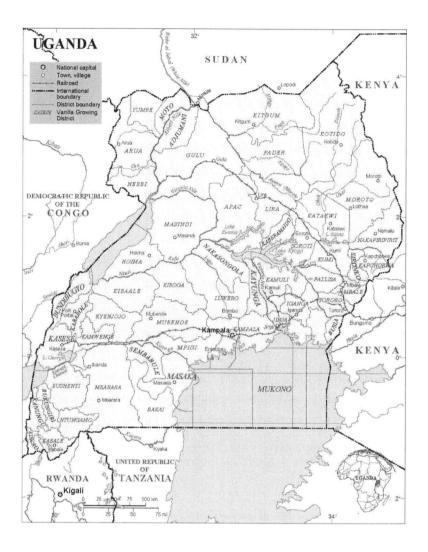

FIGURE 4.10 Uganda map, vanilla growing regions
Source: www.un.org/Depts/Cartographic/map/profile/uganda.pdf

Distinctiveness holds intangible value that translates into higher income. Distinctiveness can be assessed by product characteristics. It also involves analysis of consumer preferences; market trends; and retail price point analysis. The goal is not merely to rule in a product strategy, but to rigorously rule out those products that are unlikely to benefit from the IP positioning model. That is because it is transformative to move producers closer to retail markets with positioning strategies such as ownership of an import company, intensive brand and marketing work, and stakeholder ownership. It also has a cost.

The cost of a full IP business positioning strategy ranges between $1 million and $5 million. This generates substantial revenue, but products and situations should be carefully selected. For example, in the case of Ugandan vanilla, a branded Ugandan-owned wholesaling company as envisaged ultimately would return $48.5 million to Uganda per annum versus the Ugandan current income of about $5–6 million. This 8–10 fold increase suggests it is worth raising a solid impact investment or other financing.

The case of Ugandan vanilla demonstrates a truly distinctive underlying product. When the six-step method is considered, assessing distinctiveness is foundational, and the remainder of the IP business positioning strategy pivots on this foundation.

In the following chapter, we consider the step of selecting the correct IP tool, relative to the product, context, and overall strategy. We will explore trademarks, licensing, certification marks, and geographical indications and their advantages and challenges.

Notes

1 R. Layton and M. Brindle, "Distinctive values in Caribbean exports," OAS, 2011.
2 L. Brindle-Khym, "Power searches with Google," unpublished study for Quest Research and Investigations, New York, 2010.
3 Layton et al., "Distinctive values in African exports."
4 J. MacKay and R. Sisodia, "Conscious capitalism: Liberating the heroic spirit of business," Harvard Business School, 2014.
5 Amadeus Vanilla Beans website (www.amadeusvanillabeans.com/store/uganda/uganda -gold-normal.php), accessed May 2016.
6 Chef Hugh Fearnley Whittingstall, London, website (www.ndali.net/chefs-foodies.htm l), accessed June 2, 2016.

5

THE POWER OF INTELLECTUAL PROPERTY TOOLS

What are effective Intellectual Property (IP) tools?

IP tools such as trademarks, geographical indications, copyrights, patents, or licenses are important business tools. IP tools are generally assumed to be the domain of lawyers. However, IP tools are a critical component of business strategies. IP tools must be accompanied by a full business strategy and like any tool must be used in context to be effective.

In addition, Intellectual Property tools are part of the missing ingredient for low-income producers. As just one example, in a country considered to be rising toward middle-income status, Malaysia remains a net importer of Intellectual Property and pays the United States $1.4 billion in royalties, yet receives only a fraction of this amount or $101 million in royalties. The US has mastered IP business, despite a continual challenge with counterfeiting and earned $125.3 billion in royalties in the year 2013 with ongoing exponential increases. It would be misleading to take IP tools out of the larger business context. To be effective, IP tools should be part of a larger, more comprehensive IP business strategy. However, LDCs and rising middle-income countries can use IP tools more effectively than they have thus far.

We endeavor to demonstrate how to do this and change the perception that IP is a legal strategy predominantly for developed country companies. IP tools can be part of a robust business strategy. We also seek to counter the myth that IP is out of reach for the poor, but rather aim to show how IP business can be accessible for low-income producers with some demonstrable successful case studies.

In this chapter, we will:

- Describe the importance of IP tools as part of an inclusive IP business repositioning strategy

- Show the impact of IP business for successful companies.
- Describe several Intellectual Property tools: trademarks, certification marks, geographical indications, and licensing and how to use them.
- Provide insight from an interview with David Cardwell, the licensing agent behind the most successful licensing strategy in Europe – Star Wars.
- Illustrate successful IP licensing strategy for LDCs and distinguish merchandise licensing from franchise licensing.
- Compare and contrast the most effective IP tools for IP business positioning.

Intellectual Property tools are growing in prominence as a tool for developing countries. At the same time, many mistakes are being made. IP is ineffective in isolation from a complete business strategy. Just as a tool does not build a city, an Intellectual Property tool such as a Trademark does not equate to success or a full business strategy. An Intellectual Property tool used ineffectively is similar to using any tool ineffectively. In this next section, we will describe several dramatic success stories that illustrate the value of learning and applying IP tools.

First – IP strategies are not mysterious!

Let's first consider a success case from the United States: Coca-Cola. It illustrates an IP strategy plus a complete business positioning strategy as one of the largest and most lucrative brands in the world.

"(From holding) value of $41.41 billion US dollars in 2006, Coca-Cola reached the value of $83.84 billion US dollars in 2015."[1] According to the US Patent and Trademark Office, the Coca-Cola Trademark alone is worth $65 billion, while total assets are of course higher.[2]

Though estimates of IP valuation vary, one consistency is the IP is always valued beyond what would seem reasonable for a drink, a soda that also receives fairly consistently negative press in medical nutrition studies, reports, and popular media.

We can all agree that Coca-Cola has a remarkably successful IP business strategy. For a product that has proven to be unhealthy, and had humble beginnings, a brand value over $83 billion is impressive. If a relatively unhealthy product, one that is non-essential and less than a century old can be valued at $83 billion, what is the secret? Can the success story be replicated for low-income farmer/producers?

Consider the history of Coca-Cola, and replicable elements as an IP business case.

Coca-Cola was first produced as an experiment in a pharmacy from Coke syrup that got its name from mild amounts of cocaine in this drug. Coca-Cola is now found in the most remote regions of the earth. Of course, Coca-Cola never leaves home without its signature and trademarked bottle or can, and even when served by fountain or sold from a wooden shack on a remote mountain road in Kenya, its signature branding is consistent.

In the early 1900s, Coca-Cola expanded into the Caribbean with distribution outlets. It also set up bottling plants and distribution in Africa during World War

II, all the while maintaining diligent control over its brand and quality. Now, Coca-Cola is global (and also the largest employer in Africa), propelling the brand of simple fizzy water from its origins at a soda fountain in Atlanta, Georgia, USA to one of the world's most successful generators of income.

What was Coca-Cola's strategy?

1. Begin with a distinctive product – a recipe for Coke.
2. Manage the brand by selling more than a drink, but a well-designed marketing strategy such as: Coca-Cola is intent on "bottling happiness."
3. Develop Trademarks and (franchise) licenses for local distributors to sell.
4. Own many local distributors and control the rest through the terms of franchise license agreements.

Consider the example of Coca-Cola, worth nearly $85 billion just for intangible assets, the brand, and associated aspects such as the logo, name, and script. But the obvious logic is that the logo and brand alone (not to mention a myriad of IP lawyers) are not the full story. The story is the well-executed business strategy wherein IP is a critical aspect, alongside ownership/control of the supply chain, excellent market positioning, and including the IP. In essence, Coca-Cola followed the IP business method advocated in Chapter 4 of this book.

Coca-Cola is an example of a positioning strategy that employed Franchise Licensing, that is, the licensing of all distributors not owned by the corporation. Merchandise Licensing, in contrast, is the licensing of companies ("licensees") to use a brand or symbol on a specified agreed range of products made by the licensee.

Another example is Nike, the Oregon athletic shoe company that has expanded to the point of dominating global sportswear market shares.[3] Nike allegedly bought its first logo for under $50.00. According to Forbes, the ubiquitous Nike brand is now listed on the *Forbes* Fabulous 40 as one of the most valuable brands in sports.[4] In addition, Nike continues to build on its brand with new positioning, and partnerships. As *Forbes* Sports Money expert Mike Ozanian explains, "Nike's basketball shoe deal with Michael Jordan has been extremely lucrative for both parties. Nike owns the basketball shoe market in the US with a 95% share, including its Jordan brand subsidiary, and its stock has trounced the overall stock market during the past year."[5]

How brands are evaluated

The way brands are evaluated, is fairly simple. According to those who rank brands at Forbes, the simple formula is, "the brand value is the difference between the estimated enterprise value of the business brand and what the value of a similar business is worth."[6] "So, when valuing the Nike brand, the value is found in the difference between the value of a company *with* the Nike brand minus the value of an identical company with a different name."[7]

This is similar to the way we think of intangible value and how distinctive products retailing for say $15–20.00/lb, as Ethiopian fine coffee does, exceed the retail price of generic or commodity priced coffee. The difference would be the brand value.

If we compare an athletic shoe that is not branded such as a generic men's shoe, the cost in an American city is about $30.00. A very similar shoe, branded Nike, can sell for two–three times the price, depending on the market. While Nike would argue that it protects quality and is indeed a finer shoe, one could trace many such shoes to the same sweatshop manufacturer. In the case of Nike as in many brands, the brand name is worth more to Nike than the physical shoe. This works for Nike because they own the brand, the image – the IP effectively. An important additional step is they have positioned the product in retail markets very carefully, and they also own the distribution. To be sure, theirs is also a story of enforcement, with lawyers guarding the brand.

Interestingly enough, the third and fourth most valuable brands in sports are also on relatively basic athletic gear. With no offense to Adidas or Under Armour, athletic shoes and clothing are not complex to make, but these businesses require a keen understanding of market demand, positioning, and brand ownership. We have visited Nike factories in Africa where the products are made cheaply with low wages, a story for another chapter. What are the IP tools that are foundational?

IP tools: trademarks and certification marks

Of a range of IP Tools, two principal tools here are trademarks and certification marks. As a consequence of developing, registering, and owning these, the owners will enter into a range of agreements with users – licenses – and generate revenue (royalties, fees, profit share, etc.).

Trademarks

A Trademark (^{TM}) is a "source identifier." It indicates that the product is only made by a particular company. The TM owner controls the quality of the goods sold under the trademark, even when these are being manufactured or produced by others.

According to the US Patent and Trademark Organization (USPTO), a trademark is defined as:

> Any sign or combination of signs capable of distinguishing one good or services from another undertaking shall be capable of a trademark. Such signs, in particular word, numerals, names, letters, figures, colors or combinations or signs or shall be eligible of being registered as a trademark.
>
> *(From the World Trade Organization on TRIPS*
> *[Trade-Related Aspects of Intellectual Property Rights])*[8]

The functions of trademarks include the following:

- Trademarks help to eliminate confusion for consumers.
- Identify and advertise.
- Provide assurance to consumers and reduce consumer search cost
- Signal and encourage quality control.
- Align consumer expectations.
- A private property right.
- Investment by TM owner – valuable business assets that can be bought or licensed.

In essence, brands are protected by registration as trademarks. Trademark registration needs to be secured in each country that the owner wishes to have branded products sold.

As noted above, Coca-Cola is the most valuable trademarked brand and is alone worth $84 billion, holding its position as the world's most lucrative TM for seven years in a row.[9]

International recognition of Trademarks

Historically, international agreements for recognition of foreign trademarks were only signed in the late 1800s, a little over a century ago, following the establishment of registration systems under the laws of several developed countries. The United States corporations have mastered this tool alongside the business strategy, so the US earns billions in intellectual property exports, and almost every country engaged in active trade is trying to catch up.

It is interesting that in the US, the first trademark to earn really appreciable merchandising licensing income was Tarzan. Edgar Rice Burroughs created the fictional character and acquired a trademark. Mr. Burroughs was also a businessman. In 1923, his company used the ownership of the trademarks relating to the character to control the production of media using its imagery. He also licensed the character for use in other works, which was a precursor to the modern concept of a media franchise. It is interesting, as we describe below, how the Walt Disney Company actually earns more revenue on merchandising and licensing than on films.

Although English courts had recognized the principle of trade names for centuries, in the UK, a triangle for Bass Brewery Ale was the first registered trademark in 1876. In the US, the first trademark to be registered under the Trade Mark Registration Act of 1875 was actually a picture of an eagle and ribbon, with the words, "Economical, Brilliant," filed by the Averill Chemical Paint Company on August 30, 1870 but it was later found to be unconstitutional.[10] And, the oldest US Trade Mark still in use is a symbol of the biblical figure Samson, wrestling a lion, still in use by a company manufacturing rope.

And, in Germany in 1875, the Krupp steel company registered three seamless train wheel tires stacked on top of each other, under the German Trade Mark Protection Law of 1874.

Under registration systems worldwide, applicants for trademarks need to state the product range that the trademark applies to. For example, Apple Computers owns a number of trademarks for electronics but does not own the word "apple" in all possible uses. A car rental company called Apple can register trademarks in the business category that it operates but cannot own the word "apple."

These brief historical notes illustrate the importance of symbols and depictions that were used to help sell products, even from their earliest days more than 100 years ago. Why was the biblical character used to sell rope, and a symbol of Tarzan popular? These, as trademarks today, call upon the company's desire to speak to characteristics sought after by consumers – Samson, Tarzan, Eagles sell.

Case study example: Sunkist oranges

How did Sunkist take a common orange and turn it into a billion dollar brand?

Sunkist Growers, Inc. was a cooperative created by independent farmers who banded together in 1893 to garner more profit from their produce. By the mid-1980s, Sunkist developed a profitable licensing program that included royalties. This change contributed to growth in revenues over a 10-year period from $13 million to almost $1.2 billion.[11]

Sunkist is an IP business positioning success story. It took a series of IP business strategies beginning in 1893 to rocket the orange company to success. Ownership of the trademark for Sunkist was secured in 1926, and in decades to come, Sunkist opened distribution companies in many countries, quite far from their original California home farms. Now, the producers control the Sunkist brand in 45 countries.

The remarkable thing about Sunkist is that while it is a lovely name for oranges, the name is also used on dozens of other products that are not oranges. For example, there is a vitamin line called Sunkist – drawing on the meaning of freshness and health, the meaning behind the branded word. And, there is a soda pop line. There is sufficient, generally accepted information that soda pop is not healthy, but soda pop that is (artificially) orange in color and labeled Sunkist sells well in consumer markets. Where shoppers make instant grocery-level decisions, Sunkist, as a marketed trademark, sells well as the Sunkist intangible value of reputation overrules other consumer rational decisions.

We find the Sunkist story valuable because the orange farmers were not always wealthy. In fact, they were very poor for generations. And, while oranges and orange juice are currently highly popular products, considered almost essential to myriads of parents, this was not always the case. Prior to Sunkist and post-World War II, orange juice was not widely known – it took nutritionists popularizing the notion that orange juice, as a source of vitamin C, was an almost essential part of every child's breakfast. The poor farmers of California, setting in motion effective IP tools coupled with business strategies, marketing, branding, that meant the positioning was right. From this strategy, Sunkist managed to acquire name recognition in 45 countries, alongside an effective set of IP tools. If Sunkist farmers and the Sunkist cooperative can do it, poor African farmers can do it, too. Clearly, the growth of Sunkist benefitted from collaboration of the farmer cooperatives and farming businesses, a lesson of considerable value for Africans in the twenty-first century.

Trademarks

Note that Sunkist registered for a trademark in 1926. It did not immediately become a household name. Sunkist opened distribution companies in many countries. It was not the trademark ownership alone. The IP tool – the trademark – combined with control of the supply chain, and positioning of the brand in the right consumer framework that came together to bring the orange farmers to success. We note that it took about 60–70 years for Sunkist to become a household word, but now that it is in that position with IP ownership plus control over supply chains, it is sustainable for the long term. This is our vision for African LDCs: It is not easy, magic or a three-year aid project, but once created and managed, the increase in income is dramatic and can be sustained over the long term.

The United States Patent and Trademark Office (USPTO)

From humble beginning in the late 1800s, the largest Intellectual Property organization in the world is the United States Patent and Trademark Office (USPTO). It is located in Alexandria, VA just outside of Washington, DC, as a sprawling building complex. According to the USPTO website, there are 11,035 active agents and 33,089 active attorneys licensed to practice before the USPTO.[12] The sharp point are there is a plethora of attorneys acting to preserve IP rights for US-based clients.

The definition of a TM, according to the WTO, is very simple,

> Any sign or combination of signs capable of distinguishing the goods and services of one undertaking from another undertaking shall be capable of constituting a Trademark. Such signs, in particular personal names, letters, figurative elements, colors and combination of colors and combinations of any signs shall be eligible of registration as a trademark.[13]

It is also worth noting that the original spelling of trademark (today's spelling) was Trade Mark. "Trade Marks" were always intended to designate the mark of one's trade, intended as business strategies, not initially legal ones.

And, on a global scale, the World Intellectual Property Organization (WIPO) is the largest multilateral IP organization offering registration of trademarks. As a United Nations agency, WIPO provides training to IP offices in developing country governments, including those in Africa. Trademark registration needs to be secured in each country that the owner wishes to have branded products sold.

Certification marks

A certification mark can indicate the source of the product or that the product meets certain criteria developed by the owners of the mark, frequently trade associations of many companies or producers. Anybody can make a certified product provided that they meet the criteria and are approved by the owner to use the certification mark on the product. A certification mark system can be used on a very wide range of products. The "certification" status of the product might be shown to the consumer by a symbol or graphic that needs to stand for something quite specific.

The importance of certifications in the twenty-first century relates primarily to ethical trade, health, or environmental standards and to geographical origins (see geographical indications below).

Fame

There are also standards for demonstrating ownership of IP based on "fame," i.e. achieved recognition. Fame is usually reserved for well-established brands that have existed for a long time. For example, brands like Coca-Cola where there have been substantial advertising investments, and recognition levels are high. These must usually be backed up by significant consumer research. The world-wide visual recognition of the Maasai might meet this kind of test, although undertaking the wide-ranging research to evidence this might be costly.

Trademark Fair Use

This is based on the right to free speech, and, therefore, gives somebody the right to use words/symbols/logos even where these have been protected and are controlled through trademarks. So, for example, Apple Computers is a trademark, but Apple Computers cannot prevent people using the trademarked word or symbol, apple for actual fruit or completely different products when it has other meanings or senses.

Licensing

Trademarks combine with licensing. When a brand is owned by Trademark registration, it can be licensed for use, and advance the owner's opportunity to receive income. The details of how this works are provided below, but first, a few examples that illustrate the value of the Licensing strategy.

The Walt Disney Company is one of the genius brand and licensing strategies of the twentieth and now twenty-first centuries. Once a cartoon animator, Walt Disney became known for drawing a mouse, and bringing him to life as what is now instantly recognized as the most famous mouse in the world – Mickey Mouse. Walt Disney moved from cartoon animation to hosting a weekly Sunday evening show, and later to theme parks.

Although Walt Disney, for example, is well known for movies and theme parks, the company actually earns more money via its licensed merchandise products. While *Cinderella* and now *Frozen* are well known and loved movies, the assets in licensing outpace the characters. For example, blockbusters like *Frozen* and the *Despicable Me* series helped drive $107 billion in retail sales for the entertainment-based licensing business in 2014.[14]

More recently, *Star Wars: The Force Awakens*, a film released in late 2015, was predicted to earn $500 million in box office revenues in its opening weekend. Analysts predict Star Wars merchandise will generate some $3 billion in sales in 2015, and $5 billion over the next 12 months as this book goes to print.[15] As we can see from these few examples, the ratio of income earned by the most visual product – the film – pales in comparison to the income earned by merchandise licensing.

The good news is that low-income producers can learn, use, and control IP strategies for their brands. The bad news is that IP strategies are sometimes dictated or imposed on poor people, telling them to brand or acquire IP tools and similarly dramatic results will follow. As we lay out the basic IP tools and show how the IP tools can become part of a full IP business positioning strategy, let's consider more about licensing because licensing can work for poor farmers and producers, too.

Licensing has propelled companies such as Walt Disney into billionaire status. However, licensing is not complicated. Licensing means the trademark owner (the licensor) grants a permit to a third party (the licensee) in order to commercially use the trademark, legally. The essential provisions to a trademark license identify the trademark owner and the licensee, in addition to the policy and the goods or services to be licensed. According to the Thomson Reuter's report of May 5, 2015, licensing revenue accounted for €10.8 billion in France alone.[16]

In addition to films, a common example that illustrates the way licensing works is in the sports industry. Licensing revenues are a significant source of revenue for the National Basketball Association, National Football League, National Hockey League, and Major League Baseball. These organizations grant permission to third parties, such as apparel vendors, to use teams' logos in video games, on clothing and on other merchandise. The vendor keeps part of the profit for its role in producing and selling the apparel, but the sports association also earns money in exchange for granting the vendors the right to use the teams' logos. In 2010, the

MLB sold licensed merchandise worth approximately \$2.75 billion.[17] More recently, in 2015, the Major League Baseball's Internet/Technology arm alone was calculated to be worth \$2 billion. "MLBAM's brand value increased more than three-fold from last year, to \$2 billion."[18]

Sports and collegiate licensing continues to be among the most reliable sectors in the licensing industry. As quoted by Forbes, the sports category grew for the fourth consecutive year with \$698 million in royalty revenue on retail sales of \$12.8 billion, while a separate collegiate category also displayed growth with total revenues from licensing estimated at \$209 million, or \$3.88 billion at retail.[19]

Total sales from licensed products based on sports, colleges, and corporate logos amounted to \$241.5 billion. Of this, \$13.4 billion was from royalty revenue. Of course, in Europe, licensing is earned by sports teams of all varieties, and anyone watching an international soccer match has become accustomed to a plethora of licensed images competing for stadium space, and television audiences.

It would be reasonable logic then that the owners of products or processes developed over centuries such as Ethiopian fine coffee, or a cultural brand that speaks of strength and vigor, such as the Maasai, should also be entitled to licensing income for their brands. Yet, audiences of westerners are often surprised when it is first presented that the Ethiopians or the Maasai seek licenses, with the presumption that licenses are out of their domain. If it is okay for a Penguin image in hockey, or a Cardinal bird adorning a baseball hat to earn licensing revenue (a cumulative \$13.4 billion in royalty revenues just for sports teams), and indeed we generally agree it is, we do think a Maasai image augmenting road vehicles adding value with images of strength, courage, and tenacity is also worthy of licensing. The surprise *should* be that Africans haven't been earning licensing revenues. The opportunities to do so are certainly ripe.

Licensing in the real world

We think of licensing as appropriate to physical products, such as the license to use photos, or distribute films, or in the case of coffee, a license to benefit from the efforts of the special components of Ethiopian coffee, perfected over many centuries; licensing in the twenty-first century has become very dramatic. For example, there have been countless science fiction films, and films with magical or fantasized characters, but Star Wars has been a most unusual phenomenon, surpassing even the expectations of George Lucas who recently sold the Star Wars franchise with George Lucas films to Disney for \$4 billion.[20] Notably, while the Star Wars films earned \$8 billion at the box office, the licensing franchise earned \$27 billion, about three times higher revenue than even the much-loved films. Much of this was due to successful licensing.

Mr. David Cardwell was a leader in licensing Star Wars and has been responsible for many successful licensing strategies in the UK and Europe including Tom and Jerry, Pink Panther, Teenage Mutant Ninja Turtles, the Flintstones,

Star Trek, My Little Pony, Spiderman, and X-Men amongst others. He was the recipient of the UK's first Lifetime Achievement Award in 2002.[21] He now operates Cardwell Consultancy, a company that acts as a consultant and mentor to both licensing agencies and brand copyright owners. He is the founder and managing director of David T. Cardwell Consultancy in London.

Q: Can you explain licensing in your own words?
A: The basic answer to what it means to "license" something is taking an image already popular in one medium e.g. a film, TV series, books and transferring those images to separate licensing products. An obvious example is "Star Wars." The original (and subsequent) movies were so successful on a global scale that manufacturers (licensees) were enthusiastic to put the Star Wars images i.e. actors' faces, the Star Wars logo, on a vast array of products that ranged from all manner of apparel, e.g. shirts, T shirts, pajamas, hats, through to wallpaper, bedding, computer games and, of course, toys in dozens of different formats.

  Almost unique was the reaction of fans to the movies. They believed and still do, that there was some hidden meaning in the films beyond just being good movies, from moral issues about the good defeating the bad, to deeper views that there was some religious background, including a "God" type link. Most fans could not articulate what these hidden meanings really meant, but it has ensured that legions of fans worldwide continue those beliefs. More startling is that the films have a cult following that transcends age groups. Children as young as six or seven up to and adults surpassing their sixties continue to see the films and buy all the products. Original products still in their original packaging sell for many thousands of dollars on various websites.[22]

Q: Do you think licensing is a mystery to most people?
A: I don't believe licensing is a "mystery" to most members of the general public. I think most people understand that something already popular in one medium can be transferred to another product. However, most members of the public do not know (or frankly care) about the details regarding copyright, trademark protection, etc. I think most people know that if a company like Yves St. Laurent is known for fashion clothing, that it makes sense that fashion sunglasses bearing the YSL logo will be related and similarly to fragrance.

Q: Is it possible to say in simple terms how licensing a popular product like Star Wars is different from licensing, say, Ethiopian coffee?
A: With a Star Wars concept you have a multi-million dollar series of films with global success backed by even more millions of dollars of marketing spend, both by the film studios themselves as well as advertising dollars by the licensees. With Ethiopian coffee that licensing program worked because the

general public had some knowledge of the brand of coffee and that it was unique to Ethiopia as a country. But it was Light Years IP who turned that knowledge into a commercial success. It was then supported by the public when they saw the media coverage about how much revenue was generated by the coffee sales and how little of that revenue found its way into the pockets of the Ethiopian farmers themselves.

However, and it's a BIG however, there has to be some intrinsic or unique link to every concept before it can be turned into a separate licensing success. The Maasai are a good example. Most of the general public have heard or seen documentaries on TV about the Maasai tribes over the years. They also know that the Maasai are very colorful people who wear colorful clothes, wear very stylized jewelry and are tall, athletic and good looking. That is sufficient for a limited and successful licensing program. What you cannot do is try to spin off licensed products that have no relationship to the people and their attributes such as fridges, bedspreads, toys, etc. In short, the general public are not stupid.

Q: Do you think poor producers can learn to be successful at licensing?

A: I do not think "poor producers" can learn to be successful at licensing with the caveats I mentioned above. One needs to have a huge knowledge not only of how licensing contracts work, but about different manufacturing skills, distributors, etc. One also needs a large network of contacts and a good understanding of copyright, trademark, and design protection. In short, you cannot take an African tribe and simply say let's license this. If that tribe does not have any specific identity that is obvious to the general public and, of course, to the licensees, it simply isn't going to work.

Q: Yet, some products that originated with poor farmers did acquire successful licensing strategies. Examples include French champagne and oranges from California, now successfully licensed as Sunkist, for vitamins and soda pop. If poor farmers with simple products can earn their owners billions of dollars, it would seem there is hope for low-income farmers. What do you think?

A: Yes, that is very interesting. We also did My Little Pony TM that ended up with films and many versions. Licensing has some important basics. The first is that you must have some connection to the consumer and, at all costs, avoid over licensing by going too far. Examples of success that show how wide licensing areas can be is the Harley-Davidson spinoff licensing created by one of my rivals Mike Stone. He created a very successful licensing pro-gram with Harley-Davidson (HD) by ensuring that all the products he licensed had a "natural" fit to the HD bike owners, e.g. leather jackets, gloves, etc. The licensing became so successful he opened a store in central New York! You must create a connection to your consumer, and avoid over-stepping by going too far.

Our strategy is to focus on 10 products that really relate well, but once you step over the line, or take it too far, things die. You can create competition within your own brand that starts to be self-defeating, such as what we are seeing with My Little Pony. This has been very successful, marketed almost 100 percent to girls, and has a TV series from Hasbro, but you cannot add too many new products, or you begin to kill off your own brand.

I believe this is why the Maasai *will* be successful – there is a strong connectedness already in the market place and people grasp what the Maasai stand for such as strength, athletic qualities, and my prediction is, it can last for a long time. It does not require an army of lawyers. Trademark protection, on the other hand, does require a lot of lawyers and is, frankly boring. But, in licensing, if a concept takes off and is unique, it will work for the long term.

If anyone should understand that, it is Mr. Cardwell, a legendary licensing success story.[23]

What does it mean to earn a license for a producer?

While licensing for Star Wars and now famous toys seems often to be the domain of wealthier countries, that is a myth to be changed! As we outlined in Chapter 2, the brilliance behind the positioning strategy for Ethiopian fine coffee and its advance to return an extra $101 million for the Ethiopian fine coffee sector was to apply complete positioning, including trademarking and franchise licensing. This appreciably improved the negotiating power for Ethiopia.

The field of social entrepreneurship has evolved over the past decade. Its initial focus was on the achievements of individual social entrepreneurs. Books such as David Bornstein's excellent *How to Change the World: Social Entrepreneurs and the Power of New Ideas* captured some of these stories of individual entrepreneurs.[24] The field more recently includes a greater acknowledgment of collective action, with somewhat less focus on individuals alone.

In the case of Ethiopian coffee, one critical element of the Ethiopian Fine Coffee Initiative was the role of several social entrepreneurs who set out to make a difference in the coffee industry exports. First, Ron Layton and Getachew Mengistie, followed by Tadesse Meskela, and now Eleni Gabre-Madhin. Two Ethiopian men, one New Zealander, and one Ethiopian woman – together there's power!

As Ethiopians, three were cognizant of the role of coffee in Ethiopia, and the dire situation of millions dependent upon coffee for their life, livelihoods, and that of their children. To change the export and producer prices, another social entrepreneur who is head of the Oromia Union of Cooperatives, Tadesse Meskela, took action. Tadesse understood that setting up the network of licensed distributors had strengthened his negotiating position by March 2007. He refused the same foreign offers based on world commodity prices and set out to negotiate the doubling of the export prices for the three fine coffees distributed through the new network. This step could not have been accomplished without IP positioning. However, Tadesse was then able to increase the export price paid to Oromia which led to increases in the farm gate price, affecting members of 600 coffee cooperatives in the Oromia Union. The other Ethiopian producers who were not in cooperatives also benefitted as the export prices rose, led by Tadesse's higher prices.

A further valuable step was taken by a fifth social entrepreneur, Eleni Gebre-Madhin. Eleni established a new exchange that improved product flow within Ethiopia and greatly improved transparency, certainty, and delivery quality for the domestic supply chain handling coffee (see *Addis Life* magazine, Vol. 3).

What the Ethiopian TM and licensing initiative did not do

The international lawyers of Arnold and Porter, working pro bono to advise the initiative, proposed a trademark strategy. However, as argued earlier, a trademark alone accomplishes little to improve income – alone is the operative word. In this case study, we see that the Ethiopians had been out-powered concerning their very own fine coffees. Harar, Yirgacheffe, and Sidamo are regions in Ethiopia. Nevertheless, due to the way trademarks work, a large, powerful company, Starbucks, had registered these marks, and when challenged, believed they could withstand the legal challenge.

Why would Starbucks argue to hold onto a trademark that is the region of someone else's country? To Starbucks, the trademark has value. Howard Schultz is a smart businessman who recognized that selling coffee may be mediocre, but selling Yirgacheffe coffee has a name and brand recognition that sells for higher amounts at New York City coffee bars.

In the international development world, many say the key need is infrastructure to solve the issues of poverty in Africa. Others would say, improve agricultural support service first. However, we would argue that these are strategies that put the cart before the horse. If negotiating positions can be strengthened first so higher and more secure export prices can be achieved first, the related components will be much more effective and can ultimately be funded within an export sector better positioned to succeed.

For example, in Ethiopia, the EU had invested €53 million in Ethiopian coffee production, with little to no improvements in income, as noted by the European Ambassador publicly in 2006. However, the trademark and licensing strategy involved an investment of $2 million to yield $101 million and by contrast, once more secure income was acquired through IP business, and the sector itself was incentivized to address quality control and related components. This model is more likely to succeed in supporting an integrated approach to community poverty alleviation than the mere infusion of agricultural support.

A case of extreme isolation – Niue

Ethiopian coffee may resonate as an IP licensing strategy, given our increasing collective love of coffee, but does the combination of IP tools work for other countries?

What are your trade options if you are an island in the South Pacific of about 1,400 people, and your main export is passion fruit? To export passion fruit is to transport 1,000 miles to New Zealand. That was exactly the situation for Niue.

Niue is a small self-governing island country in the South Pacific, 2,400 kilometers northeast of New Zealand. Its land area is 260 square kilometers, and its predominantly Polynesian population is around 1,400.

Ron Layton worked in the Foreign Service out of New Zealand as an economist in the 1970s. The problem this small country had is the same as many small island countries. They didn't have products to export outside of the commodity markets. They would grow passion fruit, but other countries that were larger and more advanced could beat them competitively. They tried limes, but other countries that were faster and better at producing the limes would jump on this and beat them, too.

So, what does a small country do that is so extremely isolated from global trade?

There is global business of creating special postage stamps for collectors made in small quantities, so they become collector's items. Only a jurisdiction can issue official postage stamps. Niue licensed international companies to print stamps for philatelic use (i.e. for collectors).

Stamps are issued for the Queen of England's birthday, or an event in America, or to celebrate the Eiffel tower – not much that was related to Niue. But, the stamps held Intellectual Property value and could return income to Niue. Stamp licensing became a primary source of income for Niue and remains so in 2015. If you take a look at a search engine and look for stamps from Niue, you will find a wide variety of stamps made in Niue that belong to them, as intellectual property assets.

Two values of Intellectual Property are that IP can transcend the problem of distance from markets, lack of rainfall or climate change, and tends to increase as a revenue producing asset over time. We can see then how Intellectual Property can be a powerful tool when combined with a business export strategy in licensing for remote producers in Africa. And, we can see how the creation of IP assets and strategy works where there has been no specific prior export product, such as in Niue.

The importance of both examples of licensing is that in both cases, low-income people have learned to use a relatively simple IP tool and succeeded. This dispels the mythology that licensing of IP is for the wealthy, the creative such as musicians or the film industry, and established corporations such as Nike, Walt Disney or Coca-Cola. It is for farmers. It can be used successfully for any group willing to engage technical specialists to create much improved Positioning through IP and business strategy.

Geographical indications

An IP strategy that has been widely applied, involving millions of producers in wealthier countries, and modeled by lower income countries is an IP tool called geographical indications (GIs), promoted by the European Union and by the World Intellectual Property Organization (WIPO). Herein, a geographical place that can demonstrate that a product is grown or produced solely in a particular geographical place can acquire a legal IP mechanism called a GI or appellation of origin.

GIs are defined by the USPTO: "Geographical indications and trademarks are distinctive signs used to distinguish goods or services in the marketplace. Both enable consumers to associate a particular quality with a good or service."[25]

The best-known example is French champagne, followed by Scotch whisky – the fifth largest export from the UK. Other examples include Roquefort and Camembert cheese, Ceylon tea, Thai Doi Chaang coffee, Thai rice, and many others. Indeed, Thailand alone had over 40 GI applications in its pipeline according to the Thai IP Office as of 2014. The US government focuses some resources on enabling global IP offices to support such initiatives. The EU policy strongly advocates for GIs.

In a study conducted for the US Trade Representative's Office, assessing 10 success and failure cases using the geographical indication, we found that the GI alone was not the operative factor for success. Rather, the successful cases, defined as those with appreciable income improvements and earning higher value than similar non-GI labeled products, had the following features:

- A history of earning a distinctive recognition, such as French champagne, and Port Wine of Portugal or Scotch whisky
- A well-developed branding strategy that is recognized in the marketplace
- A product that is well positioned for consumers
- Strong enforcement and advocacy
- Well-trained producers practicing excellent quality control
- Government support[26]

The IP strategy "GIs" does not increase income, anymore than a hammer and saw, necessary for building a house, can build the house. The analogy to champagne is problematic, as champagne also carries with it a nearly 200-year history of processing based on a process perfected over time, and a marketing strategy with definitive brand recognition and French control. A concern is that the GI strategy is being promoted without acknowledgment that a full business strategy is needed, and what has worked for French champagne is not likely applicable to less specialty products such as coffees, rice, cottons, and more generic goods even if they are generally associated with a particular region. A full IP business strategy is required. While the GI may induce country level pride, such as Jamaican Reggae is associated with Jamaica, or Thai Rice is clearly of Thailand, country pride and GI alone are insufficient to improve income.

Learning from failures

For example, Malaysia has invested in its Sarawak Pepper, a black pepper that now holds a GI distinction. Malaysia has spent 14 years on the process, setting up a black pepper board, engaging the farmer/producers in quality control and is very proud of its GI achievement. Vietnam, however, not limited by years spent on a GI, has been out-producing black pepper and achieving far greater market success without the GI. This is largely due to a stronger market positioning, competitive production. Vietnam has achieved success without the GI, or the expense of the GI and rocketed ahead of Malaysia.

Our study found that Malaysia was not only lagging behind Vietnam in volume, sales, and income for black pepper, but was actually earning less income AFTER the GI than prior to the GI, as their export volumes fell precipitously.[27] This was most likely due to higher quality control, inherently a good thing, but arguably the levels of controls resident in achieving the GI have caused Malaysia to fall behind Vietnam in market presence, a situation from which it will be difficult to recover.

We will delve into these cases in detail in Chapter 9. The main point is not to criticize early beginnings or start ups, but to note that the IP tool, itself, is not a panacea. It is not helpful to LDC producers to over-inflate the value of what a particular IP tool can do, without considering the larger picture, as is sometimes done by eager, sincere aid workers, entrepreneurs, and international development experts.

Many developing country producers have been led down an unfair pathway involving considerable effort without income reward. Having been told to just "get the trademark," or to spend years of effort applying for geographical indications, and then to face decreased income is indeed more than unfair. There are monetary costs, as well as the cost of effort coupled with failure. The goal is to utilize a full method that *does* bring income improvement. As described in our chapter on methods, there is no one size fits all in IP business, and the selection of the correct IP tool involves the full IP business positioning strategy.

For example, one country that has grown fascinated with the potential of what the GI label can do for its exports is Thailand. Thailand, a country that seeks middle income status, and has many sophisticated trade strategies, had registered about 46 products, 38 Thai and 8 foreign. "The total number of applications in the pipeline (in 2013) was 93; 79 of which are Thai products and 14 foreign products."[28] Examples include: Thai products such as silks, specialty rice, pottery, and coffee.

According to WIPO (the World Intellectual Property Office) Thailand has entered what they are calling phase two of GIs. The goal is to further integrate Asian countries into the world economy and reduce poverty. Thailand was selected by WIPO to be a pilot GI program for three products: a famous silk, brocade, and wicker product and has become the poster child for GIs.

As the concept goes, GIs enable a country to claim exclusivity rights to a product, modeled after the French champagne case. To be sure, developed countries have advanced income with specialty cheeses such as Roquefort or Camembert of France as described above. However, as our research shows, the success cases for GIs are typically advanced within correct Positioning: that is, combining other IP tools such as trademarks, extensive marketing efforts, and incentives for quality with control over distribution channels.

Another poignant example for Thailand is Doi Chaang coffee, made famous by the use of a GI in recent years. Our research found that the coffee is actually shipped to Canada where it is roasted and branded and trademarked, under a Canadian business-man and exporter with significant business acumen. We salute the business strategy demonstrated here that appears to be beneficial to Thailand. However, again, it must be noted that the IP Business Positioning strategy involves more than the GI. In this case, positioning Doi Chaang coffee closer to higher priced markets; roasting the coffee outside of Thailand; and marketing it as Doi Chaang rather than Thai coffee have all contributed to a successful IP business positioning strategy.

Lessons learned from IP failures

Sometimes, the IP tool may be correct; however the value of the IP still accrues to the importer or retailer. In this situation the developing country producer holds no power in the supply chain. This was the case in Mozambique cashews described above, though multiple millions were invested in helping the roughly 1 million cashew producers.

A second common failure is that the IP tool or trademark can be a bland name with little to no consumer recognition. We have found it very typical that IP offi-cers label their export products with country brands. The name Ghanaian cocoa or Zambique cashews had little market recognition, and can be a losing strategy for developing country producers. As described, the large-scale project in Mozambique involved about 1 million cashew farmers and the creation of a new brand, but the brand was not secured at retail. The importer reportedly removed the nuts from the Zambique branded large-sized packaging and was re-packaging them under a brand owned by the importer. As we have shown with Ghana, branding the chocolate bars as Divine was a better idea than calling them Ghanaian. Similarly, Sunkist oranges used the name Sunkist rather than California oranges.

Third, the focus on the IP tool rather than a full strategy has been the issue for many Thai products that may not be truly distinctive from competitors, such as Thai fabric, or teas.

Finally, IP tools without effective enforcement are also problematic for country producers. In the case of Sri Lanka, and its rather famous Ceylon tea, the product is protected by a GI; however about 70 percent of Ceylon tea is said to be counterfeit. There are nearly 2 million Sri Lankan tea farmers who could be assisted with a better IP positioning strategy, whereas the GI is not serving them well.

Summary

- Intellectual Property tools carry power – the power to bring a distinctive product into powerful ownership by the rightful owner. We define rightful owner as the person, group or company that has produced the product, be it via farming, production, creativity or intellectual capacity.
- IP tools are not mysterious and can be learned by LDC farmers and producers.
- The use of trademarks and licensing brands ranging from Coca-Cola to Nike, Disney, and Star Wars has generated billions of dollars in income for the owners of these brands, beginning in the twentieth century with Tarzan, or more recently with licensing items from movies such as *Star Wars*. The burgeoning sports industry licensing is a clear demonstration of the value of symbols and images to a widening array of clothing and artifacts with multi-billion dollar revenue streams.
- The IP tool alone, be it a trademark, license, certification mark, or geo-graphical indication (GI) does not hold the power, but rather it is a combi-nation of using the tool or tools appropriately, and including the tool as part of a full IP business positioning strategy.
- IP tools are used in isolation, and have failed to return income or improve the market negotiating position for several million producers. "Zambique" cashews of Mozambique; Malaysian Sarawak Pepper and Ceylon Tea, despite significant amounts of money spent to train developing country producers in IP and promise results, have not proven fruitful. The result is oftentimes disillusionment, and a sense that the "western" value and application pro-duced failure. We have witnessed this in both Africa and the Caribbean where branding has been over-romanticized, and presented as a panacea. There is resistance then, and even kick-back toward creating a full strategy, whereas if the IP tool were coupled with an effective business strategy, the result could be dramatically different.
- In developing countries, IP is the domain of the government IP Office (IPO) with a tendency to promote geographical indications (GIs). The latter pro-motes country origin, and is popular for inducing patriotic responses intern-ally, but does not envision the branding according to the preference and demand of customers in developed country markets. In many, if not most cases, the GIs even after 10–12 years are not advancing income. In worst case

scenarios, the GI designations end up faring worse in foreign markets than countries selling similar products without the GI. This is not merely unfortunate, but affects millions of producers.

- A full IP business strategy, by contrast, considers the end in mind – the import and retail market, and aims to create producer-owned import companies; meaningful brands and higher prices. The strategy is then to utilize the IP tool that will enable most effective producer ownership and best response from customers.

Next steps

At this time, it is useful to turn to the Intellectual Property tools workbook accompanying this text (see workbook included on companion website). The following chapter explores the role of IP enforcement, advocacy, and education. IP tools must be coupled with support and enforcement and the next chapter describes how this can be promoted for LDC farmers, producers, and cultural brand owners.

Notes

1 Statista: The statistics portal, 2015. https://www.statista.com/statistic-portal, accessed March 24, 2016.
2 T. Hickey, United States Patent and Trademark Office, Website training video (www.uspto.gov), accessed March 2, 2016.
3 "T. Team, earnings review: Nike continues its strong run," June 29, 2015 (www.forbes.com/sites/greatspeculations/2015/06/29/earnings-review-nike-continues-its-strong-run/#6aa8c0787030), accessed March 2016.
4 M. Ozanian, "The Forbes Fab 40: The world's most valuable sports brands 2015," *Forbes*, October 22, 2015, p.1.
5 Ibid., p. 1.
6 Ozanian, "The Forbes Fab 40," p. 1.
7 www.forbes.com/sites/mikeozanian/2014/10/07/the-forbes-fab-40-the-worlds-most-valuable-sports-brands2014/#130790541676.
8 USPTO Training films (www.uspto.gov).
9 Toni Hickey, USPTO, Global IP Academy e-training module on Trademarks, accessed March 2, 2016.
10 However, in the *Trade-Mark Cases*, 100 U.S. 82 (1879), the U.S. Supreme Court held the 1870 Act to be unconstitutional.
11 R. Layton and M. Brindle, "Caribbean opportunities for higher income," Organization of American States (OAS), Washington, DC, 2010, p. 6.
12 USPTO website, Division of Enrollment and Discipline, https://oedci.uspto.gov/OEDCI, accessed March 3, 2016.
13 Toni Hickey, USPTO film on Trademarks, USPTO website, 2011.
14 "'Frozen' helps drive $107-billion year for entertainment licensing." Ryan Faughnder, *Los Angeles Times*, June 9, 2015.
15 Forbes, December 16, 2015, "For Disney, Biggest payout isn't at the box office but in merchandising." http://www.forbes.com/sites/natalierobehmed/2015/12/16/how-disneys-star-wars-merchandise-is-set-to-make-billions/#2ec156fb41a4.

16 PARIS, May 5, 2015 /PRNewswire/ – A joint study revealing the state of IP licensing in France by Licensing Executives Society France (LES France), and the Intellectual Property & Science business of Thomson Reuters. The study's results feature trends, practices and motivations behind IP licensing, as reported by senior IP professionals across the country.

17 Licensing Revenue Definition Investopedia, http://www.investopedia.com/terms/l/licensing-revenue.asp#ixzz3pVnvfNCU.

18 Ozanian, "The Forbes Fab 40," p. 3.

19 "Sports licensing soars to $698 million in royalty revenues," *Forbes*, June 17, 2014.

20 www.businessinsider.com/george-lucas-says-he-sold-star-wars-to-white-slavers-2015-12.

21 Formerly co-founder and Executive Chairman of the Copyright Promotions Group, the largest independent licensing agency in Europe with offices in every major European capital.

22 J. Nilsson, "The ten most valuable Star Wars action figures," *The Richest*, September 9, 2014.

23 Mr. Cardwell was awarded the first lifetime achievement award by the licensing industry in the UK in 2002. Interview conducted in London, March, 2016.

24 D. Bornstein, *How to change the world: Social entrepreneurs and the power of new ideas*, New York: Oxford University Press, 2007.

25 T. Hickey, USPTO Training film, accessed March, 2016.

26 M. Brindle and R. Layton, "Successful and failed cases of IP business using geographical indications," Study for the US Trade Representatives Office (USTR) and United States Patent and Trademark Office (USPTO), January, 2016.

27 Ibid.

28 Data from the Thailand Intellectual Property Office, presented at WIPO, 2013.

6

THE POWER OF EDUCATION AND ENFORCEMENT

Malaysia, for example is a net importer of Intellectual Property paying the US $1.4 billion in royalties and receiving $101 million itself in royalties in 2013. By contrast, the US is a net exporter of IP, earning 125.3 billion and paying 39.5 billion [in royalties].[1]

How is it that a country such as Malaysia is considered a "net importer" of IP, whereas the US is defined as a "net exporter" of IP, with radically different outcomes? There are two key reasons: The first is that the use of Intellectual Property as a full business strategy including positioning and marketing may be less advanced in Malaysia, and the second is that enforcement and advocacy are lagging.

Considering successful product export strategies over time, there are few products that have achieved long-term success without enforcement, advocacy, and IP education. Owning a trademark for a brand conveys to a business the power to control the use of the brand, but lack of enforcement is simply giving away that power!

This chapter builds on the power of Intellectual Property tools, such as trademarks, licensing, and geographical indications. These IP tools are critical, but do not automatically change low-income farmer/producer income without enforcement. In this chapter, we describe how Intellectual Property tools and effective positioning require support, advocacy, education, and enforcement as well. Since farmer and producer ownership is integral to our model, and advocacy often emerges from the farmers or producers, and focuses on their success, appropriate education in Intellectual Property business is vital.

This chapter illustrates:

- The value and criticality of collective, support organizations with historical examples of success

- The role of power and collective advocacy
- The purpose and vision of the African IP Trust, a support organization
- Specifics of how support organizations should be formed for new entrepreneurial businesses
- The role of education and a model for a curriculum for stakeholders, exporters, and governments
- An interview with Attorney Dick Wilder, Associate General Counsel of the Bill and Melinda Gates Foundation, and former Director of the Global Intellectual Property Issues Division of the World Intellectual Property Organization.

Advocacy and enforcement is an integral part of a full business strategy for many lucrative brands because engaging in IP in a halfway manner fails. Many such failures line the highways of international development and trade, alike, such as the IP tool of a trademark without concurrent advocacy and enforcement. One such situation involves over 2 million tea farmers. Ceylon tea from Sri Lanka is a fine tea brand with a geographical indication but over 70 percent of the product sold under this name is counterfeit, that is, it is not actually the product of Sri Lanka.[2] The tea farmers then created a distinctive product with a recognized brand and IP tool, but have insufficient enforcement.

Enforcement is critical to a lucrative brand such as Nike. The Nike brand value increased from a brand valued at $7.5 billion in 2007 to a brand value of $26 billion by 2015.[3] This did not happen without diligent enforcement. Although Nike's logo is a simple check, first purchased by the company for a legendary $50.00, no other company can add this logo to its tennis shoes, t-shirts, or anywhere. Interestingly enough, as a logo attached to a relatively basic commodity – the athletic shoe – it would be quite simple to replicate the Nike brand from a production point of view. Unlike unique agricultural products that require special soil, climate, and unique knowledge, athletic shoes can be manufactured almost anywhere, transported and sold. Nevertheless, the ubiquitous check represents protected IP, and to be sure, Nike would not permit the check to be used without taking action.

For example, the chief general counsel for Nike, Mr. Nick Carter, was overseeing about 100 lawyers in 2009, many working on enforcement, while the Nike brand value increased precipitously. He complained that counterfeiting also plagues Nike.

"We obviously invest a lot of money over time to build a brand," he says. "So it's potentially very damaging to a brand to have a product sold with unknown quality, material content and manufacturing conditions."[4] In other words and simply put: Enforcement matters and quality matters.

Obviously, this company producing athletic shoes owns a branded product that has only been popular for a few decades and has the income stream to work hard to protect and enforce the brand and its value. We advocate that African producers of distinctive products involving more specialized knowledge and unique conditions also need to protect and enforce their specialized knowledge.

How does Nike have the revenue stream to enforce its brand? Simply, the company started with the end in mind. The business plan included ownership of the retail brand and control of the use of the brand through careful selection of retail stores and full control of all parts of the supply chain, outsourcing several parts but keeping complete control. A retail store that sells genuine Nike shoes and counterfeit shoes would not be allowed by Nike to continue.

For producing businesses like the Ceylon Tea Board to reduce counterfeiting is to move to being better positioned like Nike. The example of Nike shows a correctly positioned producing business that started with the end in mind, including the following:

- Ownership of the retail brand through extensive use of trademarks, effective and timely IP tools
- A positive cash flow that funded enforcement and control of distribution keeping counterfeiting down to a low enough level that revenue stream is good
- Complete control over the supply chain to the door of the retail stores

Ten cases of success and failure enforcing IP

The authors of this book undertook a study for the Office of the US Trade Representative. Under this study, we reviewed five success cases, and five failed cases of IP strategies involving about 20 million producers. We posed the question: What variables were most important in generating the success or failure of agricultural products, when producers used an IP strategy such as a geographical indication or trademark?

The products analyzed involved nine countries, and seven product sectors involving several million farmers and producers over time. Products originated at various periods from 79 AD (Roquefort cheese) to the twenty-first century. The research compared products such as Ceylon tea, through more recent branded products such as Colombian coffee, Argan oil, and Malaysian Sarawak Pepper.[5]

The major areas of comparison were: 1) the role of stakeholders; 2) the export and retail price patterns; 3) the IP tool; and 4) the role of advocacy and enforcement. We defined success by the level of price differential in the final consumer markets from generic products that did not have an IP strategy. For example, comparing Malaysian Sarawak Pepper, which uses a GI strategy, to that of generic pepper. Or, Colombian coffee, protected by its IP, to commodity priced coffee. Did the IP tool matter? This was the simple question.

We found variance in the IP tools and variance of products. The IP tool was not the pivotal factor of success or failure. Neither was the type of product the key differential, as products ranged from tea to cheese, coffee and spices, oils, wines, and spirits. These product categories are exported and imported prolifically with enormous competition. The success was not determined by country, though to be sure, producing businesses with longer time periods to build up protection, alongside revenue streams generated by good positioning fared better. We note that the producers of champagne grapes and Scotch whisky were also once in deep poverty, and emerged from it.

There was also variance concerning time of origin with Roquefort cheese originating in 79 AD, but Columbian coffee emerging in the late twenty-first century. Too, the producer group sizes also varied, as producer group size ranged from over 1 million, in the case of Ceylon tea, to fewer than 5,000 in the case of Roquefort cheese, demonstrating that producer group size was not the pivotal variable predicting success either.[6]

Rather, the study showed the most critical factors to be the combination of:

• The positioning of the product and producers with marketing, branding, and retail market focus to earn sufficient income
• The appropriate IP tool to enable sufficient protection; coupled with
• Effective support, advocacy, and enforcement.

If we consider industries throughout recorded time – the automobile or industrial organizations, manufacturing, service or education – the organizational trajectory has been one of foundation, growth and scale via resources, organizing, and enforcement. The word management in fact derives from the root word, "maun," from the Greek, meaning to bring into alignment. To "maun"-age or manage then is to bring resources into alignment, to organize, to reinforce, and enable within boundaries.[7] Mere exploration of the Greek origins of words aside – management matters. For example, while branding has swept the world with laudatory promise, the reality is that brands must be managed, and this involves enforcement mechanisms.

IP tools such as trademarks, licensing, geographical indications, and certifications are important, but the tools, like any tools, are only part of building the house. And, while individual entrepreneurs are often the spark that puts ideas into motion, to move those ideas into successful enterprises in a sustainable and scalable way, nearly always involves some form of support, advocacy or enforcement organization that serves to sustain the enterprise and enable wider scale.

In practical examples, successful use of Intellectual Property over the past few hundred years shows over and over that Intellectual Property tools, coupled with support and enforcement, have made the pivotal difference for millions of poorer farmers.

The challenge for poor producers

It is easy to talk about creating and engaging support organizations if you are Nike, with a brand value more than sufficient to make enforcement a natural outgrowth. However, for newly emerging groups of producers and those who form large organizations of stakeholders who are developing new business capacity – how do you begin to enforce your IP? For example, there are 2 million Ceylon tea farmers. With enormous counterfeiting and caught in a circular problem – widespread counterfeiting diluting the brand and contributing to low income – the will to enforce their intellectual property may be strong, but they lack the necessary resources to do so. Over time, a trademarked brand that is not enforced can be considered "in the public domain," wherein it becomes much harder to regain lost control.

This is a real problem for developing country farmers and producers with large consequences. It is also why IP in isolation, or branding in isolation, or developing increasing production of distinctive products in isolation fails for developing countries. A fully developed positioning strategy that appreciably and dramatically improves sustainable income for the long term is needed.

As many LDC producers are realizing the value of brands, given the plethora of brands across their country and widespread advertising into emerging markets, it has led to a somewhat misleading picture of what a brand actually can do. A brand is only as valuable as it is well positioned, marketed, and enforced. Trade strategy focused on only one or two pieces, such as a country brand without marketing and positioning, or a brand without enforcement, is likely to fail and create disappointment.

Where support organizations *do* exist, they tend to be on the wrong side of power or lagging behind power. For example, in a game of football or soccer, the goal line is the strategic goal. So often in African situations, the stakeholders are aligned as cooperatives and cooperatives can be aligned in unions, a good first step, but aligned on one side of the field, and not reaching the end goal effectively.

Importing companies working with poor farmers and producers do not always have the poorer farmer and producers' best interests at heart, of course. Merely to form cooperatives, unions, or associations without full transfer of power is another partial solution. The cooperative, union or association cannot obtain and sustain power unless it is part of a truly empowered solution chain involving ownership and positioning through to retail.

Finally, in some cases, LDC government offices control the functions of support, advocacy, and enforcement of IP within the country but not in final consumer market countries. An IPO (Intellectual Property Office) may consist of a skeleton staff and a few lawyers for a country with millions of producers. The government office may be tasked with enforcement and often overwhelmed with the tasks at hand. Often government IPOs are more interested in and rewarded for promoting the country name, and thus buy into branding with country names such as Ugandan vanilla or Mozambique cashews.

Generally, government officials are not well trained in business. This has not been their focus, understandably. Lest we paint a dismal picture, the next section describes a farmer-owned cooperative that did create effective enforcement. We revisit Divine Chocolate to highlight the enforcement and stakeholder support aspects behind this fine brand. And, for producers building IP strategies that require an advocacy/support group, we highlight the African IP Trust (AIPT). This is an organization of high-profile leaders committed to assist African producers as they develop IP trade strategies, or in some cases, attempt to regain control of their Intellectual Property.

Divine Chocolate: a successful cooperative-owned business changing power

There are success stories of advancing farmer/producer ownership coupled with advocacy, enforcement, and education across Africa and LDCs. One example we have described earlier is Divine Chocolate. The emphasis here is its support organization that can be modeled – Divine Chocolate supports the successful union of cooperatives in Ghana that produces the cocoa. In the 1990s, Ghanaian farmers set up their own cooperative called Kuapa Kokoo, which then helped to establish the chocolate marketing company, Divine Chocolate, Ltd.

Divine Chocolate was developed with support from Twin Trading, Christian Aid, and the Body Shop. Kuapa Kokoo is currently the largest cocoa cooperative and Divine Chocolate now successfully markets the Divine brand in the UK, US, and other countries. The Ghanaian union of cooperatives is empowered, on the other hand, because the union owns 45 percent of the import/marketing company. The brand is positioned in higher end markets under a name that resonates with consumers – Divine. The Ghanaian roots via Adrinka symbols are displayed prominently on the package, while marketing communications emphasize the quality of the cocoa.

Here, the cooperative receives income from the import company, owned by the farmers, thus enabling a more fluid, seamless transfer of profit. Too, Divine enforces the IP rights, controlling use of the brand, which helps the company to grow more profitable over time. Enforcement serves the cocoa farmers well, enabling higher incomes and providing transparency. In this success case, support and advocacy is part of a full business strategy.

The power of collective action

Stakeholder organization with self-government is critical to IP business positioning success. The ultimate goal must be kept in mind – stakeholder ownership for the long term. Second, stakeholders must achieve a sustainable income that scales to include wider numbers of farmers and producers. While stakeholders are forming and being trained to look outside their borders and to learn the value of Intellectual Property business positioning, it is also important they learn the importance of collective action outside of LDCs. This should be coupled with strength, advocacy, support, and enforcement in developed country markets where the import companies will be located. New brands always face competition, but new brands along with IP ownership by African and LDC producers and import company ownership may encounter additional challenges. In the following sections, we will discuss various forms of traditional advocacy, and some new forms of IP advocacy such as the African IP Trust (www.africanip trust.org).

Trade Associations are a form of advocacy with a long-standing history. They are defined in the US by the Internal Revenue Service (IRS) as a group of persons banded together for a specific purpose.[8] Associations are not new. Early American settlers formed guilds, patterned after British custom to support lifestyle and mostly to support work. Even Alexis de Tocqueville commented in 1830 about America: "The new nation seemed to be succeeding at democracy, in part because Americans of all ages, all stations and all types of dispositions were forming associations."[9]

Both Thomas Jefferson and John Adams were members of associations. Entire histories have been written about secret societies that held power, some of which clearly influenced trade. Many historians believe these were pivotal in creating and sustaining powerful elitism upon which the tide of history has revolved, particularly in trade terms. In fact, the Carpenter's Union was a trade union in Philadelphia at which early plans for the American Revolution were laid. The revolutionaries seeking independence did so for trade reasons as much as loftier reasons.

While a history of associations is beyond the scope of this book, a point to be made here is that the presence and role of associations and the volumes of people belonging to them is not widely understood as one of the reasons America and the UK have been so successful at business. Trade prowess and collective ownership shifted power to the side of societies free to engage in collective activity.

There are, for example, over 1 million charitable organizations that sometimes are included in the count of associations, and millions of individuals belong to associations in the United States, alone. Worldwide, the numbers escalate. According to the American Society for Association Executives (ASAE), one in three Americans belong to or are involved with the association industry at some level.[10]

Collectives and associations sharing resources of knowledge and information, tangible resources, networks, advocacy, and subsequent power have been a critical factor at advancing enforcement. This opportunity has not been equally available to low-income countries. In Africa, for example, of the 54 current countries, all but one was colonized. Power was not shared; it was in the hands of the colonizing country and that country's trade associations. The shift to being free to advance collective societies, cooperatives, associations, and acquire trade power has only been realized on independence, years behind the pattern in many developed countries.

The power of collective action: types of power

The power to be found in collectives, be they trade, professional or more formal advocacy groups is not first and foremost legal power, though the laws of Intellectual Property are important. As discussed in Chapter 2, "Changing the power," if collective power and other forms of power such as expert, resource, network, and reputation power leading to advocacy and acceptance of the collective power are sufficiently strong, legal enforcement activities become less necessary. For example, consider our example of the well-known icon, Charlie Chaplin. His image and intellectual property are well understood. While counterfeiting happens widely, in many product lines, it is understood as counterfeiting, such as for Prada bags. Whereas, when indigenous peoples' IP is used by car companies, such as the Jeep Cherokee, for example, it is regarded as a marketing tool, assuming the name, Cherokee, is in the public domain.

Part of the purpose of trade associations is to represent collective interests, to lobby or to inform via newsletters, social media, industry magazines, and conferences. And, in the US and EU, trade unions served to shift the tide of workers powerless against sometimes tyrannical bosses. The ability to organize, to advocate, and to enforce union rules is collective power, that has been lacking amongst LDCs, and inhibiting their capacity to negotiate more powerfully in markets.

Expert power is an important type of power particularly when coupled with authority in the trade association. In trade terms, large associations such as the National Cattlemen's Beef Association promote positive images of beef, and the Motion Picture Association of America do more than advocate for films – they began running advertisements, against piracy on the Internet, even before the movie industry was well formed. These are just two examples of powerful trade associations that have become prolific in every industry during the twentieth and twenty-first centuries. That is because associations enable collective action in ways that individuals cannot, despite the inherent value of their products. The lack of collective action, until more recent decades in the form of cooperatives, has been detrimental to LDC producers.

The Scotch Whisky Association (SWA), founded in the earlier twentieth century, is noteworthy for bringing on average three cases per week against presumed misrepresentation or actions perceived as harming the Scotch whisky interests.[11] The highly lucrative brands of Scotch whisky joined together to support the Scotch Whisky Association, and are better able to protect the overall umbrella brand than if they had to perform this function as individual companies. At first glance, this may seem counter-intuitive, as individual brands of Scotch whisky are essentially competitors. But, as those who study network theory and organized industry show through extensive research, collectivity brings advantages that sole, individual companies lack.

What does this mean for African producers? Can we replicate collective action and the power of associations?

What do you do if you are many years behind in organizing for collective power?

You model after success. Farmers and producers, artisans and craftspeople from Africa and LDCs can model collective action for improved trade and take action, where needed. As in the full method described earlier in this book, changing power involves reaching beyond borders into the activity space where Africa's brands command the highest retail prices. While advocacy and enforcement may seem, at first glance, out of reach due to expense, the good news is that advocacy and enforcement need not be wildly expensive. As we describe with the lucrative Scotch Whisky Association a relatively small number of lawyers keep watch because they are well versed in how important their IP value and brand are. They take swift and consistent action, alongside a small team of enforcement agents underscoring their ownership by action, precedent, and a widely accepted understanding that has become normative.

Many African and LDC farmers and producers have organized into cooperatives, but they tend to organize on the wrong side of the goal. If the players are all on the left side of the field and organized, but the goal post is on the opposite side of the field, and the organization is not enabling them to move faster, better, more nimbly, smarter or more effectively, they may fail despite organization. All may be on board the ships and the ships are organized along with other ships, but if the ships are stuck in the port, the model is ineffective.

Organizing in LDCs and Africa has largely taken the form of cooperatives. While not fundamentally wrong, cooperatives organize workers. A cooperative may enable the women to share some costs, and exporters can have purchase points, and the women can be reached to participate more readily across rural areas. Women can be better educated inside the cooperatives with certain levels of quality control, such as improved nut drying and best means of storing and transport. And, there is a level of personal solidarity in belonging to a cooperative. However, the cooperative alone does not change the power balance.

Cooperatives do not change the power of the producers in the supply chain between producers and foreign importing companies, nor is producer income improved 10–20 times as is possible with correct positioning. For example, if shea butter of Uganda is sold inside Uganda or exported out of Uganda at roughly $5.00/kilogram, this barely covers the transport costs from the trees to a Uganda-based processing plant and to the export port. Organizing hundreds or thousands of shea producers may help the women in theory to command a higher price for their shea nuts. However, in reality, if the shea nuts, either sold as nuts or in final form in butter, export at low prices, the organization of women is missing the opportunity to achieve much higher income and have a much greater impact collectively. In some cases, cooperatives provide a benefit and advantage to the importing companies. For example, the importing company can buy higher quality shea from more reliable sources and gain the advantage of a reliable, quality supply by purchasing shea from the organized cooperative, rather than random individuals. Unfortunately, the import company oftentimes does not pay higher prices to the cooperative for the reliable supply. In short, the power remains with the import company as the cooperative becomes dependent upon the import company to purchase an ongoing, reliable supply.

The African IP Trust: collective action + power (www.africaniptrust.org)

One of the fundamental challenges of poor countries working in isolation is there is an acceptance and thus reinforcement of the status quo accompanied by the entrenched belief that African farmers and producers cannot collectively organize effectively to change the power and income. Disempowerment is a mythology that keeps people down. In the challenge to get products to port, and sell them, African farmers and producers accept the prices. Until recent communications, many farmers and producers, particularly those in more isolated regions, did not know what those products would be selling for in final retail markets. As just one example, the producer price for Shea nuts is $1.00 equivalent per kg in northern Uganda, whereas when positioned in small, attractive jars in a store such as Barneys of New York or a High Street store, London, the price point could be $100.00 or more per jar, or $1,000/kg. This type of information about potential prices is often a surprise to developing country producers. However, once the information is provided, and vision inspired, the women who have long sought improved internal market positions inside Uganda, are eager to turn their efforts and hard work toward reaching these more lucrative markets. Controlling the pathway to achieve higher income requires enforcement, advocacy, and education.

When we set out to secure more fine coffee export income for Ethiopia, there were as many obstacles and barriers as there are foreign coffee distributing companies and corporations. Many of these companies benefit from keeping Africans poor and disenfranchised by taking most of the value of their products in foreign market wholesale and retail markets. These groups have little incentive to shed power and control.

In the case of Ethiopia, Starbucks believed they could control the brand Sidamo, an old Ethiopian brand of wonderful coffee, simply because Starbucks filed their application for a trademark including Sidamo a few months before Ethiopia filed. The Ethiopian IP Office, upon our advice, challenged Starbucks and worked hard to secure Ethiopian ownership of three Ethiopian fine coffee brands. Initially, Starbucks held firm, believing that the collective action of the Ethiopian IP Office and Light Years IP could be overcome. Light Years IP director, Pauline Tiffen, took the campaign public and Oxfam joined in, collecting signatures. Even then, these efforts were initially disdained by Starbucks' leadership.

Catholic World Relief, students and even members of the British Parliament joined in to support the Ethiopian coffee farmers. Ultimately, Mr. Schultz conceded negotiating strength. Public campaigns routinely use the power of affecting the corporate reputation, and the threat of harming Starbucks' reputation was of real concern.

The power of experts; network power reaching large-scale collective form; authority power and reputation power are indeed powerful. Oftentimes, these forms of power are as critical as legal power, and when utilized appropriately, offset the need for the use of legal efforts. In addition, in the modern world of Internet and social media, the use of social power has escalated. Every corporate executive is aware of the damage of bad press and the possibility that a lucrative brand can be destroyed or seriously harmed in a day. Examples abound.

At the same time, while public campaigns are one level of building public support for enforcement, their results are mixed. Which injustice spawns a collective public outcry and which do not are hard to predict and replicating success is haphazard. For example, the restaurant chain, McDonald's, suffered from workers' tweets about food falling on the floor and being used regardless, whereas a similar practice likely occurs at other fast food chains without comparable social media presence, and similar practices are ignored. Nike has suffered from allegations of sweatshop labor, but has been less impacted than other firms. The unpredictable nature of public campaigns, and the challenges of the Ethiopian coffee case created the stimulus to form a more permanent organization – the African IP Trust.

How the African IP Trust was formed

The African IP Trust was formed with a mission to help African producers of distinctive products and support these producers to overcome challenges to their IP rights.[12] Its goal is to move importing and retailing businesses handling African distinctive products to negotiate with producers. The African IP Trust involves the power of high-profile individuals and social pressure coupled with mutually beneficial solutions, where possible. It includes high profile lawyers, government leaders such as Congressmen and -women, and a member of the UK House of Parliament, social leaders, and a network of partners across the globe.

How will the African IP Trust help poor farmers, producers, and artists?

The African IP Trust is based on promoting and helping African stakeholders to own Intellectual Property that is their human right to own.

The Trust will perform the following functions to enable and assist African stakeholders to own Intellectual Property:

- Concerted letter-writing.
- Coordinating Allies – groups of advocates such as OxFam; Students for Fair Trade; Church groups; and those groups concerned with the human rights violations of poverty that link closely to product IP vandalism.
- Fostering new Allies for the stakeholder groups based on AIPT member contacts.
- Engaging the African IP Trust's own networks of support in the form of powerful influencers.

FIGURE 6.1 African IP Trust in Washington, DC
Source: Sven Torfinn for Light Years IP.

- Acting as a respectable, organized, coordinated group that together can influence companies.
- Utilizing its collective skills from cumulative experience at negotiating solutions to recalcitrant social problems.
- Supporting and reinforcing stakeholders aiming to control brands and other IP.
- Reducing the protracted challenges of corporate interests via negotiating and exerting powerful social pressures.
- Developing processes for defining relevant stakeholders with a fair claim to ownership of brands and other IP instruments.
- Helping stakeholders to design organizing structures, suitable for each different situation, structuring the group ownership entities for their IP (brands, marks, designs, trade secrets, etc.), in transparent, participatory, and legally robust ways.
- Using social media to campaign by persuading opposition groups or organizations, such as exemplified in the Ethiopian coffee initiative in the successful struggle over trademark ownership with "Big Coffee" in the US.
- Negotiating across national borders, all along the supply chain.
- Providing an "umbrella" of protection for qualifying groups of owners, gradually extending this to millions of Africans.
- Facilitating the transition from dependency toward IP ownership and improved negotiating positions.

As per its mission statement, the African IP Trust will positively counter the challenge among African countries that view the IP rights system as designed and being used against them rather than for their long-term interests and the deeply entrenched view that fairness will not accompany their efforts however appreciable those efforts may be.

- The harmonious negotiation of IP conflict situations involving producers and international corporations.
- Advancement in knowledge of the economic viability of IP, across Sub-Saharan Africa.
- Improved understanding of using mechanisms such as brand management, licensing, and owning distribution outlets.
- The AIPT will provide the high profile functioning of an influential Board asserting the justice of rights ownership, made up of public servants deeply experienced in advancing the economic interests of poor people.
- Demonstrable advance of improved IP fairness wherein IP works *for* Africans rather than against them.
- Wider success in implementing IP value capture strategies, with strong enforcement, leading to dramatically improved income stability.
- The Maasai as first group to support: The Maasai people receive nothing for their IP. Their name is registered as a brand for cars, shoes, and other products and services without their knowledge, authority, or benefit. This situation is common among African tribal, cultural, and artisan groups.

How does an entity like the African IP Trust compare with other trade associations or trusts that have proven pivotal to the success of protecting Intellectual Property by advocacy, education, and enforcement?

Currently, as of the time of this publication in 2016, the African IP Trust had set a mandate to assist one African group, comprised of over 2 million – the Maasai of Kenya and Tanzania who approached the Africa IP Trust to assist them. Other opportunities are in the pipeline. The AIPT is supporting the Maasai to achieve a stronger negotiating position; intervene to reduce the use of their images being used offensively; and augment efforts to acquire licensed use of the Maasai brand with distributors. This high profile, visible case should enable other large groups of LDC and African stakeholders to find and seek out the AIPT for its assistance.

And, while farmers and producers such as the Scotch Whisky Association, or dairy farmers, and the motion picture industry have grown their collective power over decades and centuries, they also began with modest starting points, growing by successful interventions. The African IP Trust envisions growing its collective power as an umbrella organization to support sectors of African farmers and producers, and indigenous peoples' groups.

Trends working in favor of the African IP Trust success

Corporate Social Responsibility

One trend that may facilitate advocacy such as the African IP Trust is Corporate Social Responsibility. Corporate Social Responsibility has advanced consumer awareness of product origins and conditions in sweatshops and inequities.

Many organizations have legitimate ethical concerns about low-income farmers and producers and have been public about this concern ranging from diamonds mined to environmental issues relevant to their businesses. CSR has put corporations into the position of stating issues and making public commitments to consumers. However, the average CSR Corporation or company gives under 1 percent of profit to support their CSR programs. Nevertheless, the presence of CSR initiatives in most corporations underscores the need to protect the brand asset of corporations, of which they are acutely aware. It also reflects the criticality of brand management, and the importance of strong PR. In either case, CSR is a trend that facilitates advocacy and support organizations such as the African IP Trust, and is conducive to the enforcement of African IP rights.

Another positive trend is the collective action of some social entrepreneurs. Tom's Shoes, for example, began with the "Buy One. Give One" model. This business model has begun what some term, a movement. It has expanded to "Buy One. Fund One" and "Buy One. Invest One." These "BOGA" models underscore the importance consumers place on ethical business practices. And, of course, Fair Trade has been the widest social movement of the latter twentieth century that has raised consumer awareness toward ethical purchase decisions.

Is the AIPT a pipe dream or based on precedent?

It has been argued that the reason advocacy groups have been successful, such as Apple Computers, or in the film industry, is that these industries earn high revenue, and are capable of hiring legions of lawyers. "Anyone can enforce their Intellectual Property rights or sue when those rights are infringed, if they can hire a lawyer, or legion of lawyers" is common street wisdom. However, there are countless examples showing that support came *first* and the support and advocacy changed the power balance, enabling greater control over brand, Intellectual Property, supply, and revenue. For more about the African IP Trust, please see the African IP Trust workbook included on the companion website.

Intellectual Property education: what do LDC governments, farmers, and producers need to know?

An important aspect of transformational change is IP business education. To create transformational change is to educate LDC farmers, producers, artisans, exporters, and governments in IP business so the present and future generation develops capacity to understand and grasp the opportunity, engage the vision, and enact transformational change. Intellectual Property-based strategies with concurrent improved income will not be widespread without effective entrepreneurial education in IP-based strategies. What should this education look like and how is it different from the type of general business training currently under way in Africa?

Institutional capacity building for producers

One of the authors of this book, a university professor for many years, has designed an IP education curriculum for Africans and LDCs under a $1.2 m US Patent and Trademark Organization grant. This has involved subject areas such as Intellectual Property business basics; research in distinctive products; Intellectual Property tools and advocacy; and market research as well as specific education with case study workbooks for Ugandan Shea and the Maasai. The authors have a combined 40 years' experience carrying out training in these methods in Africa and LDCs ranging from the Caribbean to Asia. Some of the lessons learned from training large numbers of LDC farmers, producers, artisans, and owners of cultural brands such as the Maasai and other indigenous peoples are summarized here.

Who needs to be trained to carry out effective IP business strategies?

There are three groups that need to be trained in order for effective IP businesses to develop: 1) Stakeholders of farmers; producers; artisans or owners of cultural IP;

FIGURE 6.2 Maasai "mamas" at a Light Years IP training session in Longido, Tanzania with Meg Brindle
Source: Sven Torfinn for Light Years IP.

2) Government-level trade ministers and Intellectual Property officers; and 3) The export sector. We begin with the stakeholder level, because this group is crucial as they will own the business, control the supply chains, and own import companies – a very different model than the bulk of education currently under way in Africa.

The majority of business education conducted through large international development agencies is focused on agri-business with markets inside the country borders, such as street business, or improving quality for exporting. We applaud these efforts as they have improved production, quality, and street business opportunities. The education we advance, however, is focused on creating vision *outside* of the borders toward final retail markets with commensurate detailed knowledge to reach those markets, alongside building strong internal stakeholder organizations. Stakeholders need not become advanced in legal knowledge, or market positioning, but do need to understand the basics.

Stakeholder formation and organization training

A critical component of a successful business positioning with IP strategy is successful stakeholder group engagement, design, formation, and implementation to create a viable institution with strong values within a country's legal framework to own, manage, govern, and sustain the gains achieved by IP value capture strategies.

IP business positioning for stakeholders involves serious education with the following aspects:

1. In-country workshops to determine interest and capacity of farmers, producers, and general acceptance by African governments. It is important to engage established NGOs and institutions. For example, in creating a new shea butter model in Uganda, the existing shea butter cooperatives are vital to engage. Similarly for coffee, or tea farmers or artisans, engaging local producers brings knowledge and perspective.
2. Awareness raising: To engage interest, and reach beyond existing cooperatives or more distant producers, we have also used radio broadcast for awareness raising and announcements in more remote rural areas.
3. Engagement: It is important to engage with and train significant numbers of farmers and producers to build representativeness and a critical mass of trained stakeholders. In the case of Ugandan Shea, there were 22 points of training and engagement across the shea growing region. We hired local trainers with a Train the Trainer model enabling the Ugandan women to be trained and they themselves conducted further workshops across northern Uganda. While a western model might be to hold training workshops in urban centers, it is vital to reach out to where the stakeholders live, often spread across wide areas. There are countless large, international development agencies holding trainings in capital cities like Nairobi and Kampala on any given day. However, given the rural road system, and busy daily lives of low-income

farmers, and women in particular, many have never been to the capital cities, and the barriers to attend training, more than a walk, short bus or bicycle ride from home assures they will be left out of the training, with serious consequences. Though this may seem obvious, to overcome rural marginalization requires taking the training *to* the people.

As the map in Figure 6.3 illustrates, the 22 points of training had the intent of reaching 700 women across northern Uganda and into South Sudan.

4. Representativeness: It is important to consider whether stakeholder training is representative. It is relatively easy to assume representativeness as an outsider, but hard questions should be asked. Are there a representative number of women, for example? Are various education levels represented? Are we reaching the most remote stakeholders, or enabling a small group to hold power that may or possibly may not be representative of the group? Our experience has been that there are sometimes "false starts" in training. That is, training attendance can be incentivized by stipends paid and given the vastness of large international development agency training programs, care must be taken to avoid creating incentives for stakeholders to attend training who may lack motivation to take projects forward, a much harder task.

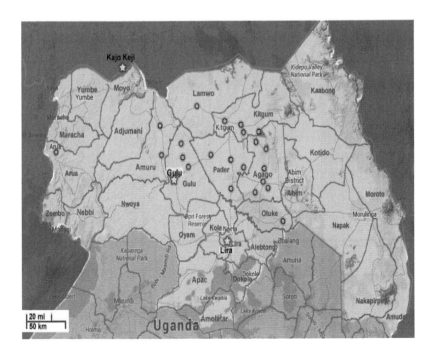

FIGURE 6.3 Maasai regions of Kenya and Tanzania
Source: Light Years IP.

Another issue revolving around representativeness concerns large groups. For example, there are approximately 2 million Maasai spread across two countries – Kenya and Tanzania – with a number of leaders and elders who are recognized in the culture as decision makers. It was clear that we could not reach *all* 2 million Maasai on our budget. Learning and listening to Maasai leaders was essential to develop understanding of who truly represents the Maasai. At the point of forming a viable Maasai stakeholder group, we invested a lot of time in careful planning to reach, train, and engage a majority of the recognized Maasai leaders. We also engaged in training via radio broadcasts in the Maa language on a popular show, which helped to build greater awareness across the Maa-speaking or Maasai regions.

In addition, representativeness matters particularly when dealing with Intellectual Property as ownership issues are central. For example, it is relatively easy to "help" a small group of Maasai mamas crafting beadwork to seek better markets, but in Intellectual Property, we are also mindful of IP ownership. How will income return and be shared equitably? This involves reaching larger populations with awareness-raising. For the Maasai, we have reached about 1 million Maasai with general training, and more specific training is focused toward leadership.

The map in Figure 6.4 shows the Maasai districts of Kenya and Tanzania as of 2013. To be representative, training needed to reach all of these districts effectively and would be lacking if training only focused on the cities of Nairobi and Dar es Salaam, respective capitals.

5. Creation of a stakeholder constitution: It is important that LDC farmers and producers receive education in building their stakeholder organizations, complete with robust constitutions. The women's constitution for the shea butter company is provided online on the companion website. It highlights the importance of building a stakeholder constitution that is simple, but covers essential areas. At the onset, only core areas need be included to avoid creating an overly complicated document. When constitutions are overly complex, for example, just as any legal document, it signals a complicated, and sometimes foreign document. The goal is to create a document under local country law that can be and *is* very much owned by the stakeholders.

Stakeholder constitution

It is important to highlight key areas such as:

- Membership
  a   Who can and cannot be members
  b   How membership is defined
  c   If there are dues or no dues (although there is debate about charging low-income participants dues, our experience is that a very small amount of dues helps to build commitment and ownership)

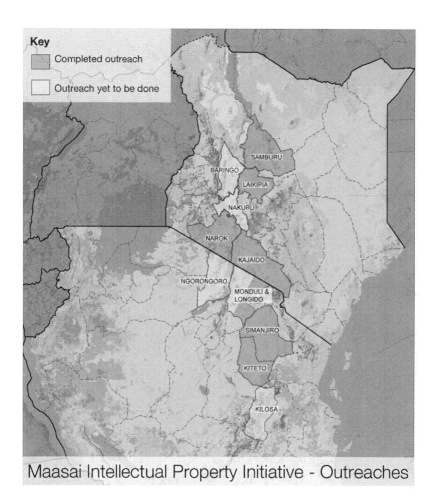

FIGURE 6.4 Northern Uganda training map from Light Years IP shea training
Source: Light Years IP.

- Operating rules
  - a What can members do
  - b What members cannot or will never do – examples include actions such as where shea nuts will be collected, and that members will not sell the company out
  - c The rules should be simple but define the boundaries so that a constitution has meaning, and most importantly, protects the stakeholder organization from outside buyers, and enables the stakeholders to fully understand processes

    d   There should be rules around the intersection between the country stake-holder organization and the import company, also owned by the producers

- Purpose and goals

    a   It is important to specify why the constitution is being built in the first place
    b   Goals are collective and augment commitment to the stakeholder organization

- Steps and processes

    a   It is important that the steps and processes of the stakeholder organization be clearly written
    b   Low-income producers need assurance of what to expect and when

While many LDC cooperative businesses create complex constitutions, we emphasize once again that keeping this constitution simple, clear, and producer/farmer-owned is as critical as the words comprising the document. Each member of the stakeholder group should have a copy of the constitution in their own language. Care should be taken to avoid adding too many rules, or legal language beyond what is necessary for ownership and practical utility. Also, building and maintaining trust is critical. Complex documents immediately signal division, and can appear imposed.

Changing systems is never easy for anyone, regardless of where they live or what the change involves. Becoming a member of a stakeholder group that has a membership and boundaries, alongside a clear, specific, tangible constitution with definitive membership helps to build commitment to the concept and reality of change. It should be taken very seriously in training. Please see the Women's Owned Nilotica Shea company constitution included in the WONS training workbook on the companion website for more specific examples of an effective constitution for stakeholder groups embarking on owning their own companies.

6. Leadership Emergence and Selection: In any stakeholder organization, leaders will emerge. Our view is that sensitivity to local norms is imperative. In the Maasai districts, for example, leadership involves a deeply entrenched seniority hierarchy. As outsiders, we would be disruptive to ignore this and favor the selection of new leaders. For example, a particularly bright, young entrepreneur surfaced as a leader during our early training sessions, and continued to demonstrate leadership talent over several years of training. However, to the Maasai elders, this young man had not come of age fully in Maasai tradition, according to centuries old Maasai culture to favor elders. It would have been harmful to promote the young leader, despite our western norms favoring young, social entrepreneurs.

In Uganda, women leaders are elected from all of the training areas to represent the women. The area of leadership selection involves, above all, awareness of local norms and practices. For a stakeholder group to be ultimately successful requires leadership, and it is not a favor to the group, or the leaders, if they are selected from an outsider's imposition. In sum, taking time for the process to mature is worthwhile, and avoiding the tendency to select or affirm the first emergent leaders generally proves worthwhile. To marry the two – the need to have leaders for the LDC stakeholders to begin to own the process, and coordinate trainings and the many on the ground activities needed, and avoiding premature selection, sometimes involves having temporary leaders or, as we call them, Acting Leaders pending time for the process to work and leaders to be voted upon via the constitutional rules.

IP business education

What are the most important aspects of IP business that Africans and LDCs need to achieve scale?

A well-trained, comprehensive, and wide-reaching collective of African stakeholders will ultimately receive, own, and manage the ongoing income and benefits from the Intellectual Property value of their distinctive products and improve the sustainability of that income over the long term. To summarize the importance of IP business education and show the reader how the method has been transmitted, the following has been a way to conceptualize and enact IP business training.[13] It illustrates a new wave of awareness and transformative education.

Course progression

IP business 101: IP business fundamentals

This course provides the fundamentals of how to engage an IP business strategy for positioning producers closer to final retail markets. Participants are instructed in the six-step method including: 1) analysis of the products' distinctiveness and intangible value to consumers; 2) wholesale and retail price gap across final markets; 3) supply chain analysis; 4) legal and business strategies to intervene appropriately in the supply chain with a variety of IP tools, including licensing, certification marks, trademarks combined with business strategies such as creation of import and export companies, and marketing tools relevant to the supply chain analysis; and 5) fundamentals in forming relevant stakeholder organizations.

Though this level of training is sophisticated, it is within the capacity of LDC farmers and producers to fully grasp. Many, if not most African farmers and producers are engaged at some level with business. A fundamental understanding of selling, customers, prices, inventory, competition, and record keeping is well entrenched.

FIGURE 6.5 Women leaders in Gulu, Uganda for Women's Owned Nilotica Shea
(WONS) training
Source: Light Years IP.

As in any training, building on what is known and describing the next level is solid pedagogy. We add to the farmer/stakeholder's present knowledge, the vision to see and comprehend what prices really are in markets outside of their local street markets. Case studies are an important part of this training, to fully appreciate the success and scale of other sectors. With vision comes eagerness for knowledge to understand how to reach beyond their borders effectively.

Building vision is productive education. For example, showing the 700 women located so remotely from lucrative markets, that many have not been to the capital city of their own country, building awareness of market prices; showing displays; and what products can be purchased for in cities such as Paris, New York, or London is like turning a light on. Once vision is centered, the stakeholders become highly motivated and incentivized to learn how to reach these markets.

IP business 202: Stakeholder organizations

At this level, participants get involved in taking products forward into implementation involving the support of additional experts in marketing and law. In addition, stakeholder organizations such as cooperatives form and advanced training is provided. Stakeholder organization is critical to ensuring full ownership of the rights and benefits of the IP transferred back to rightful owners and producers of the distinctive products.

Again, stakeholder formation is not new to African farmers and producers. They have been forming cooperatives and gaining understanding in the power of collectives for some time. Indeed, tribal people and Africans are considered far more communal in their lifestyle than westerners. The power of the group and the power of effective stakeholder organizations are readily grasped.

What is different here is transmitting knowledge to own and operate their own companies with greater understanding of supply chain ownership; advanced understanding of import companies outside of Africa; and IP business tools and strategies. It is also important to overcome a certain cynicism by some who have witnessed far too many western aid trainings and cooperative formations, only to see little personal gain from these initiatives. For the Intellectual Property to be owned effectively is to create sustainable stakeholder organizations wherein the IP is collectively owned, managed, sometimes fought for, and income is farily distributed to keep the stakeholder organizations intact.

IP business 303: Train the trainers

To transfer knowledge and engage most effectively with local stakeholders, trainers are trained and certified in IP Business specific to projects. The local trainers work hand in hand with our trainers to plan training in scope, content, and reach across farmer and producers. Train the trainer models have been widely recognized as effective, as they engage with and demonstrate cohesiveness with local farmers, build identity and inclusion, and enable the stakeholder groups to truly own the training, and the entire initiative going forward. Our favorite train the trainer's model operates in Divine Chocolate of Ghana. The farmers' cooperative now involves over 80,000 farmers in Kuapa Kokoo.

As described on Divine Chocolate's website:

> With thousands of farmers in village societies spread over all the cocoa-growing regions of Ghana, training and educating farmers about cocoa quality, Fair-trade standards, health and safety presents a big logistical challenge but one which Kuapa Kokoo has managed well. There is an outreach team responsible for dissemination of news and latest updated techniques and farming practice, there are regular meetings at village, district, regional and national level, and the AGM (annual general meeting), all of which aim to ensure views are heard, and Kuapa Kokoo's principles are adhered to. Kuapa Kokoo has its own Child Labor Awareness Program promoting its policy of not tolerating the worst forms of child labor, and ensuring all members understand how to make sure their children avoid any hazards on the farm, with emphasis on ensuring they go to school. Kuapa then works in partnership with local NGOs on monitoring and remediation.[14]

As this excerpt from Divine Chocolate illustrates, a train the trainer's model has the added purpose of ongoing training. Topics such as ongoing quality and supply, adjustments as they occur in the local stakeholder and import company relationship and coordination, and distribution of income will occur at the local organization level. The ultimate goal is for those who have begun the initiative to fade in importance while local stakeholder leadership assumes increasing responsibility.

Incremental levels of training and engagement: engaging the government

It is critical to the ultimate goal of returning more income to low-income farmers and producers that African government and ministerial levels become engaged in the training process for ultimate success.

IP business training is intended for:

> Ministers and permanent secretaries
> Intellectual Property offices
> Stakeholders who lead implementation of large-scale IP business strategies
> Government support staff
> Farmers, producers

Ministers, permanent secretaries and leading parliamentarians

The training focus for farmers and producers was summarized above, and is included in more detail in the workbooks included on the companion website. The training needs at this level differ from training in products and focus instead on IP policies including introduction of the link between African IP in foreign markets and government responsibilities for support and enforcement of all IP in domestic markets. The focus is to integrate IP Business into economic development at the national level.

Government support staff

The training needs here are in IPVC 101 and 202, described above to enable mid- and senior-level staff from the various departments to support IP business initiatives.

Government staff and the higher level government ministers such as the trade minister and IP officers are always included in our trainings. It is important to achieve transparency and inclusion early on in the process, to avoid problems further along the road.

In many cases, the country radio and newspapers have covered trainings as the opportunity for improved income is also a reinforcement to government-level servants and workers that products they have long known have been undersold and will have a brighter potential. The challenge at the government, trade minister, and IPO levels includes a cautionary need to reflect accurate time frames and expectations. For example, a full IP business positioning opportunity involves investment. For the social impact investment or other funds to be raised requires a level of in-country engagement, stakeholder formation to assure ongoing supply and quality, and government assurance. The time frame for income improvement is generally four–five years to achieve scale and appreciable income. This often seems like a long time to government workers whose own terms and evaluations may be measured in shorter time periods.

Training at the government level includes case studies and numerous product analyses to demonstrate what will and is unlikely to work well for an IP business positioning strategy. We include the workbooks on case studies as well as the "Research in IP business: determining distinctive products" workbook on the companion website. It is vital to prevent governments from chasing the wrong opportunities that are predicted to fail.

Levels of education and training include: IPVC 101 & 202, plus Sector Training.

Summary of business positioning with IP education

The IP business method is best learned comprehensively, both in training progression, as well as inclusion of broad ranging but clearly defined and relevant groups. As in any training, it is good to organize the training in progressive levels of content and projects as well as consideration of specific audience needs and differences ranging from the farmer/stakeholder level to the government and ministerial and permanent secretary levels.

We find that the most motivated students are those who see the goal. When the opportunities are presented to LDC farmers and producers, they are keen to learn how to acquire better prices, higher income, and more sustainable livelihoods. This motivation overcomes many other barriers. Indeed, some of our most successful trainings and resultant leadership emergence have taken place in open air classrooms complete with babies in arms, and goats and roosters walking through, even if the space lacks electrical power. Posters and roll up photos, diagrams, and movement, song, and dance are our choice for presenting concepts.

The ultimate goal is to see Africa and LDCs realize successful and comprehensive IP business strategies for the long term that hold genuine and substantial income generation for future generations. Poverty alleviation is not going to reach Africa via aid, but rather via the same way western countries moved out of poverty into wealth generation – through vision, business ownership, and effective business education.

To further emphasize that low-income farmers and producers can successfully achieve stronger stakeholder organizations and enforcement and thus improve

FIGURE 6.6 Zanzibar government training
Source: Light Years IP.

their income and sustainability of that income, we summarize several case studies wherein low-income producers have done exactly that.

Case studies

The following section summarizes a few case studies where low-income farmers and producers demonstrated formidable capacity to organize for support, advocacy, and eventual enforcement of their Intellectual Property. The thrust to advocate, protect, and enforce their rights went hand in hand with marketing and business strategy. French champagne, Scotch whisky, Colombian coffee, and Sunkist oranges have historical roots as begun by poor farmers – very low-income farmers and producers who disrupted the power balance, formed organizations under challenging conditions and were highly motivated to protect their product secrets well before the words brand, IP, and marketing were common place words, or indeed, even in the vernacular. Their stories are told in greater detail in a later chapter, regarding "the power of history," showing that IP business strategies are not new, but are summarized below to emphasize the stakeholder organization, and advocacy power.

Colombian coffee

Columbian coffee is an agricultural product with a fairly recent successful advocacy and enforcement agency as part of its success story. Coffee is an important example, as there are millions of coffee farmers in developing countries. As described in the Ethiopian case study, there are 4 million coffee farmers and alongside their families (assuming a small size of three), at least 12 million people dependent on coffee for their livelihoods in just one African country. The African IP Trust, for example, could become an umbrella enforcement support agent for multi-country coffee farmers such as in Rwanda and Uganda, who are also producing fine coffee.

In Columbia there is a smart retail focus, and an example of support, advocacy, and enforcement. What can be learned by other coffee farmer/producers for a model of support and advocacy? Colombia's average annual coffee production of 11.5 million bags is the third highest total in the world, after Brazil and Vietnam, though highest in terms of the Arabica beans. The beans are exported to the United States, Germany, France, Japan, and Italy.

Most coffee is grown in the Colombian coffee growing axis region. In 2007, the European Union granted Colombian coffee a protected designation of origin status. In 2011, UNESCO declared the coffee growing region a World Heritage site.

A business and enforcement strategy: The Juan Valdez marketing campaign

A key part of the history is the creation in 1927 of the Federación Nacional de Cafeteros de Colombia ("FNC" or National Federation of Coffee Growers of

Colombia). The FNC is a non-profit business association, popularly known for its "Juan Valdez" marketing campaign. The federation is a business cooperative that promotes the production and export of Colombian coffee. Membership exceeds 500,000 producers, most of whom are small family-owned farms.

The Federation was founded with three objectives: 1) to protect the industry, 2) to study its problems, and 3) to further its interests. However, unlike many African coffee cooperatives, the Juan Valdez marketing campaign of the National Federation of Coffee Growers of Colombia has a strong handle on the retail sales context, or end in mind strategy. How is this more powerful? Part of the answer lies with the history.

The policy context: a strategy for distinctive Colombia fine coffees

In June 2005, "Café de Colombia" became the first product from a non-EU nation to apply for the Protected Geographical Indication recognition to the EU.[15] To qualify for a protected geographical indication in the European Union, uniqueness of the product is required. Café de Colombia was therefore defined as Arabica coffee produced out of a maximal six different varieties with different characteristics and origin.[16]

The Juan Valdez branding concept was developed in 1981 to distinguish 100 percent Colombian coffee from coffee blended with beans from other countries. High recognition factors for "100 percent Colombian" have been recorded among North American consumers. "100 percent Colombian" authorized roasters and authorized brands are distribution companies that have each signed a "Conduct Agreement" with FNC. For example, "Ralphs" is an authorized brand; "Royal Cup Coffee" is an authorized roaster.

The Conduct Agreements are an example of power applied by the FNC over retail companies handling their product. The power derives from Ralph's perception that customers want the 100 percent Colombian branded coffee and FNC is using its ownership of the brand to set terms with the supermarket chain. Ralph's also made the judgment that FNC could stop the sale in the supermarkets if the Conduct agreement is not signed. This is enforcement without litigation and only possible because FNC owns the mark in the US and is present in the US market.

There is evidence that the investment in the promotion of 100 percent Colombian has contributed to the price margin for Colombian mild coffees on the global commodity market.[17] Vigorous investment in promotion to consumers of commodity coffee under a trademarked or registered brand would be an essential part of this success. This example by Colombian coffee farmers is noteworthy as a demonstration that the power of the brand was coupled with strong advocacy, support, and enforcement, even while Colombia was becoming a more popular coffee. This model of the FNC is replicable by other coffee producers.

French champagne

Another example of the importance of enforcement is evident in the well-known French champagne product. While we think of French champagne as an excellent marketing and business strategy, the success is actually due to a combination of marketing, business, and enforcement. France established a system to impose criminal penalties against violators of GIs even in the nineteenth century!

Toward the end of the nineteenth century, France produced further international legislation to protect geographical indications via the Paris Convention for Protection of Industrial Property (1883) and the Madrid Agreement for the Repression of False or Deceptive Indications of Source (1891).

In addition to legal protection, France also set up international lobbying groups to enforce champagne's GI in 1947. Of course, in 1947, the French had extensive challenges, such as rebuilding after the destruction of World War II, and revitalizing their damaged economy. Yet, despite these challenges, an international lobbying group was created to enforce their Intellectual Property business strategy, a priority that had significant outcomes. French champagne stands as an historical example of formerly poor farmer/producers gaining an IP business strategy. The French champagne case is particularly poignant as champagne did not actually originate in France, but is a lucrative, well-protected brand with sustainable revenue that is at least as much reflective of a fine product, as it is the fierce protection of the brand.[18]

Scotch whisky

Scotch whisky and the Scotch Whisky Association case demonstrates a successful enforcement agency, propelling Scotch whisky to be the fifth largest export of the UK.

This case is described more fully in the historical precedents of Intellectual Property business strategies. The Scotch Whisky Association (SWA) has been powerful since its roots in 1912, achieving greater power in 1942. As of 2013, the SWA has imposed legal action against more than 1,000 brands and has opposed almost 3,000 trademarks worldwide.[19]

Scotch whisky is a well-protected brand and its advocacy, support, and enforcement agency, the Scotch Whisky Association, has earned the nomenclature, "watch dog," as it does not sleep, or allow any intrusion, near intrusion, or conceptualized intrusion into its brand space! It is impossible to tease out how much the enforcement has contributed to the success; however, it is not coincidental that Scotch whisky has developed into one of the key exports of the UK, ranking in the top five of exports with approximately $6 billion in export sales reported, and accounting for one in 50 Scottish jobs.[20]

While French champagne, Scotch whisky, and more recently, Colombian coffee are demonstrable cases of IP enforcement coupled with careful marketing and positioning alongside brand management, the results involve billions of

FIGURE 6.7 Shares of French champagne retail prices by export producer and retailers
Source: Carita Marrow for Light Years IP.

dollars in improved income from their origins as barley processing; grapes plus processing; and coffee. These are agricultural products processed into infamous brands.

If formerly poor producers could turn barley, grapes, and coffee into household brands and engage enforcement, even during the struggles of World War II in France, poverty conditions in Scotland, and low income in Colombia, we advocate that LDC countries with far more distinctive products can follow a pathway toward successful enforcement, as well. The role of advocacy, support, education, and enforcement is evident in these well-organized stakeholder groups.

To gain a first person point of view on the criticality of advocacy, support, and enforcement concerning Intellectual Property rights and practical application, the following interview with Richard Wilder lends insight.

Interview with Richard Wilder, Esq.

Richard Wilder, who is Associate General Counsel at the Bill & Melinda Gates Foundation, has been a strong proponent of the African IP Trust in his personal capacity.[21]

Q: Mr. Wilder, you have been Director of the Global Intellectual Property Issues Division of the World IP Property Organization (WIPO). How do you see the role of support, advocacy, and enforcement for Africans in creating and owning new businesses? More specifically, do you think the African IP Trust can help?

A: There is value in having an organization that can help African farmers and producers. There are several ways that I believe the African IP Trust can be helpful:

1. It can help in education, to train farmers and producers to understand Intellectual Property business. There are many millions to teach and further train.
2. The African IP Trust can engage with governments through the high profile connections, as well as regional links to aid. A key question that can be posed to governments is: What can you do to better support your people? How does it link to aid?
3. The African IP Trust can provide links to global consumers of those products.
4. Governments try to help both internally and externally. The African IP Trust can help them take advantage of the IP rights they already have. The AIPT can demonstrate examples, such as by supporting the Maasai – the AIPT is demonstrating a viable use of IP that is in motion. This should prove stronger than theory and lecture, or conferences.
5. The African IP trust could also play a role in helping to identify markets outside of local ones.
6. Sometimes, one person or group of people really get it. They come to learn and understand how to use Intellectual Property. They can then serve as a lifeline to others.

Q: What is your opinion about the utilization of IP enforcement by poor farmers and producers? Are there any types of cases and situations that you see as worth learning from, either because they were disasters or successes?

A: I think the Ethiopian Fine Coffee (EFC) case was a good example. The EFC is useful because at the end of the day it was successful establishing an effective licensing strategy. There are many examples where the brand represents outsized value in comparison to the goods, such as Red Bull – that is a simple drink and the company has done well commercially with the branding and trademark. Also, Darjeeling Tea of India where the Tea Board of India has responsibility for enforcing it on a global scale. I am not sure how successful the Tea Board of India has been, but they may have been more so if they focused more attention on trademarks than GIs.

Q: If you were a company who was using or perhaps infringing on African farmer/producer rights, would you think that the presence of the African IP Trust would concern you or cause a change in actions?

A: The important thing is not so much to scare but a precedent of taking action. You don't need a large legal team as much as you need credibility. You need legal authority, which the AIPT has now with the Maasai, and a track record. This track record of managing IP resources can be in another domain, but you do need a track record to be credible. You can leverage that track record or reputation to bring the parties to the table. You may also enlist the government to bring pressure on recalcitrant parties. It is helpful to have global litigators with a track record of success.

Q: When we consider that Nike, a relatively recent success story has recently been awarded the distinction as the most valuable sports brand, I am struck with two things: 1) An athletic shoe is not hard to manufacture and the Nike swoosh was apparently purchased for $50.00. That this brand has soared to be valued at $26 billion is rather amazing. Yet, Nike has over 100 lawyers working for them, and a well-established network. And Microsoft has over 1,000 lawyers – many of whom have a role in protecting the IP of the company. In short, they have the resources and subsequent network enabling them to protect their brand.

A: Their example repeats itself amongst many, higher end brands. On the other hand, we see the Scotch Whisky Association has only a handful of lawyers, but they are very diligent, so it seems it is not volume of lawyers, but smarts and education to understand the how to. It is also important if you have limited resources to pick your fights well – either those that will lead to promising deals being done or those that will send a message to others of your seriousness – or both.

This relates to my earlier answer about establishing credibility and a track record. The African IP Trust should be able to help with this.

Q: Some people question how African producers will ever get there. In Zanzibar, for example, the office where we meet with the IPO is very small, cinder block and dirt entrance. At the same time, Zanzibar grows distinctive spices that are arguably harder to "create" than a Nike shoe. Spices require specific growing conditions, processing, etc. to produce their distinctiveness.

What is your opinion as to how Africans and LDCs might catch up with enforcing their IP rights and realize that IP is conducive to income?

A: What we are talking about here is launching a number of different startups, building businesses with IP tools and support and advocacy. The key is identifying what is valuable (or potentially valuable) in the countries or regions you focus on and identify the role IP plays in capturing that value. One example comes to mind from when I taught law in the 1980s in Malaysia. A very popular local performer, Sudirman, advocated for strong copyright protection for music. I was on the committee drafting the law. When it was done local banks showed interest in investing in production studios as there was a potential revenue stream for music in the local language. This is an example of a local "resource" for which IP helped to capture its value. In parallel to capturing IP value, as we have discussed, you need to adjust your ambition with the resources you have. So, it may be a matter of starting small and locally to build the base before branching out globally. So, yes, LDCs can and will make smart use of the IP system to capture value in a way that increases the wealth of nations, communities, and individual people.

Lessons learned and relevancy for advocacy and support organizations in LDCs

- Successful cases of Intellectual Property business always involve active support and advocacy, alongside enforcement from bottom-up education, and organizations, along with networks of support and upper level laws, rules, and policies.
- Successful IP enforcement is not merely the domain of lucrative industries such as computers, film, and higher end companies, but *can* be achieved by otherwise low-income farmer/producers. The same tools, processes, and tenacity that enable successful enforcement for Nike, the world's most valued sports brand, can be appropriated by poor farmers and producers. History has proven this, both in centuries past and recently in the twenty-first century.
- Successful support and advocacy involves various forms of power. Most typically, expert and authority power; network and relational power; and in the modern era, the fluid power of the media affecting reputation power with the consumer.
- IP education and the formation of educated cooperatives and stakeholder organizations is critical to forming effective IP business in LDCs. Critical components include representativeness; local leadership; stakeholder group formation with effective, clear constitutions; and local ownership.

- Legal power is important, but is most effective when coupled with other forms of power, such as network and reputation power, education, and advocacy.
- Poor farmers and producers have changed the power balance through such enforcement and advocacy arrangements as evidenced by previously low-income Colombian coffee growers; French champagne growers, and Scotch whisky producers now representing several million farmers and producers.
- Lower-income farmers and LDC producers cannot wait to *become* rich and then implement advocacy, but need to see advocacy, support, and enforcement as part of a business strategy. Power is not always about numbers but about practices of social, collective support.
- How to organize, create, and maintain solidarity in stakeholder organizations, and take collective action should be part of IP business training for poor producers. It should be built into the overall strategy, as stakeholder ownership is the goal.
- The African IP Trust will serve as a role model and umbrella of support and advocacy to LDC producers.
- The African IP Trust endeavors to model as an umbrella of advocacy and support for millions of low-income producers. The model is based on IP tools alongside the historical precedent. Advocacy and support does not require copious legal fees, or large, bureaucratic structures. Advocacy and support is often conducted by small, efficient but effective groups of committed individuals.

Notes

1 OECD report, Malaysian IP, p. 24.
2 M. Brindle and R. Layton, "Five cases of success and failure with geographical indications," The US Patent and Trademark Office, December 2015
3 Ozanian, "The Forbes Fab 40," p. 1.
4 Susan Hauser, "He just does it: Jim Carter defends the Nike brand," Super Lawyers, Corporate Counsel Edition, March 2009, p. 1.
5 The authors wish to thank the USPTO and Attorneys Deborah Lee and George York of the United States Trade Representative's Office for supporting this interesting study, forthcoming USPTO publication, 2016.
6 Brindle and Layton, "Five cases of success and failure with geographical indications."
7 M. Brindle and L. Mainiero, "Managing power through lateral networking," New York: Quorum Press, 2001.
8 "The power of A," The Center for Association Leadership website, www.asaecenter.org, January 2016.
9 The Center for Association Leadership (asaecenter.org, January 2016, FAQ).
10 ASAE website (www.asae.org) as viewed, May 2016.
11 As reported on the Scotch Whisky Association website, www.scotch-whisky.org.uk, January 2016.
12 The idea to form the African IP Trust, a more permanent support organization to help African farmers and producers was conceptualized by Light Years, with a grant from the US Patent and Trademark Office, under a Fair International Intellectual Property RFP.

13 M. Brindle, "IP Education for low-income stakeholders," The United States Patent Trademark Office, 2011–2014.
14 This excerpt is taken from the Divine Chocolate website, viewed March 2016. www. divinechocolate.com/uk/about-us/research-resources/divine-story/kuapa-kokoo.
15 FNC (translated, National Federation of Coffee, 2007).
16 Tipica, Caturra, Colombia, Borbon, Maragogype in a limited production area. Out of the total coffee production area of 7,300,000 hectares (representing 6.4 percent of the total area of Colombia) 12 percent (869,158 hectares) are defined as GI "Café de Colombia" area. The GI area includes 590 districts in the regions of Antioquia, Boyaca, Caldas, Cauca, Cundinamarca, Huila, Magdalena, Cesar, Guajira, Narino, Norte de Santander, Quindio, Risaralda, Santander, Tolima, and Valle.
17 The erosion of this margin in the last two years may be due to increased supply, meaning that the strategy is succeeding in achieving sales at an expanded volume.
18 The nineteenth century saw an exponential growth in Champagne production, going from a regional production of 300,000 bottles a year in 1800 to 20 million bottles in 1850.
19 A. Park, Worldwide Symposium on Geographical Indications: Marketing and Protecting Geographical Indications Around the World – The View From The Scotch Whisky Association, from the World Intellectual Property website, viewed March 2016 (http://www.wipo.int/edocs/mdocs/geoind/en/wipo_geo_bkk_13/wipo_geo_bkk_13_17.pdf).
20 Ibid.
21 Mr. Wilder was previously Associate General Counsel for Intellectual Property Policy at Microsoft Corporation, as well as a former Director of the Global Intellectual Property Issues Division of the World Intellectual Property Organization, a specialized agency of the United Nations in Geneva.

7

THE POWER OF THE BRAND

The Maasai Intellectual Property case study

Purpose matters to us as human beings because we have the desire to contribute and belong to something bigger than ourselves. When a brand offers an idea beyond the actual product or service it brings to this world, the brand will build stronger connections with the people sharing this vision.[1]

Innate Motion

Intangible value and wealth generation

The two simple sentences quoted above from a major branding firm, Innate Motion, have meaning for millions of producers. These sentences capture a sea change in the world of branding – a world where purpose, values, and emotional experiences associated with a product may be more vital than the product.

To understand branding, we build on our discussion of intangible value, described earlier as growing in importance. Intangible value is defined as that part of a product that is not about the physical part of the product, but about the intangibles, the feeling or emotion one has that is associated with the product. Intangible value can also be the experience or perceived value associated with the physical product. Consider, for example, a Lexus car. This car has a chassis that is identical to the Toyota, but is more expensive, and considered more valuable.

A Prada purse may be of similar material – fine leather – another, non-branded purse, even perhaps of greater size, using more of the leather than a smaller Prada bag priced 10–20 times higher. The sense of value, the emotional satisfaction, and the connection to a culture or group identity of those who may also purchase a Prada bag involve intangible value. What then is the logic of buying a Prada purse perhaps with less leather than a generic purse, using more of the physical product? As any fashion-minded woman would know, the value is in the brand and the association – the identity with haute couture.

Applying this concept more widely than Prada bags, intangible value is driving value in nearly every industry sector. In recent decades, the intangible value of products in developed country markets has overtaken the physical value as the main source of corporate income.[2] At a corporate level, intangible value is defined by the value of a product to a firm not accounted for by current earnings.

There are profound implications beyond corporate walls to this sea change in the world of intangible value. Intangible value may impact many millions of low-income producers. For the most part, this change is only now beginning to be comprehended by international development that has been more concerned with commodity products than higher end products.

This chapter will continue to build the IP business positioning model with:

- A review of intangible value
- Examples of intangible value translated into high earnings and hence high brand value such as Charlie Chaplin, Prada, and Samsung
- How brand value can translate into income for LDC producers
- The Maasai IP Initiative (MIPI) case study – a brand built by using indigenous peoples' culture of strength and courage and used by over 1,000 companies
- A detailed method for translating brand value into income for the Maasai
- Implications for indigenous people of improved brand value

Although intangible value was described earlier, it is so critical to an understanding of branding for LDCs we reiterate that intangible value has grown in value. In 1982, 62 percent of the market value of Standard and Poor's 500 companies could be attributed to tangible assets – that is physical assets such as factories, properties, equipment, etc. – and just 38 percent to intangibles. By 1998, only 15 percent of the assets of S&P 500 firms were considered tangible, while 85 percent were intangible. This shift in the value of assets reflects the ability of these intangible assets or IP to generate income. In a mere 16 years, the brand value of companies listed on the S&P 500 outpaced the value of their physical assets by 4:1.

The management of intangible value in the form of Intellectual Property (brands, designs, patents) is a priority activity for all western companies. It is not just a "legal issue" delegated to the legal department to act upon infringement, but the brand value usually sits at the heart of a company's overall business strategy. Though the legal department acts to protect IP assets, and the marketing department may best promote the brand, brand value is also part of quality control, human resources, distribution, and positioning. In short, a brand value, rather than being a mere noun or one time decision, as in "to brand a product," meaning to select a name, is an activity affecting the whole company. As Anne Belec, former marketing manager at Ford Motor Company puts it: "A branded company needs to reflect the brand promise at all touch points with the public."[3] If a company has a human relations challenge, or a story of untoward labor practices, a quality issue, or notorious delay in service, the brand value is affected.

What is a brand? Why are brands or sub-brands valuable?

A brand is a name, symbol or a sign that represents a physical product or service. It is usually in the form of a word, or several words, the letters (font and style) are distinctive and the design is memorable. Or it can be in the form of an image or shape. Examples include the "Hershey kiss," or the American firm, Target's bullseye. The colors and presentation do not vary, so that over time the brand becomes recognizable to the person who sees it.

A good or effective brand, and the design around it, may also tell the person something about the product or service that it represents just by looking at it: it is tasty, or inexpensive, or luxurious. Brands can even convey geography and origin, for example, by including or inferring the colors of a national flag, or the contours or outlines of a map. There are many products which have features of the American flag within their branding, for example, and the use of the "stars and stripes" conveys the "authenticity" or the "traditions" or "style" of that product.

Germany is famous as a producer of cars: six brands of cars are among the most valuable in the world including Mercedes, Audi, and BMW. Germany and the German language is often featured in the promotion of these types or makes of cars. The country of origin is often used to differentiate brands owned by companies and to reinforce the price premium and exclusivity, when the association with that country adds something to the reputation or image of the product.

Anybody can create a brand and assert ownership of it. Brands can be the property of multi-national companies. Equally though, farmers can own valuable brands. For example, Coca-Cola, owned by the Coca-Cola Company, is the fourth most valuable brand in the world, considered to be worth $58.2 billion in 2008.[4] As an example of value and continual increase, the Coca-Cola brand value continued to increase between 2006 and 2015, with a value of $41.4 billion in 2006, $58.21 billion in 2008, $67.99 billion in 2010, $78.42 billion in 2012, and was valued at $83.84 billion in 2015. Despite renewed interest in health and many publicly voiced concerns associated with sugar and soft drinks, the Coca-Cola brand nearly doubled in value from 2006 to 2015.[5]

Despite the dramatic growth in Coca-Cola's brand value, it was surpassed by Apple which became the most valuable brand in the world in 2013, valued at $93.3 billion according to Interbrand, a corporate identity and brand consulting company owned by the Omnicom Group. As the firm's global chief executive, Jez Frampton, wrote, "Every so often, a company changes our lives, not just with its products, but with its ethos. This is why following Coca-Cola's 13 year run at the top of Best Global Brands, Interbrand has a new No.1 – Apple."[6]

Obviously, not all brands in any specific industry advance and some fail. When Chevrolet, the car company brand made the coveted top brand list, the global head of Chevrolet at GM attributed the success to making a conscious effort to globalize the brand, selling in 140 countries, but also to playing up attributes such as, "value for money and designs that move hearts and minds."[7] The focus was on humanizing the brand, rather than the technology.

Sunkist Growers, Inc. which was founded in 1893 by independent citrus fruit farmers, now owns a globally recognized brand which covers orange juice, and, under licensing agreements, many orange flavored products (from children's snacks, to vitamins and cough medicines). We have discussed Sunkist at several points in this book. The following quotation from their 2008 annual report shows the importance of their brand value, with accrued licensing and royalty revenues:

> Sunkist ranks number 25 in the list of the top 100 licensing companies. This new ranking, in License! Magazine's recent global edition is a big step up for a company built on growing a fairly common commodity product – the orange. The growth of Sunkist's licensing business demonstrates the value inherent in the brand. The program generates millions of dollars in advertising and billions of consumer impressions, enhancing the brand worldwide at no cost to growers. It also returns substantial amounts of royalty income to Sunkist.[8]

Sunkist is still a collaboration of orange growers' cooperatives and businesses, one hundred years later. In 2015, Sunkist announced its fifth straight year of billion-dollar revenue growth and payments to growers of $1.1 billion in 2014, up from $873 million since 2013.[9] In 2014, Sunkist branded, but counterfeit, oranges were being sold in Hong Kong, wherein 5,000 oranges were seized by authorities, along with over 100,000 counterfeit labels revealing that the counterfeiters have copied the Sunkist label for oranges that were not Sunkist.[10]

It is interesting that Sunkist now covers many products that have little to do with the orange. For example, Sunkist candy brands and soft drinks such as soda pop have zero orange product in them, other than orange artificial coloring, but moms will purchase the soda pop because of the association with the Sunkist brand, considered healthy, wholesome, and authentic. When a brand is successful, the values associated with that brand may transcend facts.

How does IP generate wealth?

Over time a brand, when it becomes recognized and associated with a specific product or service, is an extraordinary, valuable asset. Why? Because it helps people – the consumers – select that one particular product or service from the many competing ones that might be available in the same category and, in this way, provides a more certain source of future revenue and income.

Social psychologists who have studied human decision making affirm that reducing uncertainty may be the single most influential variable in human decision making. People tend to place a high value on familiarity and consistency. People also tend to favor building commitments when those commitments are built on consistency. A related concept underlying decision making is "social proof" – choosing actions based on what similar others are choosing and selecting.[11]

Consider Harley-Davidson, a very lucrative brand concept involving higher engineering for motorcycles. The motorcycles are expensive at $20,000 and upwards. A unique culture with several elements has developed around the product and the brand. Some part of the Harley-Davidson culture overlaps with working class imagery, particularly pickup trucks, leading to the superb design of a collaboration of brands by Beanstalk, a New York brand extension firm hired by Harley-Davidson.

- In 2000, Ford and Harley-Davidson signed an agreement to associate their brands under a design by Beanstalk.
- Harley-Davidson provided its own culture to paint and fit out the standard Ford F-150 pickup truck as the "Harley-Davidson Edition," increasing the retail price from $24,000 per truck to $42,000.
- The two companies shared the increased revenue.[12]
- Between 2000 and 2014, over 8,000 Harley-Davidson Edition F-150 trucks have been sold, for total sales of $336 m.[13] What changed between the Ford truck and the Harley-Davidson version? If you guessed $18,000 in price differential, alongside Harley-Davidson's paint, logo, and fittings – that is right. The brand value is clearly high. Harley-Davidson has earned that value and lawyers and most observers would say that is clearly their asset, and along with ownership rights should convey to financial gain.

Brands however do not remain static. While continuity and trust are valued and brand loyalty works to protect consumers and shield consumers from what would be an overwhelming number of everyday choices via trusting reliable brands, consumers also value improvements, and new experiences.

A special opportunity in time – many corporations and corporate brands are unpopular

Only 28 percent of European consumers report that they believe that established brands add value to our quality of life and wellbeing. The strong and escalating reaction to corporate tax evasion will deepen distrust in corporate brands. Trust in established brands is collapsing and purpose is now a critical element of brand loyalty.

Some part of this opportunity can be captured for products from Africa and LDCs, reflecting perhaps a better opportunity than at any time in the last 50 years. Most African distinctive products have a human story that resonates with the values of consumers, and transparency in supply chain ownership and financial disclosure is of greater importance. African brands can provide:

- Truth in transparency on the share of the retail price that reaches African countries and, in particular, poor farmers and producers.
- Heritage products, particularly women's heritage such as Argan oil and Shea butter.
- Pure qualities without manipulative additives like sugar.

There is some tendency for LDCs to brand their products after country names, such as Zambique cashews, or Ugandan vanilla, Kenyan AA coffee, and Zanzibar Cloves. This only works if that brand resonates with consumers, which Zanzibar does but many others don't. We have described chocolate made from Ghanaian cocoa, branded as Divine Chocolate, a product that has done well in the twenty-first century because the brand resonates with consumers and is well positioned.

Reflecting the need for brands to keep pace with consumer changes and volatility in preferences, in 2015, Unilever, one of the world's most lucrative brand owners, began reworking 400 of its brands. As Marc Mathieu, former Senior Vice President of Global Marketing for Unilever and currently Chief Marketing Officer, Samsung, described it:

> We helped Unilever build and execute "Crafting Brands for Life" (cB4L), the most ambitious marketing change program in Unilever history. B4L embarked 7,000 marketers on a journey to put people and purpose at the core of 400 brands. Innate Motion provided thought leadership, developed and rolled out new tools such as the Brand Deep Dives and the immersions, guided the internal change storytelling, and ran positioning work on dozens of brands to, in the words of Paul Polman, "bring the passion for brands back to the company."[14]

This serious investment by Unilever reflects their awareness that consumers change.

The challenge and opportunity for the developing world

In the absence of awareness and knowledge, significant levels of misappropriation of the developing world's IP are taking place. To name just a few examples: Ethiopia faced down a global Trademark application including the coffee brand name Sidamo which would have meant significant problems in the future usage of this coffee brand by Ethiopians. Similarly, specialist Kikoi cloth producers in Kenya were assisted by a UK fair trade organization in forcing a UK company to withdraw an application for cloth that was similar to Kikoi. Bogolan producers of Mali, West Africa face constant misappropriation by an extraordinary range of companies: from interior design items, e.g. wallpaper, to Nike running shoes who use their famous Bogolan Mudcloth designs. And, the Tuareg, a nomadic and ancient people of the West African Sahara, are explicitly referenced in a range of products designed for high performance in "rugged" terrain such as a popular family Volkswagen car model, brands of motorbikes, and bicycles. A global brand of walking shoes and boots has been rapidly built based explicitly on the Maasai name, called MBT or Maasai Barefoot Technology. There are countless examples of African names being used for lucrative gains by global companies.

The pattern of corporations appropriating African symbols, names, words, and products for added brand value to their products has become so commonplace that it is taken for granted. As an example, when Starbucks was challenged for applying for a trademark for the Sidamo brand, as Sidamo is an Ethiopian fine coffee, the company at first stood on the legal point of view. That legal view is that whoever applies for a TM for a product first is likely to achieve legal rights to use the name ownership.

We assert that the pattern should begin to run the other way. Just as, in the end, Starbucks recognized the value of an Ethiopian coffee brand and claimed it before being challenged, Africans holding distinctive products should own their product lines and achieve higher income by learning to brand and reposition those products in a manner appealing to higher end consumers who are mostly resident in developed countries. This will involve significant training and education, and also recognizing and publicizing successful models.

There has been a common misperception that Intellectual Property is a concept that is too difficult or inappropriate for LDC farmers and producers. This is part of a mindset in which the norm and roles are understood as Africans produce, and developed country corporations own brands and distribute products. And further, that developed countries take the benefit of the intangible value of those original, and hard-earned products from African and LDC farmers and producers. This is changing.

Corporations generally discount the distinctiveness and unique attributes of many products coming from Sub-Saharan Africa as belonging to or attributable to the producers who generate this distinctiveness. Where the uniqueness relates to a collective legacy – heritage textiles like Kente cloth, for example – the picture is even more ambiguous. Fortunately this is beginning to change. There are some notable success stories from Africa and corporations and the development community are beginning to take note. Africans need to develop IP business strategies to gain the "intangible value" associated with their exports. This is not merely to catch up, but because millions of dollars of additional revenue is available every year through IP strategies including smart branding as part of correct positioning.

Brands and corporate reputations have never been more important as a cause of profitability. While successful brands assure their products will be selected and generate revenue, companies need to watch out for their own reputations and values. Attacks on the latter can reduce the attractiveness of the former. The Nike Corporation, the number one sports brand, now valued at over $20 billion, just for the brand, and 33rd most valuable brand in the world according to Interbrand, has found itself under relentless attack in the last decade over its use of sweatshops to manufacture goods.[15]

As stated earlier, Nike is a corporation that started with the end in mind, correct positioning in all respects. Its brand is not secure because it missed an important component, putting trust and credibility at risk among the fast growing numbers of consumers with awareness of unfair treatment of factory workers. Perhaps, the company felt that rich consumers would not care about poor factory workers?

In sum, Sunkist orange growers have moved from a group of farmer cooperatives to a collective corporation, achieving ownership by very poor orange growers from southern California, just since 1926, to having a brand value of over $1 billion, with their name recognized as the brand on over 700 products. With 49 licensees in total, the Sunkist brand is used to market approximately 700 products in 77 countries.[16]

If Nike can sell a basic athletic shoe transforming a commodity product to a brand valued at over $20 billion, and Charlie Chaplin's family can own and manage the brand of a poor English boy who perfected a certain walk, comedy, and cultural iconic sphere, what are the implications for African products that are truly unique and developed over centuries of time, infused with knowledge, culture, and skill?

Implications for brand value in Africa

As we described earlier in this book, the major challenge concerning brand value in Africa is that while African producers might brand their products, the value of the brand is often taken from them – as the importers outside of Africa understand IP tools, supply chain ownership, and consumer positioning, enabling them to benefit from the brand.

While learning "to brand" is not "brand" new to Africa and has become almost faddish in international development circles, the big challenge is that the brand does not make it across the goal line when products continue to be marketed to low-end markets. More often than not, when a product is considered sophisticated enough to brand, the value accrued from the brand is taken by the importers outside of the country with little return to the African farmer/producer.

A UK chocolate company partly owned by Ghanaian cocoa cooperative, Kuapa Kokoo, did things differently. Rather than market chocolate made from their cocoa as Ghanaian chocolate, they have a name that resonates well with consumers – "Divine Chocolate." Kuapa Kokoo own 45 percent of the import

FIGURE 7.1 Maasai Mama photo
Source: Light Years IP.

company so considerable brand value from Divine in 13 countries accrues back to the Ghanaian cooperative owners. One can find Divine Chocolate positioned with the finest chocolate bars at high end retailers such as Whole Foods. While the packaging holds Ghanaian symbols, the brand name resonates with consumers who buy chocolate which could be heavenly.

The Tramp, a cultural icon with commercial value

In 1914, Charles Chaplin created a unique character for his globally popular silent movies called "The Tramp" or "The Little Tramp." The Tramp was extremely poor, but kind and optimistic, leading to highly favorable recognition for over 100 years since Chaplin first introduced the character to audiences.

Developing the character meant that audiences knew the Tramp's values and culture, so he inspired people to overcome hardship at a time that was recognizably poorer than the twenty-first century. The massive loss of jobs during the 1930s with unemployment rising from 5 percent to 20 percent meant that the Tramp's positivity meant very much to millions. With humility but dignity, the Tramp endured and kept going.

Chaplin created a character over 100 years ago with a distinctive look and a unique way of walking. The "Tramp" or "The Little Tramp" became an iconic figure that leading companies could not use without the permission of the Chaplin family. IBM secured a license to use the (Little) Tramp in the 1980s in an advertising campaign to promote the simplicity of IBM personal computers, a new concept at the time.

The parallel between the Tramp and the Maasai is clear – there is also uniqueness and long-lasting value in the Maasai cultural brand. In the next section, we will describe the cultural brand of the Maasai tribe of Kenya and Tanzania who number about 2 million and have a brand that will generate licensing revenue. This case study holds implications for indigenous people who equate to approximately 6 percent of the world's people.

The Maasai Intellectual Property Initiative (MIPI)

We have been working with the Maasai of Kenya and Tanzania since 2008. As gaining value from cultural brands is not widely or well understood, we will describe in great detail how a cultural brand valued as being worth $25 million per year can be used by the Maasai for community development and poverty alleviation.

Background

The Maasai are an indigenous people with traditional knowledge. Within Kenya and Tanzania there are an estimated 2–3 million Maasai men, women, and children.[17] However, certain regions are known to be "Maasai."

The Maasai as a people have achieved phenomenal renown throughout the world, and a wide penetration in consciousness of their existence and attributes and visual recognition. Some assert that fewer slaves were captured from Kenya, for example, as the Maasai protected their borders fiercely. Other legends present that the Maasai were required to kill a lion with few tools to help as proof of manhood, though this practice has ended as lions have become more protected. While legends vary, they combine to create an image of the Maasai as strong beyond human norms, brave, courageous, and more than slightly exotic. A simple Google search of Masai, Maasai, and variations is revealing in the enormous scope of material available:

> Maasai – 1.5 million references
> Masai – 6.11 million references
> Masai Mara – 1.1 million references

In just Internet images alone, there are more than half a million images of the Maasai. What is clear is that the Maasai are not alone in being used to imbue commercial products on the market with the attributes of a tribe or ethnic group and its culture and traditions[18] There is a significant body of literature on the Maasai culture, traditions, diet, and history. The Maasai culture and tradition is imbued with a great deal of "traditional knowledge" which is defined by the United Nations Educational, Scientific, and Cultural Organization (UNESCO) as follows:

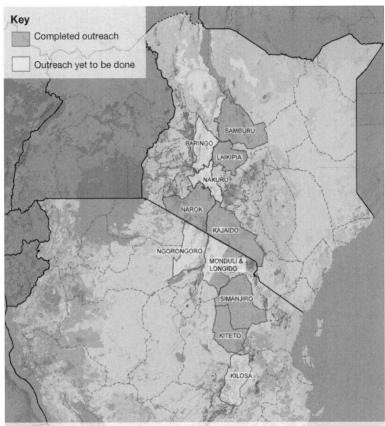

Maasai Intellectual Property Initiative - Outreaches

FIGURE 7.2 Kenya/Tanzania map of outreaches to Maasai communities conducted by the end of round 1 and before round 2

Source: Light Years IP.

Living in and from the richness and variety of complex ecosystems, they [indigenous communities] have an understanding of the properties of plants and animals, the functioning of ecosystems and the techniques for using and managing them that is particular and often detailed. In rural communities in developing countries, locally occurring species are relied on for many – sometimes all – foods, medicines, fuel, building materials and other products. Equally, people's knowledge and perceptions of the environment, and their relationships with it, are often important elements of cultural identity.[19]

What is clear, though, is that these frameworks have not or have not yet been used effectively to protect indigenous people from straightforward commercial exploitation. Nor do they – or the UN bodies responsible for IPR (Intellectual Property Rights) – offer a platform, specific tools or approaches that can overlay the assertion by companies which undermine or appropriate the IP assets of indigenous peoples' trademarks including the tribe or ethnic group's own name.

When one thinks of Intellectual Property and business, the Maasai tribe is not typically the first image that comes to mind. Rather, we tend to think of wealthy westerners endeavoring to preserve ownership of artistic work with copyrights or patenting inventions; or to claim company names and trademarks such as Coca-Cola and Apple Computers. There is a collective understanding that IP laws and norms alongside plenty of rules and international laws govern the use of IP for the wealthy.

However, the Maasai name, image, and heritage have been used by over 1,000 companies to increase the market and financial value of items and services ranging from cars such as Maasai Landrover, to brands such as Louis Vuitton, who hosts a Maasai fashion line. There is also a category of services such as Maasai management consulting suggesting a certain natural intelligence, strength of leadership, and exercise clothing line drawing on the physical, intangible value of the Maasai.

IP recovery attorneys whose professional living involves licensing and estimates of license value, Jeremiah Pastrick, and Karl Manders, CEO and President of Continental Enterprises, estimate the Maasai name and image is worth about $25 million per year – adding value to a plethora of companies using the Maasai image, reputation for strength and courage.[20]

While it is interesting to assess the value a tribal people may bring to corporate brands, it is a rather useless exercise unless the tribe can acquire a measure of ownership. Can a legal system designed to protect IP in products be applied to a cultural asset such as a tribe? Can IP now considered potentially in the public domain be brought back to achieve income for the 2 million Maasai?

The history of the Maasai IP Initiative

The Maasai IP initiative began in 2010, to empower and enable the Maasai to gain more control over their own IP, increase respect for their culture, and to achieve reasonable, sustainable income for the Maasai people. The Maasai had developed a growing sense that their name and image were being used without their permission, not only to make money for foreigners, but in many cases, the use was offensive to the Maasai.

For example, Maasai images in the form of tourism posters were literally plastered over the Paris subways in 2010, and applied haphazardly to all manner of products including shoes such as Maasai Barefoot Technology who claim you will "walk like the Maasai" when wearing their shoes which sell for as high as $300.00/pair.

FIGURE 7.3 Maasai Intellectual Property Initiative Trust, Ltd. logo
Source: Light Years IP/ Maasai IP Initiative.

In 2009, Maasai elders contacted the authors of this book to ask for help – is it possible to gain more control over their IP and limit offensive use? Light Years IP had recovered important IP for the Ethiopian coffee farmers, enabling the farmers to reclaim more control over their fine coffee Trademarks and take on big coffee giants such as Starbucks with income return of $101,000,000 for about 1 million coffee farmers.[21] The Maasai wanted to do the same – regain more control over their own IP, and if possible, to create sustainable revenue. There was no point in merely complaining about the misuse, but to turn it around for sustainable revenue.

How does this work?

First, we considered *why* the Maasai IP is valuable. Consider Disney or Star Wars images. Why does a child want "Disney" merchandise, or an adult want a Harley-Davidson? These images enable a person to associate with the qualities of Disney princesses, or with the courage of Star Wars, or the bravado of the Harley-Davidson culture. For these firms, the IP value of their firm is worth more than the tangible assets. It stands to reason that if firms that were created in this century have IP rights and protection and value, so should a tribe that has built its cultural heritage for centuries. And, if Charlie Chaplin's family can protect and continue to receive income from Chaplin's iconic image and walk, reason tells us that the Maasai should be enabled to do so, as well.

To begin an IP business positioning strategy for a cultural group, such as the Maasai, there were some core questions to ask:

1) What is the attraction of the brand?

It is first important to consider why a company would add a tribal image to their product. Just as Ford determined what the value would be of partnering with Harley-Davidson, many companies obviously believed the Maasai image would be useful to advancing their brand value. According to Marc Mathieu, Senior Vice President of Global Marketing at Unilever, the companies using the brand seem to be attracted to different elements of meaning of the Maasai: Authenticity, Strength, and Courage.

2) What is the brand valuation of existing users? Or, how does the use of the Maasai add value in numeric terms?

A more in-depth brand valuation considers the size of the market. Research indicates strong demand in the marketplace, with over 1,000 companies using Maasai Intellectual Property to sell their products. A number of large corporate users have Maasai-related sales of over $100 million per year each. Maasai Barefoot Technology alone has sold over $1.5 billion in Maasai-branded shoes.[22]

The goal is to achieve licensing revenue, and sustainable income based on a similar licensing process used by other famous, iconic brands due to high recognition among consumers who value being associated with the culture. For example, Charlie Chaplin and Harley-Davidson add significant brand value to a wide range of merchandise, and achieve sustainable licensing revenue, worth billions. This is true for Charlie Chaplin branded products decades following his death, and for a motorcycle brand. Why should licensing revenue not be obtainable by African tribal brands that are also valued by consumers?

The Maasai are now represented by an organization created through the traditional decision-making structure of the culture and also hold legal standing as the owner of the brand. For the first time in history, corporations wishing to use the Maasai brand have an authority to talk with and know where to apply for a license. It is notable that Jaguar Land Rover immediately responded positively and practically to a request to respect the Maasai ownership.

3) What would the correct IP tool be in this situation?

As described in Chapter 4, IP tools vary according to the situation and Trademarks are appropriate in some situations, whereas licenses and a combination of trademark/licensing is more suitable in others to yield income. Typical license royalty deals are: 5 percent of the gross sales for users, in this case Maasai Barefoot Technology; and for new licensees. This is industry standard.

How does licensing work?

The Maasai initiative will receive income via three main ways that are standard in licensing strategies:

1. Achieving licensing revenue from the many companies who already use the Maasai name and image at an estimated 5 percent royalty;
2. Creating licensing deals for companies not yet using the Maasai name and image, but who wish to do so given the attractive brand value, for 5 percent royalty; and
3. Increasing the value of the Maasai brand by building a pro-active brand for several products.

How can the Maasai protect the brand?

We are doing what a company would do. Consider, for example, that I began to sell something like "Charlie Chaplin shoes" and promised that you will walk like Charlie Chaplin if you wear these. Well, since Charlie Chaplin is an iconic figure, his family would have something to say about that. They might write me a letter and ask me to stop, they might enforce their rights, or they might like a Charlie Chaplin product idea and ask/demand licensing fees. Charlie Chaplin's Little Tramp has been in public knowledge for 100 years. The Maasai have a longer history and are instantly recognized.

Challenges for the Maasai and challenges for indigenous people groups

The Maasai must overcome a few challenges that any group or company would need to overcome to gain, or in this case, to regain control over their IP. Their two main challenges are presented below along with strategic actions to address these common challenges:

1. Prove legal standing: The Maasai must prove they have a legal entity to "own" the IP. The Maasai are spread across Kenya and Tanzania, organized into districts and governing bodies with well-established, recognized effective leadership.
2. Public domain: When IP is used extensively without formal complaint, it is sometimes considered to be in the public domain. This implies that it is used so frequently that it is no longer owned by anyone. However, IP recovery attorneys have frequently recovered IP from the public domain when a legal entity proves its ownership and mounts an effective case. Even the VW company enlisted IP recovery lawyers, when their classic VW beetle shape was being used generically.[23] The VW bug was argued to be "in the public domain." The lawyers who accomplished this for VW – acquiring the ownership of the VW bug for VW, and out of "the public domain" – are also working for the Maasai. For the Maasai, the ethical framework is that the Maasai have developed their culture for centuries and collectively want control over how it is used by companies everywhere. This is not hard to understand. If the Maasai were a modern company such as Apple Computers, Disney or Coca-Cola, these trademarks, images, reputation, and intangibles are much more recent, but people cannot use these images without the permission of the company, of course.

The following diagram illustrates the seven-point plan strategy for the Maasai with the circle illustrating the seven areas of activity, overlapping as these strategies are done in concert.

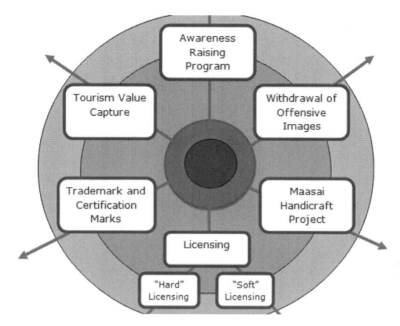

FIGURE 7.4 The Maasai seven-point plan for IP recovery
Source: Light Years IP/ Maasai IP Initiative.

1. Awareness raising program
2. Withdrawal of offensive pictures
3. Maasai mamas handicraft project
4. Hard licensing program
5. Soft licensing program
6. Trademark and certification
7. Maasai tourism value capture

These seven areas are seven strategies for building the Maasai brand into income. The concentric circle illustrates that the seven areas overlap and are engaged, simultaneously.

1 Outreach and awareness raising

The first area is the Awareness raising program. This involved a training program to create a Maasai training team capable of reaching the Maasai to teach them about their cultural brand as Intellectual Property. Many Maasai travel, and acquire information, see travel posters at airports, and are aware of the use or misuse of their brand, but of the approximately 2 million Maasai across Kenya and Tanzania, the overwhelming majority of Maasai needed to learn about Intellectual Property and how IP could be turned into a revenue stream.

Our operative goal was to educate the elders and leaders via the Maasai traditional organizational structure. We created workbooks, brochures, handouts, and power points, along with a website and Facebook page. Then, through the elder, Isaac ole Tialolo, we began mapping an outreach strategy to reach *all* of the Maasai districts and regions and to train the Maasai leaders to better understand IP. It was important to hold large-scale meetings, radio broadcasts, and listen to what was offensive to the Maasai and what they wished to accomplish.

Creation of a Maasai Intellectual Property Initiative Trust Limited (MIPI), supported by the Maasai and recognized in Kenya and Tanzania

The MIPI constitution ensures that no Maasai individual can take control of the organization or its revenue. The constitution also requires that the revenues are transparent to representatives of all Maasai districts, clans, elders and leaders, and all Maasai NGOs and Community Based Organizations in order to provide checks and balances on the use of revenues. The MIPI board declared that it would have equal numbers of Tanzanians and Kenyans and must include Maasai women.

A goal of the Maasai Outreach has been to build the General Assembly of all Maasai leaders and elders from Maasai communities across Kenya and Tanzania, to:

1. Show the world that the Maasai are united by demonstrating that this work follows the will of the Maasai people.
2. Direct the board of MIPI and executive staff on their work to recover the Maasai brand and other IP, particularly in directing MIPI on what commercial use of Maasai images is acceptable to the Maasai.
3. Select a Welfare and Development board to distribute income earned from the approved licensing of the Maasai.

MIPI is pledged to regain the Maasai cultural brand and return income for the Maasai with the values of: transparency; representativeness; unity; inclusion; accounting; a strong board; and cooperation.

A challenge faced by indigenous people subjecting them to greater exploitation is having no representative body that speaks for their rights. For example, the 1.5 million Tuareg have no formal structure to discuss, and then represent their rights. These semi-nomadic people live across at least five sovereign boundaries complicating this as it is difficult for a single government to act on their behalf. The similar situation of the Maasai people has put the onus on MIPI to develop a credible trans-border, representative structure to assert its rights and impose either a legal or a political obligation on users (existing and future) of its name.

Creating a legal entity across two countries has been a careful and painstakingly detailed process.

As a Maasai representative entity, the members have made the following priorities for income:

- Maasai child education
- Maasai mamas, advancing Maasai women's capacity in building handicraft businesses and other businesses
- Advancing Maasai knowledge of the value of IP and capabilities to acquire further income gains in IP-related businesses
- Natural resource management: adapting to climate change
- Food security

The Maasai are not seeking to grow wealthy with their IP. They are, however, seeking to build greater respect, and to enable an income stream for community projects to advance the Maasai welfare.

2 Withdrawal of offensive images, respect

The Maasai were concerned about the plethora of offensive images used without their permission, and oftentimes splattered across the Internet, or shown in photos. As the team gathered offensive images, these were shown to the Maasai elders and leaders and decisions were made about what was offensive. The Maasai then engaged in a letter-writing strategy to offending companies. The Maasai engaged in extensive letter writing to inform the 20–30 most offensive users that the misuse of their images was against their will.

3. The Maasai Mamas Handicraft Project

Since 50 percent of the Maasai are women, it is important to assist the women to improve their income from their main livelihood – making handicrafts. Yet, the challenge of handicrafts is there is an abundance of supply of handicrafts and most are sold at very low prices. For example, there is a famous market in Nairobi, the Masai market where the Maasai mamas compete with non-Maasai to sell handicrafts to tourists. Though remarkable to us, tourists have an expectation of acquiring products at low prices, and seem to take a pride in negotiating prices downward.

Our goal is to create a certification mark that will enable the Maasai mamas to attract a higher price for authentic handicrafts. A challenge is they are positioned in a low-end market with abundant supply. Our first project was to create higher end products and sell these in the US for $79.00 each, rather than the local $29.00 by marketing the items as certified, one of a kind. The pilot project was successful.

There have been others who have endeavored to help the mamas. For example, Walmart via their CSR program engaged in training programs and marketed the Maasai handicrafts at their stores. However, the majority of Walmart shoppers do not come to Walmart for high end products, but rather for bargains. This project was admittedly a failure by Walmart CSR individuals, though they tried.

For the Maasai IP initiative, we believe the mamas can fare better once the Maasai have regained ownership of their brand, and will earn more income from the IP revenue. In sum, the pilot project was intended to engage the mamas and train them.

4 Soft licensing

The idea behind soft licensing is to offer licenses to 10–20 friendly companies who are willing to acknowledge Maasai ownership of their IP. Many companies with valuable brands often recognize that in today's highly visible Internet world, "doing the right thing" is also about protecting their own brand from negative press, and are willing to agree to a licensing agreement. The Soft Licensing strategy begins to establish the precedent of licensing.

5 Hard licensing

We call this part of the strategic action, "hard licensing," because we anticipate that not all companies currently benefitting from the Maasai brand will be enthusiastic or willing to obtain a license to use the Maasai images. These companies will require a harder approach beyond letter writing and negotiation. We anticipate the African IP Trust, as an advocacy organization, will be engaged to bring pressure, public and legal. Modeling after the Ethiopian Fine Coffee Trademark and Licensing Initiative, the first licensees are most difficult, and then establish a precedent.

6 Trademark and certifications

Research and file trademark applications for the certification mark and the "Maasai" and "Masai" word trademarks in Tanzania and in available categories in a number of target countries. Follow this program with requests for cancelation of trademarks owned by existing non-licensed companies.

7 Maasai tourism

Many people associate Kenya with the Maasai, as the Maasai are frequently shown on Kenyan tourism posters. In Tanzania, the Maasai have many tourism companies. Our view is the Maasai could earn more income on tourism, but we see advancing tourism as a future goal, once the legal precedent is established publicly in countries that are the origin of tourists.

What IP Recovery and Income means for the Maasai

As noted above, the Maasai population is approximately 2 million people, and about 70 percent live below poverty levels for Tanzania and Kenya. The Maasai are very much affected by climate change and are livestock dependent as a source of income, along with handicraft sales and tourism. Their financial and living hardships have grown more difficult with the loss of land and access to water, so they have experienced much loss over the past few years. However, their hard-earned cultural brand has been developed over centuries and can prove to be a source of sustainable income. For the Maasai to regain their cultural IP has implications for creating a sustainable revenue stream.

For the Maasai mamas, their situation of poverty is quite difficult as the Maasai are often in polygamous situations, and the women are not able to attend school as regularly as the young boys, are typically married young and often in pre-arranged marriages, and have sparse opportunity to earn income outside of their fine handicrafts. The mamas' handicrafts are sold locally for very low prices despite the intricate skills to fashion them. Thus, poverty gets passed down by generation.

The Maasai IP initiative will help the mamas in three ways:

1. As income is returned to the Maasai via licensing agreements, local projects such as schools and education improvements will enable a ripple effect to aid the mamas;
2. The mamas' handicrafts currently have no authenticity marks, but as the Maasai IP initiative gains momentum, we envision authenticity marks being helpful to the mamas' handicrafts, enabling them to certify the distinctiveness for higher prices; and
3. As the Maasai forge relationships and win–win situations with lucrative firms, we envision a brighter spotlight toward the mamas and their welfare.

Currently, our education model has reached about 1 million Maasai in varied degrees of training. As people advance in understanding of their cultural asset, we envision other opportunities for benefitting from the IP recognition and believe this will pass to the mamas and to their children. The Maasai, owners of a vital IP asset, have every ethical right to take advantage of their hard won cultural asset for the benefit of their tribe.

Some questions and answers concerning the Maasai

Q: What are the distinctive attributes of the Maasai culture and history which have IP value capture implications?

A: The color red

There is no particular shade of red associated with the Maasai. This compares, for example, to Cadbury's purple or Barclay's peacock blue which are specifically defined and protected as the company's IP in terms of widely accepted Pantone color codings. Yet, there is a sufficiently clear association with the color red in a variety of shades — derived principally from the main color of the cloth worn by the Maasai — to enhance the descriptive value of a product by using the epithet "Maasai" associated with red.

Specifically Maasai objects or symbols/form(s)

Head-dress: The Maasai tradition of using beads and glittering metal shapes to make head-dresses and other personal decorations is well known and easily transferred to clothing, jewelry, and ear-rings to add cultural authenticity. The Maasai are not alone in using beads for adornments, but there are clearly motifs and styles that are distinctive to the Maasai traditions. Necklaces of a particular style and shape are specifically Maasai, and derivations of this artistic and cultural expression can be seen in many necklaces which mimic this.

Shoes: International observers have commented on Maasai footwear that is made out of off-road tires. The Maasai call them "Michelins" or "Thousand Milers" because the part of the sandal that goes over the top of the foot is the steel belted inner tube. A Swiss company patented a shoe design that the company acknowledges was inspired by the Maasai. The founder realized the Maasai could walk and run for hundreds of miles without any back pain. In fact, the company built its sales on the slogan, "we discovered the secret of the Maasai — to walk for hours across uneven terrain without back pain." The patent may be questionable.

FIGURE 7.5 Maasai Mama during training, Simanjaro, Tanzania
Source: Light Years IP.

[Red] Cloth: Ilkarash or shúkà are the Maa words for the sheets traditionally worn wrapped around the body, one over each shoulder, then a third over the top of them. They are found in a wide range of colors and patterns, often checked but nearly always Maasai red. Depictions of the Maasai, or Maasai-related products nearly always pick up this thematic code in some form.

Association: Without knowing the specifics of Maasai history, or even the specifics of Tanzania and Kenya borders, references to the Maasai help consumers to "situate" a product in East Africa/Africa. This means that a Maasai allusion denotes "place" or, more usually, some geographic attributes of an African place, which goes beyond a depiction of "rural," i.e. without "farms." The Maasai evoke the potentiality of endless plains or savannah, wild animals, undisturbed nature, harmony with nature, a free or uninhibited lifestyle. The most widespread use, then, is unsurprisingly the tourism, travel, or hotel industry even when the tours are not expressly or specifically involving visits to Maasai regions.

Q: How are the Maasai used in the market?
A: From research and observation, the Maasai name(s) are being used globally in the following ways:

- Within or as part of a company name
- As the name, or part of the name of a particular product or model
- Through Maasai imagery (photos, graphics) to convey company or product attributes/style
- Cited as inspiration for style or content of a business venture (many types of commercial activity or specific products).

Q: What kind of positive output for the Maasai does MIPI intend?
A: For the Maasai, it is about *respect.* We also wish to see a sustainable income. The Maasai have built their culture and all that it represents and deserve licensing revenue. The Maasai are moving toward a positive outcome. Some companies have agreed to acquire a license to use the Maasai name and image. As additional companies follow the pattern to acquire a license, this will create momentum. It will also set a new norm.

This may also be good for companies, many of whom are quite high end and can afford to purchase a license to sell the Maasai name for 5 percent back to the Maasai. There are other companies whom the Maasai could decide would be good and respectful and these companies could purchase a Maasai license for 5 percent of the sales revenue.

Q: What is it about the Maasai history that is particularly distinctive?
A: The word Maasai means my people. Maa means the language. The Maasai are one of the most cherished tribes in East Africa and around the world. A noble and dignified people, they have proudly maintained their authentic traditional

FIGURE 7.6 Isaac ole Tialolo, Maasai leader of MIPI
Source: Maasai Intellectual Property Initiative.

lifestyle and cultural identity despite pressures of the modern world. They live a nomadic lifestyle, keeping cattle, sheep, and goats, wearing traditional clothes, and living in small villages called *manyattas*, which are circular arrangements of mud huts.

The Maasai Cultural Band: a tribe at the heart of the world

Maasai Mamas

Maasai mamas form the backbone of the community rich culture. Maasai women are the most enterprising members of the Maasai community. They rise early every day to milk cattle, collect firewood, prepare breakfast thereafter fetch water, launder clothes, before embarking on a busy afternoon beading and crafting. They also collect herbs and roots recommended by traditional medicine-men for young babies and also other herbs for de-worming older children. With the help of their daughters they also collect sticks, grass, and cow dung used to build the *Enkaji* (housing unit). The most interesting part of the Maasai mamas' chores is making decorative beadwork for a husband, sons, and daughters and also for themselves. After a long busy day, they prepare dinner for their families in the evening; they narrate interesting stories to tuck in their children before they get to sleep. They are the last to retire to bed and first to wake very early.

FIGURE 7.7 Maasai leaders in field with Ron Layton of Light Years IP

Maasai mamas' beading

The mamas sit together with their daughters in small groups under trees to craft the next beautiful handicraft. Young mature girls try their best to please their boyfriends by crafting the most attractive and appealing jewelry and hope that their boyfriends would like them. If one constructs a piece of jewelry that is awkward or unappealing, the other mamas might tease her and quickly point out the flaws in her work. This makes the mamas and the young mamas (daughters) learn the rules of aesthetic eye. This is essential because the color combinations and patterns in Maasai beadwork rely on contrast and balance to create pieces that are eye-catching. Colors also reflect important concepts and elements in Maasai culture. Much of the color symbolism relates the cattle, environment, and the Maasai way of life.

The warriors

Commonly known as the *moran*, they represent the young Maasai men who have undergone the rite of passage (circumcision). After their circumcision and graduation from childhood, Maasai boys become men and enter the next stage of their life, Moranhood, or warriorhood. Through traditional rituals and ceremonies, over a period of almost seven years, young men are guided and mentored by their fathers and other elders in the community on their new responsibilities as morans.

They are strong with great physique and brimming with strength, confidence, beauty, and prospects of the future. They represent the new generation, an age group and they are respected by other members of the community. They protect the community from external attacks; they also organize counter-raids to recover stolen livestock from neighboring communities. They seek strategy advice from elders and spiritual blessing from the *Olaibon* – the Maasai spiritual leader.

They wear *enkishili* around the forehead. The hair is painted with concoction mixture of red-oxide liquid and oil melted from bull's fat.

Implications for other Indigenous Peoples

There are approximately 370 million indigenous people in the world, belonging to 5,000 different groups, in 90 countries worldwide.[24] Sadly, indigenous people comprise 30 percent of the world's poorest people. Indigenous peoples' intellectual property has been widely used without any income gain. However, if the Maasai IP initiative achieves effective ownership, licensure, and income for their vital IP, we expect that other widely recognized peoples' groups will benefit from the precedent established by this initiative. There are also specific tools and tactics from which other indigenous people can benefit. To date, there have been complaints and campaigns, but most do not have a systematic strategy for achieving revenue.

In the next section we set out some similar experiences and examples.

What have been relevant or similar commercial applications or experiences of other tribal *or ethnic groups?*

As almost 6 percent of the world's population are indigenous people, the cultural brand ownership may serve as an example to other indigenous people to advance sustainable income for many millions. In many cases, as described below, indigenous peoples' images and intellectual property are used in marketing in ways that are quite lucrative for western companies who also stand to benefit in mutually beneficial ways. Some examples include the Guayaki, Cherokee, Tuareg, and Apache.

Guayaki

The Aché Indians are a traditional hunter-gatherer tribe living in Paraguay, called "Guayakí" by neighbors and in early anthropological accounts. The Aché Guayakí people have a tragic history, one that is similar to many other indigenous people of South America. Paraguay, like other Latin American countries, had a long colonial history of Indian enslavement that continued well after the official prohibition of slavery in 1869. Aché camps were systematically raided with the intention of killing the men, and capturing women and children. Aché children were sold openly in the region as late as the 1970s. Aché suffered repeated abuses by Paraguayan colonists, ranchers, and big landowners from the conquest period to the twentieth century. In recent times they have been massacred, enslaved, and gathered onto reservations where no adequate medical treatment was provided. This process was specifically carried out to pacify them and remove them from their ancestral homeland so that investors could develop the lands that once belonged only to the Aché.

"Guayakí Inc." is a thriving US herbal tea company based in California, begun as a college project in 1996. Guayakí has a mission to steward and restore 200,000 acres of South American Atlantic rainforest and create over 1,000 living wage jobs by 2020 by leveraging a new business model and the ecological passion of the founders. Guayakí founders were well-intentioned people who had not thought through the IP aspect of the issue until it was pointed out to them, and because of the important social and environmental agenda of the company a settlement was relatively easily reached. They have approached this matter through a royalty agreement with the Guayakí. They openly acknowledge the origins of their company name. "Our name Guayakí honors the Aché Guayakí people, who are native to the sub-tropical rainforests of Paraguay."

Cherokee

The Cherokee Nation is the second largest Native American tribe in the USA with about 280,000 members. Some 70,000 live within the 7,000 square miles that make up the Cherokee Nation in northeastern Oklahoma, USA. The Cherokee call themselves "Ani-Yun-wiya," the principal people. The name

Cherokee is used on thousands of businesses, casinos, sports teams, uniforms, and motor vehicles.[25]

The most significant example however is the car brand Jeep Cherokee. The first Jeep Cherokee was made in 1974. The Jeep Grand Cherokee has been in production since 1992. Since its introduction, DaimlerChrysler has sold over 4 million units, primarily in North America.

The Cherokee Group publicly owns brands that generate about $4.0 billion in annual global retail sales.

The Cherokee Group also owns several brands including Cherokee, a clothing line for men, women, children, toddlers, and infants with casual, comfortable style at affordable prices. The Cherokee brand is sold through licensed retailers including Target, Tesco, Zellers, and Pick 'n Pay.[26]

The Cherokee Nation do not benefit from the use of their name in these brands and licensing agreements!

Tuareg

Today there are 23 million Imazighen who are scattered throughout North African countries including the Tuareg, whose population is approximately 1.5 million. They are Berber people and they live in Algeria (65,000), Mali (534,000), Libya (21,000), Niger (720,000), and Burkina Faso (37,000). There are also refugees and migrant Tuareg in Nigeria (23,000) and Senegal (7,000).[27]

The Tuareg name is used on a number of products, but especially to promote tough and durable vehicles, bicycles, and motor-bikes: Volkswagen – Touareg SUV; Orbea – Tuareg, mountain bike; Aprilia – Tuareg 600, motor sport bike; Tuareg Rallye, North Africa. These products are widely distributed. The most notable example is the Touareg SUV.

Volkswagen Touareg SUV

The Volkswagen Touareg was introduced to the market in 2003. The luxury sport utility vehicle was a joint effort between Volkswagen and Porsche to create an offroad vehicle that handles like a sports car. It is marketed as a go-anywhere, rugged off-road vehicle and uses Sahara desert imagery to promote this. It is said that the Tuare tribe can battle in all weather – it is this imagery that is used to market the VW Touareg.

Orbea Tuareg mountain bike

Orbea is a bicycle company based in Spain. The company sponsors and supplies bikes to bicycle teams including a professional road racing team. Freedommachine.com describes the bike as "a fantastic entry level mountain bike that will last for years. This bike not only looks good but can take heaps as well."

FIGURE 7.8 Maasai Mama completing IP training

Orbea bikes are available throughout Europe, North America, Australia, and China. There are numerous examples of the Tuareg name being used on sports and motorbikes. The challenge for the Tuareg is they live within a half dozen countries and forming a stakeholder IP organization would be challenging, but not impossible.

In summary, it is easy to see that even at first glance, millions of indigenous people groups' names, cultures of strength and endurance are drawn upon to promote products. This is not coincidental. Creators of brands and the marketing firms that promote them, spend great amounts of time and resources to determine what connects with people in their projected markets. Brands sell products. As we see above, the Tuareg people comprise over 20 million people. The Cherokee, smaller in surviving number, are a familiar name to Americans as one of the most widely recognized Native American tribes. It is generally taken for granted that their names can be used to sell products, as these names have been used for a very long time, due in large part to the concepts they represent such as strength, courage, endurance, ruggedness, and a certain warrior connotation. The majority of time, the names and images are used without thought to the people groups behind these names.

But, as the case of the Maasai IP Initiative has brought forward, what if it were not so easy to use images representing people, particularly the millions of indigenous people, the majority of whom live at or below poverty levels? What if there were a win–win scenario that benefitted the indigenous people *and* the corporation? This scenario is not a fairy tale. It is called licensing. Individuals and firms have been using it for 100 years. Even Charlie Chaplin, an initially very poor boy from England, put into the workhouse for a season as his mother was too poor and ill to care for him, created a brandable image in the Tramp. And, we have discussed how sports firms can build substantial revenue by licensing their team's names and images. As this book goes to press, the BBC, NPR, and BusinessWeek have covered the Maasai IP Initiative, as it may be a beacon for income generation for some of the poorest people in the world, whose name, image, and culture give great value to brands around the world.

At this point, please see the Maasai IP workbook included on the companion website. It shows the many products using the Maasai name and image, and outlines the seven-point plan strategy in detail.

Notes

1 Innate Motion website (www.innatemotion.com), accessed April 1, 2016.
2 B. Lev, "Intangibles: Management, measurement and reporting," New York: Brookings Institute Press, 2001.
3 A. Belec, "Training course in Addis Abbaba, Ethiopia for the Ethiopian IP Office, July 2011.
4 L. Partos, "Coca-Cola-brand-value-tops-58.2 billion," Food Navigator – *USA.com*, May 13, 2008.

5 "Leading most valuable soft drink brands worldwide in 2015, based on brand value," Statista, 2016 (statista.com).

6 Stuart Elliott, "Apple Passes Coca-Cola as Most Valuable Brand," *New York Times*, September 2013.

7 Ibid.

8 "The 150 top global licensors," May 2015, www.licensemag.com.

9 "Sunkist announces 5th straight billion dollar revenue year" (www.sunkist.com/p ress-room/annual-meeting-release-2015).

10 Mike Knowles, "Sunkist fakes reflect brand's value," Asiafruit, April 25, 2014.

11 M. Brindle, "Games decision makers play," *Management Decision*, 1999, Vol. 37, Issue 8, pp. 604–612. R. Neudstadt and E. May, *Thinking in time: The use of history for decision makers*, The Free Press. Printed in the USA by Simon & Schuster, Inc., 1999. R. Cialdini, "Influence: The psychology of persuasion," Harper Business, February 2007.

12 Although the terms of their agreement are not published, HD are understood to have received at least $4,000 per truck.

13 To calculate royalties to Harley-Davidson, using the formula of 5 or 10 percent, depending on the type of royalty – if Harley-Davidson received a 5 percent royalty, that would be $2,100 per truck and total royalty income would be over $16 million. If the royalty rate was 10 percent, royalty income would be over $32 million.

14 Marc Mathieu, as interviewed, April 1, 2015 and reflected on the Innate Motion website, http://www.in8motion.com/clients/unilever-crafting-brands-for-life.

15 www.irtfcleveland.org/economicjustice/sweatshops/nike.gif. L. Brindle-Khym, *Quest research and investigations*, Manhattan, New York, May 2014.

16 Sunkist website, "Sunkist announces fifth straight billion dollar revenue year," www. sunkist.com/press-room/annual-meeting-release-2015.

17 Census data on the Maasai vary, as in Kenya, the rules governing census and counting are problematic. Estimates on the official number of Maasai vary from 2 million to 3 million. In this report, we use the smaller number, preferring to err on the conservative side.

18 Only the Australian Aborigines would appear to have gained wider recognition than the Maasai (more than 10 million references for Australian Aboriginals) as measured by an Internet search.

19 D. Nakishima, L. Prott, and P. Bridgewater, "Tapping into the world's wisdom," UNESCO Sources, 125, July–August, 2000, p. 12.

20 K. Manders and J. Pastrick, Esq., Continental Enterprises. Report performed for the Maasai IP Initiative (MIPI) and Light Years IP, 2013. The value of the Maasai IP has also been evaluated by Mr. David Cardwell, of Cardwell Consultancy, London. Mr. Cardwell has overseen the Star Wars Licensing and numerous other noteworthy licensing deals, and is interviewed in Chapter 5 of this book.

21 About 500 articles have been written about the Ethiopian fine coffee trademark and licensing initiative. See www.lightyearsip.net and www.produceralliance.org.

22 Reports by Continental Enterprises and Qwest Research Investigations, LLC.

23 See Continental Enterprises, IP Recovery lawyers, www.ce-ip.com.

24 "The state of the world's indigenous people," United Nation's Report, January 2010, (www.un.org/esa/socdev/unpfii/documents/SOWIP/press%20package/sowip-press-pa ckage-en.pdf) culturalsurvival@cs.org and www.eurekalert.org.

25 www.cherokeeuniforms.com, www.cherokee-project.com, www.cherokeecasino.com.

26 Countries where Cherokee is licensed: Ireland, Slovakia, Czech Republic, Hungary, Spain, Poland, Turkey, Kuwait, Saudi Arabia, Qatar, Oman, UAE, Egypt, Jordan, Lebanon, India, Bahrain, Israel, Columbia, Peru, Chile, Argentina, Brazil, South Africa. Pauline Tiffen, LYIP Desk Research, 2009.

27 Pauline Tiffen, LYIP Desk Research, 2009.

8

THE POWER OF WOMEN'S OWNED IP BUSINESSES

WONS of Uganda and South Sudan

Women's empowerment has been a central focus of the twenty-first century for international development and entrepreneurship initiatives. With women comprising 50 percent of the world's population, the enthusiastic focus is appropriate. In Africa, women make up a large percentage of farmers and farm workers – 40 percent by some estimates, or higher as a large percentage of African farmers are smallholders.

Indeed, women are the economic backbone of many African countries, sustaining families in times of war and conflict, and providing for them in times of peace. Women also carry lessons forward to their children and families and impart specialized knowledge in jewelry making and other artisan crafts, soaps, oils, spices, and processing. In the details of farming, women teach planting, harvesting, drying, storage, and marketing to their families. To empower women is to empower the continent now and for the next generation.

In addition, according to an indicator known as the rural multiplier, women in rural areas spend their income locally. Thus an additional income of $1.00 equivalent to women generates up to a $2.00 impact on local economies.[1]

New women's inspired and focused initiatives begin every day. The purpose of this chapter is not to provide a summary of women's initiatives, as books about women and women's empowerment have been penned. Rather, our purpose is to demonstrate a model of a women's owned business in sufficient detail for women producers to replicate the model and create well-positioned women's owned businesses across the continent of Africa and elsewhere.

This chapter will:

- Illustrate why women's owned businesses are the best way to lift women out of poverty in a sustainable way.

- Describe an IP business positioning strategy that is creating an income stream 20 times higher than alternatives.
- Provide a detailed case study of a women's IP business positioning strategy.
- Illustrate how a representative women's stakeholder organization was formed with a representative constitution and lessons learned.
- Outline the training that enabled the rural Ugandan and South Sudanese women to fully understand and participate in their own company.
- Demonstrate that when women's owned businesses are correctly positioned, their power is dramatically increased.
- Illustrate how women will become the transformative change agents for northern Uganda and for western and southern South Sudan.

Transformative power of women

The Millennium Development Goals (MDGs) place women centrally in several ways. The target for MDG # 3 is gender parity in primary and secondary education along with a much wider approach – addressing gender equality and women's empowerment as a requirement for the fulfillment of all the MDGs. In addition, a gender focus is central in the promotion of maternal health; in the fight against HIV/AIDS; and in conflict resolution as conflict affects women in life threatening ways across many countries and continents.

The term, "women's empowerment," is laudatory in its intention and has resulted in waves of international women's projects, particularly since the turn of the century. The UNDP (United Nations Development Program) for example reports helping hundreds of thousands of women in conflict resolution with justice systems, supporting dialogue, advancing rights of women in courts, and in working against sexual exploitation. In Africa, women's street businesses and training programs abound.[2]

The work of the Cherie Blair Foundation; Bead for Life; Thomson Reuters; Comic Relief and Acumen, among others, has shown a renewed focus on women. As just one example, Acumen has invested $86 million in 77 companies across Africa, Latin America, and South Asia just since its founding in 2001 with an ongoing continued lens on women and women's role in entrepreneurship.[3]

By Internet "measurement," a simple search online, under "gender empowerment," yields over 5 million results and when narrowed to the international arena, there are still over 1 million results for the words, "international gender empowerment." Many books focused on empowering women have been written on the topic over the past decade.[4] In traditional and nontraditional ways, advancing and empowering women has taken on new urgency and high priority. In the twenty-first century, new priorities on women in the banking and finance sector have advanced women's investment, and professional women of the EU, UK, and USA in particular have advanced gender investment turning it into a movement.

FIGURE 8.1 Women trainees, northern Uganda
Source: Light Years IP/ Maasai IP Initiative.

In 2015, President Obama pledged to invest $1 billion in Africa with half of this going specifically to women and girls.[5] This plan will expand women's entrepreneurial centers with a goal to benefit 1,600 women and girls.

"Women are powerhouse entrepreneurs," said President Obama. "The research shows that when women entrepreneurs succeed, they drive economic growth and invest more back into their families and communities."[6]

A recent report by the World Bank shows that female-run enterprises are steadily growing all over the world, contributing to household incomes and growing national economies. Africa leads in this surging growth in the 142 countries measured by the World Bank and focused on the gender gap in economic participation and measures that support or challenge women's economic participation. According to an extensive World Bank report, comparing data collected over a range of nine years, 105 countries are making progress to close the so-called and aptly termed "Gender Gap."[7]

Even though dramatic progress has been made in the twenty-first century, the World Bank report also shows that "of the 173 economies covered by the World Bank report, 'Women, Business and the Law,' 155 economies maintain at least one barrier for women seeking opportunities that does not exist for men."[8] In fact, the majority of the world's economies show at least one legal gender difference. Those with most dramatic differences defined as 10 or more legal differences defined by gender are in the Middle East and North Africa with 18 and Sub-Saharan Africa with eight major differences.[9] This is a strong reminder that progress has not, by any definition, reached as far as creating gender equality. Legal disparity affects women's ability to acquire jobs, and a great income disparity exists between men and women in many countries. The economic and legal disparity, of course, contributes to cyclic poverty.

In some African countries, such as Uganda, relatively few women run businesses and a very high gender wage gap contributes to ongoing poverty. Few women hold bank accounts, or develop income that predictably would be spent on local economies, and often perpetuate cyclic poverty, with early pregnancies and childhood poverty. In Uganda, for example, while progress has been made, few enterprises have women on boards. In terms of business ownership, only 15 percent of firms show women in top leadership. The estimated earned income for women is on average $722.00 per year, compared to the male earned annual income of $1,932 or about 60 percent lower by reporting accounts, recognizing that all income may not be reported by women due to complicated norms concerning what women are or are not allowed to formally own and report.[10] For example, in some households, all income is required to be owned by the male head of household.

Our goal is not to rehearse gender disparity, or to evaluate the varied and wide scope of gender projects. Given the wide scope and criticality of the topic of gender disparity and the movement toward gender empowerment, initiatives have been formidable.

Rather than describe what is wrong, or summarize what is going well, this chapter illustrates a successful gender empowerment project presenting a model, an explicit business method. It is a business positioning project involving over 700 women and growing to 10,000. The stakeholder organization, export and import companies are owned, led, and run by women. The method is replicable with wider reaching implications. In fact, the name reflects the key role of women –

the Women's Owned Nilotica Shea (WONS) project. The initiative involves women leaders who were former abductees, forced into lives of poverty and early marriage and are now emergent as strong, capable, determined leaders of their own business with full supply chain ownership of the brand, as well as an import company based in London.

What is the difference between the WONS model and other women's businesses?

The difference between this initiative and other business models is that rather than the women providing shea butter as an ingredient portion to foreign importers that is then sold to higher end retailers, in this situation, the women *are* the exporters, importers, and producers. This enables greater control and improved income coupled with ownership all the way along the supply chain.

There are many initiatives involving shea butter, for example where the product is sold to a larger retail brand via import. These have been in operation since the turn of the twenty-first century – at the time of this book, for about 20 years. The product may comprise 1 to 20 or even 30 percent of the product as it is sold at retail. The challenge here is that while ingredient brands may form the essential ingredient, and often serve retail companies' marketing and promoting of their brands as supporting African or LDC women, the ingredient brand, or in this case, shea butter would be sold at commodity pricing, with volatile swings and typically low prices.

L'Occitane, for example, claims to sell a product with West African shea butter as an ingredient, every three seconds. While this speaks to the volume of shea butter demanded by consumers, the women sell their shea in Uganda at commodity prices, albeit with Fair Trade incentives.

The more critical key component of the WONS initiative is business positioning, wherein the WONS women have been positioned to sell a final cosmetic consumer product at high end under a WONS-owned brand. This moisturizing product can be sold by retail stores and online for around $1,000 per kg. By owning the brand and the import/distribution company in Europe, the WONS cooperative earns far more income that is returned directly to the women. This is an example of "begin with the end in mind." Though the concept was made famous by Stephen Covey in a multi-million dollar best seller,[11] the principle applies to business.

The power of women's ownership: women's owned Nilotica shea

The case study of a women's owned business involves opportunity for hundreds of thousands of women. The women live in northern Uganda and South Sudan, and many have emerged from conflict. They are owners of their own company that creates one of the best natural moisturizers in the world.

WONS: the context

Shea butter is one of the most effective natural skin care products in the world, and it is one of the star ingredients in the ongoing "natural personal care" market expansion, featuring prominently in best-sellers by companies such as Body Shop, Burt's Bees, and L'Occitane. As reported on its website, L'Occitane claims to sell a product with shea butter globally every three seconds, though it is sourced by West Africa which is a different variety of shea bearing tree, and the shea butter product contains only 20 percent shea because West African shea is a bit harder.[12]

The worldwide "personal care" industry sector had reached $333 billion in annual sales by 2015, led by North America and Western Europe. Within the personal care industry is the "natural personal care" segment, estimated at 15 percent of the total personal care market. The "natural skin care" segment accounts for approximately 42 percent of the natural personal care segment, or a projected $21 billion as of 2015.[13]

In Europe, where WONS will be first positioned, as of 2014, the skincare segment dominated the overall personal care market, with a market share of 68-70 percent. With emphasis on more natural skincare products, the European market is likely to grow at a Compound Annual Growth Rate (CAGR) of 9.58 percent from 2014–2019.[14]

Nilotica shea is found exclusively in northern Uganda and South Sudan. It has substantially more olein content than the more common West African shea, and as a result is softer at room temperature, has a "creamier" feel, and absorbs more easily into the skin. Unrefined *nilotica* shea butter is one of the most effective natural skin care products in the world, containing high concentrations of olein, Vitamin A, Vitamin E, and healing agents called unsaponifiables.

Despite the fact that East African *nilotica* shea butter is a rare and distinctive product, the women producers of northern Uganda and South Sudan have been selling their shea into a global commodity market. In the commodity market, they suffer low prices, volatile price swings, and uncertainty about future sales volumes. In order to escape this commodity trap, shea producers must reposition their product as a distinctive retail consumer product and gain control over the supply chain.

From Uganda, the shea butter is exported for $5.00 per kg when delivered to Mombasa, whereas at higher end markets, with correct positioning, the retail value is $1,000 per kg.

IP Business Positioning

The WONS' Initiative is employing IP business positioning methods to put women shea producers in control over the supply chain in two significant ways:

- Creation of a producer-owned luxury retail brand in final retail markets
- Control over distribution, achieved through producer ownership of distribution (i.e. WONS UK).

FIGURE 8.2 WONS packaging, first version
Source: Light Years IP/ Maasai IP Initiative.

Under the WONS Initiative, the shea producers of northern Uganda and South Sudan will at long last receive a price worthy of their distinctive product, dramatically raising incomes for a large number of women in one of the poorest regions in the world. Furthermore, the new higher price will be more stable and predictable. The reason prices are less volatile is illustrated by the simple chart in Figure 8.3, comparing the relative stability of prices when there is ownership compared to when prices are set on the commodity markets which are volatile.

The importance of positioning toward higher end markets

Figure 8.3 shows the volatility of commodity markets. The frequent price swings are a product of the commodity markets with unpredictable changes. The volatility makes it hard for farmers and producers to plan. This volatility is the situation when shea producers sell their shea butter as ingredients to foreign-owned branded products, which is essentially commodity priced subject to price swings.

The data to construct the chart in Figure 8.3 is from the World Bank Monitor showing commodity prices and volatile trends for bananas, cocoa, coco oil, coffee, copra, cotton, maize, oranges, palm oil, rice, rubber, soybean, sugar, tea, and wheat. A 10-year cycle was selected to show change over time. While we

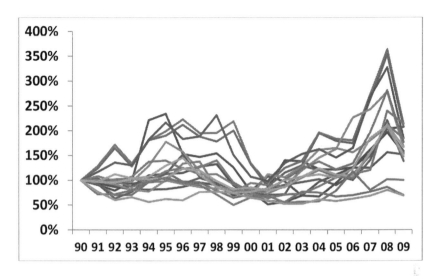

FIGURE 8.3 Commodity export price fluctuations for basket of commodities
Source: World Bank Monitor.

can see from this chart that some products retained low prices, and others rose, the common factor is the volatility. The sharp point being that even when farmers have better years, as defined by higher prices for their products at export, these are nearly always followed by price swings. This is often due to over-supply. The volatility chart also illustrates the concept of why improving production, and thus oftentimes, resultant over-supply is problematic for low-income farmers and producers, and again, why poverty is not solved simply by farming or manufacturing more of a good product. Unfortunately, as already underscored in this book, the majority of aid and development projects do focus on the supply of products, not coupled with ownership or positioning.

A comparison of commodity markets and pricing based on higher end retail price points shows greater price stability. This will be the situation for Ugandan women as their product achieves market share with the higher end retail consumer. Stability will allow women to plan for the future of their families and their business in a way that is not possible with the price volatility of commodity markets. As equity holders in WONS UK, the women will receive additional income in the form of dividends, and the value of their holdings will predictably grow as WONS UK grows.

How will the WONS Nilotica shea butter be transformational?

Light Years IP has been working closely with producers in the northern Uganda and South Sudan regions applying IP business strategies. WONS UK will be a producer-controlled, EU-based distribution, wholesale, and marketing company offering a new brand of high quality, differentiated *nilotica* shea butter moisturizing products to consumers and retail outlets in the EU and at a later stage in the US. WONS UK will build upon two primary strengths – a distinctive product with superior moisturizing and healing properties, and a strong ethical value proposition achieved through producer ownership – to offer a superior and compelling product at a competitive price. WONS will be test marketed in 2016 and launched in 2017.

The case is different because of positioning

- It involves women owning the supply chain – ownership of their own import company in London.
- The women are positioned to own an import company closer to high end consumers.
- The product is positioned at high end retail complete with high end branding, packaging, and formulation – most shea butter on the market is targeted toward low cost and lower priced markets.
- It removes women from the commodity market price swings, though they are free to participate in other models.
- The shea butter is East African shea, whereas 95 percent of the current shea butter on the market is West African. The East African, or *nilotica* shea tree only grows in East Africa and the shea butter comes from the White Nile Valley; it is softer and higher in olein content.

In addition to a healthy return on investment, this plan will provide dramatically increased and stable income to the women producers of high quality Ugandan and South Sudanese *nilotica* shea. By controlling a strategic position in the supply chain and building retail consumer loyalty through the new brand, WONS members will escape the volatile commodity market and gain control over their economic destiny.

To demonstrate the six-step method for this case study, the following section will summarize each of the six steps.

Step 1 of the IP Business Positioning method: the distinctive product

As described in the chapters "The power of the Method," and "The Power of Distinctive Products," a critical first step is to assess if the product being taken forward for an IP business positioning strategy is distinctive. It must be more than a good product, but be appreciably distinctive, with the opportunity for dramatic and sustainable income increase. Without this foundational step, the positioning strategy would have a reasonable chance of failing. Since the product forms the foundation of the strategy, it must be distinctive and hold intangible value. To this foundational, critical decision this section explores the shea tree that bears fruit for over 100 years. Though a study in trees, dendrology, is not intended, the details of the shea tree and its fruit are provided to demonstrate the level of detailed analysis required to build an initiative.

A serious challenge in LDC agri-business has been to assume that if a product grows in a region, a profitable business can be created around it. While not to be over-simplistic, the dominant thinking historically in international development has often been: "if it grows, grow more of it. If it is produced, produce more." In our model, that thinking is problematic and evidence for East African shea is strongly against such thinking. Most exporters have closed down their operations because the commodity price received from all importers is so low that it barely covers the cost of transport to the export port, Mombasa.

The positioning strategy is to build higher end brands that can last for 100 years, and these require a sufficient supply of distinctive product. The intention is not to build a "charity brand" that "helps women." The reason is that research shows cosmetic consumers are likely to buy a "charity brand" once, whereas consumers will grow committed to a brand that delivers on its promises, or in the simple vernacular – consumers want brands that work. Period.

The shea tree and shea nut

The shea tree (species *Vitellaria paradoxa*) is a perennial fruiting savannah tree indigenous to 20 countries in the latitudinal "shea belt" across Sahelian Africa. Historical records indicate a shea butter trade as early as the fourteenth century, but it first came to the attention of the western world through the travels of Scottish explorer Mungo Park in the late eighteenth century. Since that time, the scientific community has established two distinct subspecies: *Vitellaria paradoxa* subspecies *paradoxa*, found from Senegal to the Central African Republic (West African shea), and *Vitellaria paradoxa* subspecies *nilotica*, found only in northern Uganda and South Sudan (East African shea).[15, 16]

The shea tree is a significant resource to the region, and is used for fruit, food oil, soap, ointments/cosmetics, lighting oil, charcoal, and critical shade in this dry region. The trees live for hundreds of years, producing fruit after about 20 years. The shea fruit falls to the ground during the rainy season, and is harvested by women from communally owned trees, typically in managed "parklands" surrounding settlements.[17] Shea trees and nuts have been highlighted by USAID projects across western Africa, with an emphasis on protecting the trees, which is also a source of charcoal for firewood.

The primary use of the shea tree is the production of shea butter from the kernels of nuts (seeds) contained within the fruit. Most shea butter is used locally, and the higher grades are exported for use in foods (typically as a high-grade cocoa butter equivalent, cosmetics, and soaps. It is estimated that during one recent year, approximately 100,000 tons of Paradoxa shea nuts and butter were exported from across Africa as cocoa butter equivalents (CBEs) and cocoa butter improvers

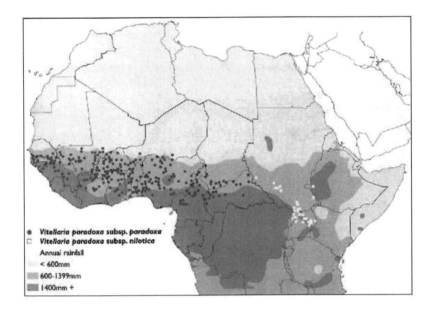

FIGURE 8.4 The "Shea Belt"[18]

Source: Boffa J.M., Yaméogo G., Nikiéma P. and Knudson D.M., (1996) "Shea nut (Vitellaria paradoxa) production and collection in agroforestry parklands of Burkina Faso". In: Leakey R.R.B., Temu A.B., Melnyk M. and Vantomme P. (eds) *Domestication and commercialization of non-timber forest products in agroforestry systems. Non-wood Forest Products 9.* Rome: FAO, 110-122.

(CBIs), and that 10,000 tons were exported to the natural cosmetics industry. The natural cosmetics industry is faster growing, more resilient, and more lucrative than CBE exports. Western Africa has a significantly more developed market, with countries such as Ghana, Mali, and Burkina Faso producing the bulk of globally traded shea nuts and raw shea butter. Large cosmetic and skin care companies source their shea butter from West Africa.[19]

Is the product superior and distinctive?

As noted, there are two distinct subspecies of the shea tree, West African (*Vitellaria paradoxa* ssp. *paradoxa*) and East African (*Vitellaria paradoxa* ssp. *nilotica*). There are many scientific papers describing differences in morphology (physical appearance), preferred climate, and genetic markers between the two subspecies. Industry specialists specify that the two subspecies are "obviously different" in a number of ways ranging from the size of the tree, to the size and shape of the fruit, to the characteristics of the butter.[20] Laboratory tests clarify the *nilotica* and *paradoxa* shea trees are noticeably different, as are the butters produced from their nuts.

FIGURE 8.5 A shea tree, shea fruit, a shea nut cracked open to reveal the kernel, and raw shea butter.

TABLE 8.1

Property	Nilotica (East African)	Paradoxa (West African)
Color	Tends toward pale white	Tends toward yellow
Smell	"Pleasant," "nutty"	Less pleasant odor
Texture	Creamier, softer	Harder
Skin absorption	Absorbs easily into skin	Absorbs less easily

Physical characteristics

Several physical differences are immediately apparent when comparing the two butters in raw (unrefined) form (see Table 8.1).

The higher the ratio of olein to stearin, the softer the resulting lipid is. East African (nilotica) shea has substantially more olein than West African shea, and this is the reason that it is closer to a liquid at room temperature, has a "creamier" feel, and absorbs more easily into the skin.

Further, shea butter has a much higher percentage of beneficial unsaponifiables than almost any other plant oil – typically 8 percent for shea versus 1 to 2 percent in other oils (see chart above). The unsaponifiables in nilotica shea include high con-centrations of vitamins A and E compared to other plant oils and to paradoxa. And there is UV protection, a low-level "natural sunscreen." Nilotica shea holds anti-aging properties, and healing properties for improved skin elasticity. The superior East African product is easy to confuse with the more widely known shea butter on the market at the lower end and as an ingredient. While this level of detail may seem unnecessary to the reader, it underscores some of the analysis needed to differentiate a commodity product with less potential for an IP business strategy from a truly superior export product. To create an IP business strategy with IP tools and positioning involves investment, and the goal is to create a strategy to overcome initial obstacles and ideally, to last for 100 years.

Step 2: what is the export and retail price gap?

In order to do justice to this important question, a thorough market analysis is needed. First, it is relatively easy to learn the export price. It is roughly $5.00/kilo paid when delivered at Mombasa in Uganda as determined by surveys of exporters and export data.

To determine the retail price of shea requires:

1. An assessment of the retail market for shea butter, and trends in natural beauty care.
2. The competitive framework.
3. The target customer.
4. Based on this framework, to provide a projected retail price point where the WONS product will fit well for expanding sales volume.

With the market analysis, recognizing that the majority of shea products currently on the retail markets are of a different quality from West Africa, and shea is largely sold as a commodity product, projections based on the overall higher end beauty market, skin care segment, and trends are particularly important.

It is critical to begin with the end in mind to determine if the end point – well-chosen retail price coupled with market demand and projections of continued market demand – is worth the investment needed to create and promote the high end brand for a sustainable longevity and income, without unrealistically building hope for those in poverty, who have seen promises without delivery throughout their lifetimes.

Market analysis

The worldwide "personal care industry" (skin care, hair care, makeup, fragrances, oral care, and other toiletries) has reached $333 billion in annual sales in 2015, topped by North America and Western Europe.[21] Brazil is a leading market and 17 Asian, Russian, and New Zealand markets had a combined cosmetics and toiletries market worth of $60 billion.[22]

Skin care is the largest segment of personal care, accounting for more than one quarter of that amount, or roughly $90 billion annually.[23] Within skin care, Europe has a 32 percent share (roughly $29 billion) and North America has an 18 percent share (roughly $16 billion).

Within the personal care industry is the "natural personal care" segment. Although there have been inconsistent standards of "natural" and a degree of consumer confusion and inconsistent statistics for volume and growth, it is clear that the growth of natural personal care continues to grow. According to the Kline Group, the worldwide natural personal care segment was estimated at $23 billion in sales in 2010, $26.1 billion in 2011, and is projected to account for 15 percent of the total personal care market (or about $50 billion) in 2015. Surpassing projections, the natural personal care market continues to grow at 10 percent per year.[24]

Natural skin care accounts for approximately 42 percent of the natural personal care segment, or approximately $21 billion in 2015. Europe has a $7.4 billion natural personal care market of which approximately $3.1 billion is natural skin care products. The shea butter products offered by WONS UK will compete in the "natural skin care" segment, and less directly in the broad skin care segment.

Market growth

The overall personal care market is projected to have a compound annual growth rate (CAGR) of approximately 8 percent with standout growth in emerging markets, natural products, and skin care for men.[25] Kline Group notes that growth in the skin care segment (which has risen from the fifth-place segment to first place among personal care segments in the past decade) is driven by aging baby boomers in Europe and North America.

The natural personal care segment (which includes natural skin care) is experiencing remarkable growth worldwide, with a 15 percent compound average growth rate from 2005 to 2009 and no signs of slowing down. A spring 2012 report by Kline Group calls natural personal care products the "little-red-sports-car of the consumer products industry," noting that "consumers have displayed ever-increasing interest in natural products, which will continue to push worldwide growth into double-digits."[26]

Forecasted market size

There are two ways to forecast the market for natural skin care in the UK – a top-down approach based on the greater sector, or a bottom-up approach based upon known trade statistics for shea nuts and butter. Employing a combination of these methods, the UK market is estimated at over 450 MT (metric tonnes) of shea butter annually. Major brands including the Body Shop and L'Occitane occasionally report their source volumes of shea butter, showing a marked upward trend. For example, a 2009 Body Shop presentation contains the graph in Figure 8.6.

The Body Shop stated that over 450 tons of shea butter were purchased for worldwide sales in 2011,[27] indicating that use of shea butter has only accelerated during the economic downturn. L'Occitane has reported similar growth and volumes. Combining these top-down amounts with known producer volumes tracked by the United Nations Food and Agriculture Organization and others, the UK market for shea used in cosmetics is estimated at about 450 MT of nuts per year, and expected to grow to over 650 MT within five years.

Body butters

An important question in market analysis research is to determine if there is a niche market. One niche particularly suited to natural and organic products is

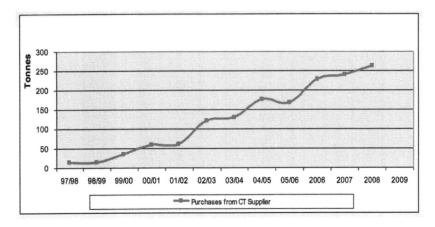

FIGURE 8.6 Shea Butter at the Body Shop
Source: Sarah Clancy-Jaiteh (2009) quoted in Chris McCormick, Business Plan, Oxford Said Business School, 2012.

"body butter." According to a Mintel report on women's body care, this segment is poised for significant growth:

> Body butters are a new category that has flourished at a time that market values have been hurt by pricing pressures. Despite a lackluster performance by body moisturizers, the emergence of body butters is helping to stimulate consumer interest in products … based on natural ingredients and shea butter used for its moisturizing properties.[28]

The easily spreadable nature of shea butter means that it can be used not only as a hand, face, foot, and body cream, but can be used as a body butter as well. Indeed, major retailers already market pure shea butter for this purpose, though their reliance on the West African variety means that their product is less well suited than *nilotica* shea. Scientific and clinical research has indicated that East African *nilotica* shea butter is superior to the West African *paradoxa* shea butter currently on the market in a number of ways.

Market trends

There are a number of significant drivers of growth in the skin care and natural skin care segments. Among them:

- General growth in middle- and upper-middle-class buying power in developing and BRIC (Brazil, Russia, India, and China) countries.
- The aging of the large baby boomer demographic in wealthy markets.

- Rapidly increasing consumer interest in what has been termed "Lifestyles of Health and Sustainability" meaning consumers desire products and purchases that are high quality, authentic, meaningful, and sustainable or ethical in a broad sense. The term LOHAS encompasses the terms "natural," "organic," "fair trade," and "farmer-owned brands," indicating the overlap among consumer motivations.
- The largest personal care companies in the world (Estée Lauder, L'Oréal, etc.) have significantly increased their presence in the natural market through significant acquisitions or new brands.
- Consumers have increased health concerns about synthetic chemicals, such as parabens, phthalates, and aluminum salts.[29]
- The likelihood that all of these factors will continue to trend upward. For example, life expectancy continues to rise among western countries; consumer concern about healthy and natural products and disdain for chemicals continues to trend upward. These factors combine to enable a predictable upward trend for the natural beauty care market.

Competitive landscape

Industry reports indicate that the cosmetics and toiletries sector in the UK has a low level of concentration, with the four largest specialty chain stores comprising only a 20 percent market share.[30] The natural personal care sector is covered by a wide mix of retailers, from large value-oriented hypermarkets such as Tesco and ASDA, to smaller aspirational and natural markets such as John Lewis, its Waitrose division, and Whole Foods market, to high street chemists like Boots, and specialty shops ranging from Lush and the Body Shop at the value end up to very expensive boutiques such as Space NK, L'Occitane, and Neal's Yard Remedies.

Consumer loyalty

Consumer loyalty is an important consideration when entering the market with a new product brand. According to brand innovators, and our partners, Innate Motion, a high percentage of consumers change brands in personal care, where consumer loyalty is ranked low. With extremely low switching costs in an innovation- and trend-driven industry, customers regularly try out new brands. This low loyalty applies to retail outlets as well – according to a Mintel report, "One in five adults shop from different retailers depending on which type of beauty/grooming products they are looking for."[31]

Retailer brands

In addition to the Body Shop run by L'Oréal, there are several other significant retail brands that demonstrate the large-scale opportunity available to develop country producers of specialty skin care products. While it is beyond the scope of this book to provide a full array of retail brands here, an example is provided below with L'Occitane, as they report selling a product with shea butter globally every three seconds, as noted earlier.

L'Occitane en Provence

L'Occitane en Provence (or simply L'Occitane) is one of the world's largest retailers of natural personal care, reporting $975 million in sales in 2011, with growth in the UK of over 20 percent in recent years, and worldwide sales CAGR of 33 percent between 2000 and 2007. It operates several dozen small boutiques in the UK, and has several store-within-a-store modes in the UK.[32] L'Occitane's focus is on skin care products from ethically sourced, natural ingredients. L'Occitane's highest-selling product is its 20 percent shea butter hand cream. L'Occitane focus strongly on shea butter throughout their product line, with large in-store displays about shea butter, and glossy materials about their long-standing ethical partnership with women's cooperatives in Burkina Faso. However, all of the shea in L'Occitane is of the lower quality West African shea. From our market analysis and competitive analysis, we turn to price and positioning.

Price and positioning

A consideration of pricing is critical to African producers. Typically, the producers price their fine products at a low point for export. However, when you consider the size and the pricing of skin care, the opportunity is much larger than is widely known to lower income producers.

Retail price

As a distinctive product, WONS UK will aim for a premium price point, above the 75th percentile of existing retail shea pricing. Personal care products like shea butter typically have a higher unit price when the packaging is smaller – the price per kilogram is higher for L'Occitane's 8 ml tin of pure shea butter than it is for the 150 ml tin of the same product. The same will be true for WONS UK.

WONS UK will sell the initial product, a 50 ml jar of pure shea butter, at a price in the $40–50 range (pending further detailed market research and pilot testing). With regular use, this quantity is expected to last a typical consumer about three months.

Target consumers

WONS UK's strategy in the UK market is designed for maximal influence on a primary consumer target. Though the strategy will achieve results with other

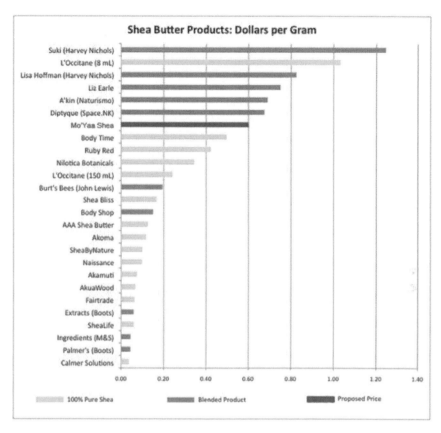

FIGURE 8.7 Shea butter price comparisons
Source: Chris McCormick, Report to LYIP, Said Business School.

demographics, this target will be the core of early sales. Using a methodology combining demographic profiling with life stage/lifestyle profiling, the primary consumer target is defined below:

- Female
- Aged 45 years and over
- Professional and university-educated
- Primarily suburban/near urban. Likely to shop and/or work in Central London
- Upper middle income or higher
- Married, with older children or empty nester/nesting
- Stronger than average tendency to engage in social media, and to use social media as a means to discover and cement their "in-the-know" credentials

Step 3: supply chain leverage

Where in the supply chain is it possible to obtain the maximum leverage for stakeholders?

This question is important because it is relatively easy to note that large western firms are buying copious amounts of shea butter for ingredient brands and that the natural beauty care market is increasing precipitously. It has been trending upward for a decade, and is projected to continue to do so, given health and aging trends, and that many companies are interested in finding their role in what has been called, "women's gold." A next critical step is to determine where producers can assert more ownership and leverage in the supply chain. To position the producers effectively is to assess the intersection of the market demand and where the producers can achieve best leverage. The African shea producers must own the import company selling to the retail stores. It must also secure the quality of supply to the import company by controlling all steps from the nut forwards.

To ascertain best leverage position requires, first, an understanding of the actual supply chain. For Ugandan shea, the supply chain looks like the following:

The Shea Butter supply chain

1 The collecting and producing

When converting from kilograms of nuts to kernels to raw butter and finally into packaged product, the following diagram is useful. A single woman in South Sudan or Uganda can collect approximately 85 kilograms of nuts per year, which yields around 9.5 kilograms of raw butter, or just fewer than 200 containers of retail product (includes wastage).

Collection

Women and children collect shea fruit several days a week in the early morning hours between April and June.[33] It is estimated that an average household (woman) can collect approximately 85 kg of nuts per season, gathered in a range extending 1 to 3 km from their residence.[34] Current estimates are that only about half of the shea is collected due to low prices.[35]

Storage

Upon return to the village, the shea fruit traditionally are removed from the nuts, or allowed to sit until the fruit naturally pulls away from the nut. The nuts are then separated by quality, dried (often by roasting), and stored. The quality price premium provided by WONS shea will encourage the use of superior methods by the cooperatives, such as drying the nuts in "solar tunnel" driers, raised above

WONS Shea (WONS-controlled distribution/wholesale/marketing company)

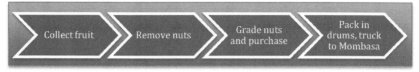

FIGURE 8.8 The East African shea butter supply chain
Source: Chris McCormick and Ron Layton, LYIP Business Plan on Nilotica Shea.

the ground, in order to reduce moisture content and the incidence of fungus while eliminating the need to procure and store firewood. The nuts can then be stored in jute bags in dry storehouses raised above the ground. These improvements will save fuel wood, increase yields via less fungal growth, and lead to a higher quality product. Dry shea nuts may be stored for up to a year without significant degradation in the quality of the resulting butter.

While some agri-business strategies in Africa assert the need to build a factory close to the production or farm, we believe that strategy is usually a mistake for higher end, distinctive products. In the case of WONS, the shea butter will be initially processed in Lira, Uganda, and final product processing in the UK.

Another common tactic in African agri-business is creating producer cooperatives; however, if the combined collection of producers join together, they may or may not end up with improved income. If prices are low, and importers control the prices as they do, cooperatives and collectives are oftentimes largely ineffective and may influence prices to be even lower as they create a stability of supply for importers or in some cases, competition amongst the cooperatives that importers can exploit.

Creating import companies closer to higher end markets is the more effective way to achieve leverage in the supply chain. Though low-income farmers and producers may be untrained in this, and the concept of organizing an import company beyond a present state of mind, it is not hard to form import companies, with adequate financing. Once stakeholders are enabled to have a vision, tools, and knowledge of the relative effectiveness of the import company formation strategy, the decision to do so is not hard.

Initial support is required. The import company can be as simple as an office near higher end markets. Distribution and marketing itself is sophisticated. However, Divine Chocolate showed that European staff skilled in distribution and marketing will work for the benefit of African stakeholders. As described later in this chapter, the effectiveness of import companies is part of the training provided to African stakeholders, so everyone understands supply chain leverage. Women learn complicated farming and processing. It is not hard for them to learn that they need to own import companies.

Two elements of this step are important: 1) The supply chain cannot be owned or already controlled by those with vested interests who will take the increased income earned by farmers and producers; 2) The income return must be high enough to justify investment. For example, in our Ethiopian coffee case repeated throughout the text as a teaching example, the income increase was $101 million.

In one case example of a project feasibility study done for Jamaican rum, for example, the capacity to earn higher income was realistically supported with market research. However, the supply chain was already controlled by a company known as Bacardi Rum. It would have been difficult to nearly impossible for producers to achieve leverage in the supply chain, or to receive added income by going around this very vested interest. Despite holding some promise, Jamaican rum was ruled out as a viable opportunity.

However, in the case of Ugandan shea, the $21 billion natural skin care market, our business plan indicates that the initiative has the potential to reach over 10,000 women in both the northern Uganda and South Sudan regions.[36] By owning the import company and controlling the interface with the higher end retail consumer, producers will escape the volatile commodity market and gain sustainable control over their economic destiny.

Step 4: Is it possible to form a viable, sustainable stakeholder organization? Can the stakeholder organization have true supply chain ownership, and be advanced from poverty into a sustainable income capacity?

The stakeholder organization for this initiative is comprised of two arms: The first is the WONS (Women's Owned Nilotica Shea) cooperative in Uganda, with a legal arm in South Sudan; and second, the WONS import company, located in London, UK. While each side has different functions, they are unified by one goal, the end in mind. As described in Chapter 6 on support, advocacy, education, and enforcement, the WONS constitution was drawn up through meetings of stakeholders. It is their document, with guidance from successful models. It is kept simple to avoid the appearance or reality of foreign imposition, but covers important topics. These include: membership, rules, processes for gathering and exporting nuts. The constitution is built on transparency. The constitution also includes a set of legal documents, called the Memorandum of Association and the Articles of Association. The women have been trained in the concepts of ownership and engaged in their cooperative.

WONS UK will enable livelihoods for 10,000 women through WONS Cooperative, as income is returned to the cooperative through yearly dividends and guaranteed higher pricing.

The women stakeholders, organized into an umbrella cooperative called Women's Owned Nilotica Shea ("WONS"), will own a share of equity in WONS UK, the distribution and marketing company. The partnership between WONS and WONS UK is being facilitated by Light Years IP and the African IP Trust.

The overall goals of IP business training have been and will continue to be:

- To enable and empower producers to understand the retail market outside of their borders and thus to reduce dependency on commodity markets.
- To educate producers to own and manage their supply chains for more control.
- To train producers in critical aspects of quality control.
- To train producers in all aspects of owning and managing their own export companies including interfacing with producers, board, and organizational management, and capacity building for long-term success.
- To train the trainers for an educated and sustainable workforce.
- To train and educate the trade and government sector to realize better long-term trade and export strategies, and to empower their producers.
- To enable the next generation of farmers and producers to understand IP business positioning.

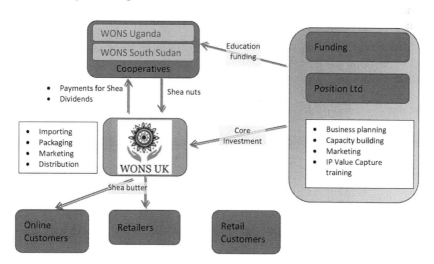

FIGURE 8.9 Investment plan for WONS shea butter
Source: Position Ltd.

Education as a component of the Women's Owned Nilotica Shea (WONS)

IP business education has been built into the business plan for WONS UK as a way of expanding the social impact of the business. It is critical that the women of WONS cooperatives understand the business method, and it is critical they understand their own company. As women are empowered to take a more active role in partnering with their import company, based in the UK, we are building the capacity and competence of WONS Uganda and WONS South Sudan, who are both producers of the product and owner-partners.

Over the course of several years (2011–2015), workshops and training have taken place for Ugandan women and have focused on moving the women from being basic producers to successfully participating in and managing a company. The training has focused on:

- Creating the vision via demonstrating the model of ownership.
- Training in the value of their product and potential alongside heightened understanding of higher end markets.
- Quality control and meeting minimal and progressive quality standards with the goal to ensure producers are fully equipped to meet standards.
- Development of a WONS constitution with bylaws and rules to best understand the ownership model, and how best to coordinate amongst the suppliers and importing side of WONS.
- Training workbooks have been produced and train the trainers workshops are ongoing with a certified core group. A second focus is on mechanisms of delivery from packaging and quality-based pricing through to payment; and a third focus is on organizational coordination across distances through cell phones.

The WONS leadership

The 25-member core group overseeing WONS Uganda have learned IP business positioning methods including advancing knowledge of retail markets, licensing, and Trademarks from marketing and branding experts. They are learning to interface with producers such as registering additional producers. They learn advanced quality control; manage supply from tree to port; and receive export company organization management in leadership, roles, and responsibilities, basic bookkeeping, board management, and conflict resolution from world-class experts.

A model we have adopted is the Divine Chocolate model, wherein the cooperative is located in Ghana (Kuapo Kokoo) and the import company has headquarters in London. A difference in the Divine Chocolate model is that the cocoa growers' cooperative was formed from existing cooperatives, pulling these together in umbrella fashion, whereas WONS has had the opportunity to draw on skilled shea producers but to build the WONS cooperative from the beginning.

This has enabled us to engage the women's input and preferences in drafting their organization's operating rules and procedures, and resulted in a WONS constitution.

The overarching goal has been to train the women to build and sustain their organization from supply to port with a focus on quality for the long-term. Education will be ongoing, and with a full curriculum of interactive workbooks created in all aspects of training, along with a core group of WONS trainers committed to train new members; sustain their organization; advance supply; and remain committed to owning and managing their distinctive brand.

WONS structure

The women stakeholders, organized into umbrella cooperatives in northern Uganda ("WONS Uganda") and South Sudan ("WONS South Sudan") will own a controlling share of equity in WONS UK (the distribution and marketing company), and will be central to decisions about how the gross margins of WONS UK will be used, for purposes including:

- A higher, superior quality price to producers, exporters, and regional processors
- Retained earning to ensure funds for the growth of WONS UK
- Servicing costs and repayment of any debt taken on by WONS UK
- Dividends to stakeholders, through ownership of WONS UK by women producers.

FIGURE 8.10 Trainers and trainees, WONS, Gulu, northern Uganda
Source: Light Years IP.

The partnership between the WONS Uganda/South Sudan and WONS UK will be facilitated by Light Years IP.

Post-conflict recovery in Uganda and South Sudan

South Sudan presents a striking confluence of challenge and opportunity, but large numbers of low-income producers, particularly women, remain unlikely to move to secure incomes derived from foreign investment in minerals, rebuilding institutions, or world commodity markets. The January 2005 Comprehensive Peace Agreement brought an official end to the longest-running civil war in Africa, one which has claimed over 2 million lives and displaced over 4 million people (nearly 80 percent of the South Sudanese population).[37] However, South Sudan faces daunting obstacles with the years from 2013–2015 marked by conflict. The Republic of South Sudan begins life as one of the poorest countries in the world, a land-locked economy ravaged by war and decades of neglect from Khartoum, with extremely poor infrastructure (with fewer than 100 miles of paved roads in an area the size of France) and a large diaspora to repatriate. Its stability is threatened by frequent food crises, poor public health, ongoing disagreements with Sudan over the Abyei region, and continuing attacks and abductions by the Lord's Resistance Army. During the current crisis of 2014/2015, another 7 million South Sudanese have suffered.

WONS UK ownership structure will ensure that Ugandan and South Sudanese cooperatives have a say in the use of profits from the distribution company operations. Through a large stake in WONS UK, the women cooperative members will have greater control over the whole supply chain. After earnings retained for the healthy growth of WONS UK, profit will be returned to the cooperatives through yearly dividends, in addition to higher nut prices with quality premiums.

A governance structure that ensures producer ownership will result in a much higher return for the women's hard work and naturally superior shea butter. The benefits of a successful company in the EU and US will be directly felt in Uganda and South Sudan.

According to British law, there is no limit on the percentage share a foreign company can own, allowing WONS to own a significant stake in a UK-domiciled company. In future, it is hoped that all high-margin stages of the value chain will be owned and controlled by WONS.

Step 6: Social impact investment

The WONS initiative is a perfect example of an impact investment opportunity. Without a bold step, the woman producers cannot sell their distinctive shea butter in any quantity. The transport cost to the nearest port simply takes most of an export price based on global commodity pricing for shea butter as an ingredient in food products, a substitute for cocoa butter and similar commodities.

Impact investment seeks to bring about positive change in the world while generating a return on investment that is adequate for the risks taken by the investor. Generally, impact investors are more patient than commercial investors and also recognize that the business they are investing in may not always be sold to an equity investor. The investor's exit is often generated by a buyout of their interest from retained earnings of the business or by the investment being made as a loan with interest. Social impact investors in Divine Chocolate included the late Anita Roddick, founder of Body Shop. Many of the investors still hold shares with voting rights being used to help the cocoa producers of Kuapa Kokoo.

WONS profitability is the source of investor returns. Producer prices have already been increased to three times the going rate prices in 2015. Continued growth and improvement in stability of producer prices will generate benefits for WONS families, while gross margins are high enough to create returns to investors.

By moving the producers out of dependency on commodity prices, investors will have impacted stability of family incomes and real incentives for quality control.

They will also have made it possible for producers living beyond Gulu and in West and Central Equatoria in South Sudan to move up to living incomes. Without investors, this would not be possible.

Summary/conclusion

The Women's Owned Nilotica Shea company and higher end shea butter embodies the IP business positioning concepts discussed and illustrated in this book. The power of the Intellectual Property business positioning is:

For the WONS Ugandan cooperative to be correctly positioned, it needs to:

- Own the shea butter when it leaves the Ugandan processing plant
- Control the product throughout the supply chain
- Own the professionally formulated consumer product
- Control the final retail packaging by a European cosmetic fulfillment company
- Own the distribution company marketing to retail stores in Europe and online.

The results of this business strategy will be:

- Income increases of at least 20 times to women producer members of WONS
- Stable pricing of nuts and
- A cash rich WONS cooperative that can invest in quality development at all stages in the process.

The women of Uganda and South Sudan have a superior, distinctive product (Nilotica shea) wherein there is a significant price gap between current export and higher end retail.

They will engage an IP tool (trademark) + correct positioning + supply chain ownership + import company ownership + investment = power.

To this we add – the significant power of women. The goal is to enable a brand supported by the correct business positioning that will last for more than 100 years. The packaging shown in Figure 8.12 was a first model of packaging. It has been updated by brand and positioning expert Megan Wood of Innate Motion. We used this packaging model in earlier training to illustrate the concept of packaging.

This is not merely Fair Trade, wherein the shea butter producers would become part of another company's successful branded product, and the shea butter would likely be an ingredient keeping the product at commodity export levels with low income. This differs in that it is women producer owned all the way through to retail with appropriate market positioning. The WONS shea butter is not a CSR, or Corporate Social Responsibility project owned by a corporation, to give a little back after buying the shea at low prices. This is not Fair Trade, nor "value-added," but rather a fully women's owned and positioned company with 700 producers, projected to advance to 10,000.

The challenge to this is that it is somewhat outside the normal mindset of those who think about Africa as most development experts think – it is Africa's role to export commodity products, or ingredient brands, and that help is in the form of creating low-price agri-businesses that at least provide jobs, albeit at low wages without much hope of change.

While we appreciate the progress made to create women's cooperatives for exporting Shea butter, and those who create agri-business or low-end manufacturing, specifically in the Shea butter production, while also providing some income for women, we believe there is a better way. It is a stronger way, a way

FIGURE 8.11 WONS packaging, first version
Source: Light Years IP.

that not only temporarily empowers women, but more predictably sustains the empowerment. The Ugandan WONS model is on the one hand, unusual, but on the other, it is simply business. It is what a corporation would do.

Essentially, unless there is a business model that enables women to rise above the low, commodity market prices with price fluctuations as difficult as low prices alone, empowerment will be in spirit and sentiment rather than in real advance in income. The only way to true, sustainable empowerment is a business model that changes the power, not for tomorrow, not for the next year, but a sustainable brand built on a superior product with full women's ownership all the way through to high end retail. That is empowerment. That is sustainable for 100 years, and more, for the women of today and their children.

Lonya Ma Tam!

Next steps: At this point, it would be advisable to review the Ugandan Shea Butter Workbook included on the companion website. This workbook illustrates the way the women of Uganda have been trained in their company, and highlights the IP business positioning training model.

The model is applicable to other African and LDC IP business positioning opportunities.

Notes

1 M. Brindle, "World Bank rural multiplier study," LYIP, 2011.
2 UNDP, "Fast facts, gender in crisis," Gender Development Programme, 2013.
3 Acumen, "Women and social enterprises: How gender integration can boost entrepreneurial solutions to poverty," Acumen publication, 2015.
4 R.K. Sumanta, ed., *Empowering women: Key to Third World development*, MD Publications, Pvt, Ltd., New Delhi, 1999.
5 B. Gitau, "Obama in Kenya: Why the US is investing $500 million in African women," *Christian Science Monitor*, July 25, 2015.
6 President Barak Obama, in Gitau, CSM, July 2015, p. 1.
7 World Bank Group, Women, Business and the Law: Getting to Equal, Washington, DC: World Bank, 2015.
8 Ibid.
9 Ibid., p. 9.
10 World Bank Group, "Women, business and the law: Getting to equal," Washington, DC: World Bank, 2015. reports.weforum.org/global-gender-gap-report-2014/economies/#economy=UGA.
11 S. Covey, *Begin with the end in mind: Seven habits of highly effective people*, Simon and Schuster, New York, 1989.
12 L'Occitane website, May 2016 (usa.loccitane.com/shea-butter-hand-cream,82,1,29193,261659.htm).
13 US Department of Commerce, Cosmetic and Toiletries Market Overview, TechNavio, 2015. http://trade.gov/industry/materials/ITA.FSC.Cosmoprof.2015_final2.pdf (2011).
14 "Big vendors are going organic to capture the European skincare market," Technavio, July 17, 2015 (www.technavio.com/blog/big-vendors-are-going-organic-to-capture-the-european-skincare-market), accessed March 2016.
15 A. M. Fati Paul, "Do not fell shea trees," Ghana Web, March 14, 2011.

16 J. Boffa, M.YaMéoga, P. NikiéMa, and D.M. Nudson, Shea nut (*Vitellaria paradoxa*) production and collection in agroforestry parklands of Burkina Faso. Department of Forestry and Natural Resources, Purdue University, West Lafayette, Indiana, USA, 1996. FAO document available at: www.fao.org/docrep/W3735e/w3735e17.htm.

17 Ibid.

18 Ibid.

19 R. Layton and C. McCormick, "Business plan for shea butter," Oxford University, MBA students in Social Entrepreneurship unpublished paper, 2012. Oxford.

20 Interviews with renowned biochemist and Shea expert Dr. Peter Lovett, who has worked with the different shea butters for over a dozen years; he asserts that the differences between the two subspecies are extensive.

21 Global Industry Analysts, 2012.

22 US Department of Commerce, Cosmetic and Toiletries Market Overview, 2015. http://trade.gov/industry/materials/ITA.FSC.Cosmoprof.2015_final2.pdf.

23 "Big vendors are going organic to capture the European skincare market," Technavio, July 17, 2015 (www.technavio.com).

24 The Klien Group, "The natural personal care market moves to truly natural products as sales continue to grow," February 2015 (www.premiumbeautynews.com/en/the-natural-personal-care-market,7769), accessed May 2016.

25 The Kline Group, "Natural personal care: Regional market analysis and competitive brand assessment," 2011.

26 The Kline Group, "Natural Personal Care: Global market brief," 2013.

27 Body Shop, 2012.

28 Mintel Report, Women's Bodycare, UK, March 2009. http://store.mintel.com/womens-bodycare-uk-march-2009.

29 C. McCormick and Oxford University MBA students, "Business plan for WONS Shea butter," unpublished by Light Years IP, London, April 2013.

30 Ibid.

31 UK Beauty Retailing, Mintel Report, January 2011, p. 1, http://store.mintel.com/beauty-retailing-uk-january-2011.

32 L'Occitane en Provence, 2011.

33 USAID report, "Rebuilding lives and livelihoods in Uganda," The Shea Project, Lira, Uganda, reported by USAID, 2007 (www.thesheaproject.org/index2.html), accessed May 2016.

34 The Forestry Working Group, 2004 (http://ufwg.envalert.org). Consultation with Peter Lovett, expert in shea butter, Geneva, Switzerland, 2012.

35 Consultation with Peter Lovett, expert in shea butter, Geneva, Switzerland, 2012.

36 R. Layton and C. McCormick, "WONS Business Plan," Washington, DC, updated 2015.

37 US Committee for Refugees and Immigrants Annual Report, UNCR, 2001 (www.refworld.org/publisher,USCRI,,UZB,,,0.html).

9

THE POWER OF THE HISTORICAL RECORD

Intellectual Property business is not new!

One important reason why Intellectual Property business positioning strategies are not more widely used by developing country farm and producing businesses is an assumption that IP is a sophisticated, legal framework, involving lawyers, expensive enforcement, specialized businesspeople or creative artists, wealthy people and well – more lawyers! The myth that IP is only for more developed countries inhibits the use of this simple, powerful, and transformative business method.

The second formidable barrier is the assumption that Intellectual Property is the domain of artists, musicians, films, and other creative products and it is simply not applicable to agricultural products. It is wrong, however, to think that African farmers and producers can only take their turn at low-income production-focused commodities and processing.

Corporations in developed countries have indeed benefitted from Intellectual Property revenue, and understand its value well. It is not only the domain of the wealthy, elite or privileged. It is fundamentally misunderstood and thus wildly underutilized by poor producers.

Using the historical record and case studies, this chapter explores four agricultural products over several centuries, showing that since 47 AD, poor farmers and producers have sought protection for their agricultural methods and unique products. In a number of cases, they were successful and produced such outcomes as French champagne, originally the product of poor peasant producers.

This chapter will show that:

- Farmed exports, not music nor creative products nor twenty-first-century brands, were the first set of products to achieve protection and thereby income improvement.

- Intellectual Property strategies have been used for centuries and IP business methods are not entirely new but have a rich, historical record.
- Tools such as the "Trade Mark," the earliest form of the word, were truly to assist trade, protect producers, and signal to consumers that the products could be trusted.
- Intellectual Property continues to create large income gains for products such as wines, spirits, and cheeses and many other agriculturally based products.

History is a master of dispelling myths. The historical record documents the engagement of hundreds of thousands of farmers, producers, craftsmen and women who have actively owned, controlled, protected, and improved their income from their distinctive agricultural products. This has included the explicit recognition that a specialized knowledge was involved in producing the distinctive product. In the case of French champagne, for example, the grapes were not unique to France, but the process, though invented in England, was first promoted in the French region of Champagne. The historical lens also enables us to see income improvements over time, advances against deep poverty among producers once very poor, and most importantly, the confluence of factors that enabled such advances. These include correct positioning with consumers and ownership of IP, stakeholder organization, plus support and widespread enforcement.

In this chapter, we show how the historical record provides themes and lessons learned from IP-based product cases. These products and more specifically, the IP business positioning strategies, have benefitted millions of producers. Moreover, similar strategies can be replicated *today* by poor producers.

One caveat – a challenge of the historical record is to summarize key points, though the historical record takes place over centuries. The advantage of the historical record is to provide perspective, and a lens for looking backward to analyze relevant factors.

The historical record presented in this chapter includes three products with long histories from the European continent, French champagne, Scotch whisky, and Roquefort cheese. We also include Sunkist oranges, a powerful branded agricultural product from the US with over $1 billion in licensing revenue, emergent from poor orange growers. The results of positioning and management of IP in the four cases are contrasted with Ceylon tea, which involves 2 million Sri Lankan tea farmers.

The successful products and their IP business development share the following commonalities:

1. Agricultural products that are currently earning higher retail prices than similar products without distinctiveness, or simply, commodity products.
2. Products that have demonstrated a measureable intangible value and successful use of Intellectual Property tools over time, that are also capable of being used by today's poor producers in developing countries.

3. Stakeholder formation for support, advocacy, and enforcement that enabled poor producers to gain control over distribution and ownership. This includes collaboration amongst producers to form not only solidarity, but real negotiating power.
4. The challenge and struggle of truly poor producers that ultimately resulted in dramatically higher income.

French champagne was first produced in the 1600s, and in fact not first "invented" in France but in England. Champagne is registered as a trademark in some countries and as a geographical indication (GI) in France and other EU countries. A GI is a form of trademark with very similar legal powers to prevent unauthorized use by non-owners. In countries that recognize GIs and trademarks, either can be used to exercise power over unauthorized use, but only trademarks have power in countries that don't recognize GIs. Champagne is now a "poster child" for those promoting the use of GIs by developing countries and LDCs.

Champagne is also a demonstration of excellent positioning including brand ownership, marketing, control over distribution, and intervention using legal Intellectual Property tools and methods. But, the champagne brand was not always protected and the French who grew the grapes from which champagne was made were peasants, and quite poor. Although theirs is a rousing success story, it was not always so – there were intensive struggles over decades to acquire the IP ownership and achieve correct positioning, marketing, and control.

Roquefort cheese was first noted in 47 AD in part of Roman Gaul (now known as France) and protected aggressively. This story shows how a product with distinctiveness, whether part mythology or true, coupled with assertive branding and distribution ownership has served a small group of producers of about 4,500, very well. While everyone is aware of champagne as it is a famous and large industry, Roquefort cheese only involves around 4,500 producers, a tiny cottage industry by twenty-first-century standards, but powerful due to effective IP positioning and management.

The third example case is Scotch whisky, a lucrative and aggressively protected brand, and the fifth largest export from the UK. The story is fascinating as it is a history of control and product ownership, alongside a strong protective association, the Scotch Whisky Association (SWA), for nearly 100 years. There are lessons to be gleaned from Scotch whisky for low-income farmers and processors, which of course, the Scotch distillers also were at one time.

These success cases, all begun by relatively poor farmers, monks, distillers, and producers, contrast with some cases wherein the IP tools being used by millions are not working effectively – Malaysian Sarawak Pepper and Ugandan vanilla, for example, alongside Sri Lankan Ceylon tea. These three products are made by millions of producers. In the case of Ceylon tea, for example, there are over 2 million tea farmers, yet a great majority of their fine tea competes with counterfeit tea falsely labeled as Ceylon tea, denying the tea farmers the value of their Intellectual Property.

The questions we will address in comparing the successes and failures are:

What is the difference between success and failure in the use of Intellectual Property? Is it the product or the ownership or the alliances and associations that protect the brand? What role has the intervention of governments played and what can we learn about the most effective use of Intellectual Property tools and positioning strategy that is applicable for today's distinctive agricultural products emergent from Africa and developing countries?

By comparing success and failures in the effective and non-effective application of Intellectual Property, lessons can be learned that are applicable to the many opportunities available now for millions of low-income farmers and producers.

The case of French champagne

When we consider French champagne, it is easy to adopt the perception that this product and its success has limited relevance for poor farmers and producers.

Why? How could a product that is obviously associated with higher end markets, rituals of luxury, and as distinctive as champagne emergent from a relatively rich western country have anything to do with poor farmers producing coffee or tea?

Consider that French champagne did not begin as a luxury item. It began with several common grape varieties with all the challenges of growing seasons that require seven years from planting to first harvest. Champagne was adopted by from unorganized peasants in a country that saw the great majority of its residents in poverty at that time in its history. Grape growing involves hazards in soil, climate, unsteady harvest, and the challenges of processing, export, control over distribution, and sales fluctuations, alongside competition, which was a ubiquitous problem for French wine. Yet, champagne now brings in substantial export income and importantly, export income is around 50 percent of retail value. If African distinctive export sectors could approach this share of retail value, poverty would be vastly reduced.

The product

Champagne comes from Marne, the French district in the northeast of France whose capital is Calons-en-Champagne. Champagne is made from black Pinot noir and Pinot Meunier grapes and also white Chardonnay grapes. The availability of these grapes in other parts of the world means that, in theory, champagne could be made anywhere.

Wine was produced in the region now known as the Champagne region from the fifth century onward – possibly earlier but this is the earliest date documented. As history records, the grapes of the Champagne region were less full-bodied, more acidic and produced a wine lighter in color than the famous wine of the period – Burgundy, located further south with a longer growing season. The attempt to compete with the famed Burgundy wine led to various degrees of experimentation, much of which is attributed to the monks of the region working in enterprises owned by Abbeys. As the famous cathedral of Reims is located in the champagne region, producing wine for Eucharist and later for religious ceremonies as well as the crowning of Kings at Reims was also an important function of the monks.

Although Dom Perignon is attributed with "inventing" champagne, history records very clearly that it was actually an Englishman, Dr. Christopher Merrett, who added sugar to the process and produced the first champagne in the mid-1600s.[1]

We highlight this fact because despite the fact that champagne was "invented" outside of France, and is actually able to be created in many countries, the Intellectual Property is owned by France on the basis of geographical origin. This may be more socially constructed than factual. In addition, the regional name, "Champagne," is not unique to France alone. A city in Spain and small village in Switzerland have the same name and were established long before the French region. Interestingly, both cities have been known to produce special varieties of wine long before the champagne-makers in the French Champagne region. Furthermore, a majority of the grapes in Champagne vineyards are from plants outside the Champagne region. Yet, the entire Intellectual Property system for champagne is based on a claim of regional distinctiveness of the terroir, the natural environment producing the specialized, unique process; and distinctive grapes.

Intellectual Property protection

So, why does "champagne only come from France" as advertised by the French Committee on Champagne? France's justification to nationalize champagne can be attributed to three major factors. First, French champagne producers in the region share a history of creating innovative solutions to produce champagne in large quantities.[2] Second, the propagation of powerful myths propelled into marketing campaigns, by champagne pioneers – from Dom Perignon to the Clicquot family house – has effectively caused the international public to see champagne as a luxurious French national product. Examples of this include the adoption of the legend of a French religious figure, Dom Perignon, into marketing campaigns directed at the French aristocracy that greatly increased the prominence of champagne as the preferred beverage of the wealthy class in France. Third, and most importantly, has been France's ability to enforce the champagne trademark throughout Europe in the past century to strengthen the ownership claims. Together these factors combined to create an increased international awareness of champagne as an exclusive product of France.

The French have maintained a diligent enforcement to protect the geographical indication internationally. One action has been to create the Committee on Champagne (1947) as an international lobbying group to enforce champagne's geographical exclusivity. The Committee greatly contributed to the promulgation of the Lisbon Agreement for the Protection of Appellations of Origin and Their International Registration (1958), which established a registration system. The "TRIP"S Agreement launched in 1994 marks the last comprehensive agreement to protect geographical indications of champagne among many others.[3]

Champagne has become the poster child for geographical indications, inspiring literally hundreds of applications for similar protection based on origin.

Currently, one can visit the champagne region, and there is no shortage of special tours that showcase the history and process. According to one champagne cave, the vineyard owners, who were once ordinary and largely poor, continued to experiment with champagne processing over a 75-year period. For example, sometimes they turned the bottles upside down, and finally found the right process to produce the thousands of bubbles that characterize the drink, though what portion of this is myth making and really contributes to the unique process is hard to distinguish. In short, the French champagne producers have created a lucrative brand, and serious Intellectual Property protection for a product claimed to be unique to France, largely based on social and historical construction. They have coupled it with solidarity among stakeholders and rigorous international enforcement.

The success of Champagne is also linked to brilliant marketing strategies throughout the history of the product. During its nascent stages, powerful Maisons (Moets, Clicquot, Roederer) centered in Marne liaised with government and other aristocratic figures as part of an imaging campaign, propping the idea of champagne as a celebratory drink for the wealthy. From Versailles, champagne spread throughout the ranks of royalty and nobility in Europe. Global leaders from England, Spain, and even the Vatican were noted to own champagne vineyards. Other aristocratic leaders including Napoleon – known for his famous quote about the beverage, "in victory you deserve it, in defeat you need it" – promoted the appeal of champagne to his subordinates, as well as foes.[4] The same marketing strategy exists in current times as leading Maisons continue to sponsor celebrities, including Winston Churchill, and even literature characters.

In addition, various European wars acted as a conduit to market champagne to foreign nations. After the Franco-Prussian War, Madame Clicquot expanded her sales as far as Russia before any of her competitors. As a result Clicquot Champagne became the leading champagne on the market in Russia. On a more populous note, champagne and toasts of champagne continue to characterize weddings and celebratory events, reinforcing its reputation as a drink of specialty, special events, promotions, and life transitions. This is positioning with style!

Revenue for France

The nineteenth century saw an exponential growth in champagne production, going from a regional production of 300,000 bottles a year in 1800 to 20 million bottles in 1850. In the last decade, annual champagne export volume has averaged around 310 million bottles per year.[5]

There are more than one hundred champagne houses and 19,000 smaller *vignerons* (vine-growing producers) in Champagne. These companies manage some 32,000 hectares of vineyards in the region.[6] And, at 310 million bottles of champagne exported per year and growing, with average export price of $25.00/bottle equivalent, revenue from French champagne has approached $1 billion/year.[7] Note that the average export price is close to 50 percent of the average retail price of champagne, depending on the variety and brand.

Lessons learned

The factors that propelled champagne to be the proverbial "poster child" for Intellectual Property, most specifically in the geographical indication, or Appellation of Origin category, can be learned and some factors modeled. These factors in addition to legal protection have enabled French champagne to enjoy success in the marketplace:

1. A distinctive product that was part truth, part social construction that created the brand story that champagne originated and can only be made in France.
2. Excellent positioning and marketing to higher end consumers.
3. Creation of quality control and incentives for quality control by revenue generation.
4. Control of supply chain by prominent brands who collaborated for advocacy and protection.
5. A pricing scheme supporting the concept of high quality product that has created demand, and concurrent interest in control over all aspects of the brand.
6. An Intellectual Property tool coupled with vigorous enforcement in the international arena.
7. Government support.

By contrast, poor and low-income African and LDC farmers and producers are often taught to sell their distinctive products on commodity markets and in some cases, to consider Intellectual Property as beyond the limits of their understanding, or to view their products as less distinctive and incapable of generating IP-based revenue models.

While it could be argued that French champagne is unique, with large-scale investments in marketing and with the benefit of two centuries of being associated with luxury, historical occasions, and fame, we underscore that it was not always so. The majority of French grape farmers were poor peasants, and the IP business positioning strategy used by French champagne is actually replicable. An analysis of Scotch whisky and Roquefort cheese illustrates further lessons in Intellectual Property business that can be modeled by low-income producers.

The case of Scotch whisky

Scotch whisky emerged from humble beginnings to take its place as the fifth largest export of the UK. Scotch whisky is a story of an agricultural product. The brand name, "Scotch whisky," is protected by law and involves cereal origination, coupled with a process developing quality. Most importantly, Scotch whisky also benefits from a powerful association that enforces and protects the intellectual property – the Scotch Whisky Association. A few interesting facts about Scotch whisky that demonstrate the industry size and success include the following:

- There are over 100 distilleries licensed to produce Scotch whisky in Scotland.
- More than 1 billion bottles of Scotch whisky are sold every year and 90 percent of these sales are outside of Scotland.
- The value of those exports in 2011 was over $6.6 billion.
- The industry is one of the UK's top five manufactured exports and it supports 1 in 50 Scottish jobs. Over 1 million tourists visit Scotch whisky distilleries every year.[8]

The product

Scotch whisky derives from local spirits, made first in the small distilleries of the Scottish Highlands. It first appears in the historical record in 1505 and was noted when the Scottish Parliament began to tax drinks in 1644. Scotch whisky achieved formal recognition in 1755 with an entry into the dictionary by Dr. Samuel Johnson.[9]

For many centuries, Scotch whisky remained a local spirit and did not achieve massive, large-scale production until the eighteenth century.[10] The advantage of 100 years was to enable the whisky producers to develop a specialized process. In addition, the largest market was close by as the majority of exports were to England during the first two centuries.

History of the policy environment

Although Scotland derived its name from a Spanish Celtic King in 1699 BC, no nation is more closely associated with a drink than Scotland and Scotch whisky.

The following history of Scotch whisky shows how the product enjoyed many centuries of development, even aided by being "underground" for a period, and fostered by the competition among tens of thousands of small distilleries. Eventually, an enforcement group begun by producers in 1900 became the Scotch Whisky Association in 1942 that demonstrates rigorous enforcement of the brand.

The word whisky (spelled without an "e" in Scotland, and differentiated from Irish whiskey, with an "e") is from a Gaelic word, "*uisge beatha*," or "*usquebaugh*," meaning "water of life." According to the historical record, the practice of distillation began with either physicians (named Mackeveys or MacVeys) or Celtic monks.[11] In Scotland, the earliest distillers were doctors who distilled Scotch for medicinal use. Indeed, the first protection of the distillation of Scotch whisky was in 1505 when the Guild of Surgeon Barbers were given manufacturing monopoly. It should be noted that barbers at this time in history were also often surgeons, and used whisky as anesthetic.

The next three hundred years were a fascinating time for Scotch whisky. First, it came under a system of fiscal control in the eighteenth and nineteenth centuries. Heavy taxation and attempts to standardize processes caused many farmers to go into underground markets and engage in smuggling. The so-called "smuggling era" lasted until 1823, when use of smaller stills was legalized, giving birth to the Scotch whisky industry.[12]

During this same period, the Royal government confiscated more than 14,000 illicit stills a year, noting that half of whisky consumption was without payment of duty.[13] The House of Lords passed the Excise Act in 1823, implementing a license fee of £10, and a set payment per gallon of whisky. Later, after phylloxera devastated the French vineyards, which led to a global deficiency of brandy in 1897, Scotch whisky was able to fill the void. In doing so, Scotch reached prominence throughout the world, giving impetus for the Royal government to protect its brand.

Organized advocacy and enforcement: the Scotch Whisky Association

The Scotch Whisky Association (SWA) is important because it currently controls industry standards, Intellectual Property, and monitors counterfeit whisky. The SWA traces its roots back to the establishment of its predecessor organization, the Wine and Spirit Brand Association, founded in 1912 to combat the threat of prohibition and government dominance of trade. The organization continued to establish measures to promote whisky producers, helping create the first definition of Scotch in UK law in 1933. The modern SWA was founded in 1942, notably during World War II while clearly other priorities existed, but the need to protect a growing export was also obviously important.

As of 2013, the SWA has imposed legal action against more than 1,000 brands and has opposed almost 3,000 trademark applications worldwide.[14] In 2009, the UK Parliament acted to further protect Scotch whisky by mandating that "Scotch Whisky must be wholly matured in Scotland." It established a more precise definition of Scotch whisky as well as the penalties for counterfeiters.

IP enforcement

In its 2013 report, we can see how strongly the SWA enforces the Scotch whisky brand. The SWA declared that counterfeiting remains a serious issue for distillers – albeit enforcement has increased immensely over recent years. Some of these issues include counterfeiters whose bottles:

- Show brands that display the name "Scotch Whisky."
- Use Scottish symbols such as the tartan, bagpiper, castles or Scottish names defined as "Mc" or "Mac."
- State "blended with Scotch."
- Depict false claims to the aging process – e.g. "aged 10 years."[15]

Interestingly enough, even bottles with plaids as labels have raised concerns for the SWA who have taken legal action against non-Scottish producers for allegedly mimicking Scotch whisky. The SWA keeps careful watch over counterfeiting. For example, the SWA will take action against any product on sale in the EU as "whisky" if it does not comply with the EU definition of whisky. The details are provided here because while seemingly pedantic, these actions illustrate how fiercely important the quality control, and product definition and control are to the Scotch whisky owners. For example, the SWA will take action against *any* whisky product sold in the EU unless it is:

- Distilled from cereals.
- Distilled at an alcoholic strength of less than 94.8 percent vol. so that it has the aroma and taste derived from the raw materials used.
- Aged for at least three years in wooden casks of 700 liters capacity or less.
- Retains the color, aroma, and taste derived from the production process.
- A minimum alcoholic strength of 40 percent.
- Contains no added flavoring or sweetening or other alcohol (Annex II(2) of EC Regulation 110/2008).

Consider the way the Scotch Whisky Association demonstrated the power of their IP protection in these cases reported in the SWA Legal Report of 2014. The SWA raised objections to 161 new trademark applications in 43 countries, according to its report.[16]

As one poignant example, in South Africa, the use of the word Highland was used, and later labeled "Clan Whiskey" to which the SWA objected, arguing that this would imply an association with Scotland and thus be under the SWA right to object, based on their geographically protected IP. The SWA argued that it was further alarmed when a photo of a Scottish Highlander was used on the bottle, again associating the whiskey strongly with Scotch whisky. The South African Ministry of Agriculture negotiated a settlement, but the South African company did withdraw the product.[17]

When a company in Taiwan manufactured and were selling a whisky not using the word Scotch or any symbol remotely associated with Scotland, the Scotch Whisky Association *still* objected, arguing that the Taiwanese were harming the reputation of whisky, since their product was inferior in process and taste.

In addition, the SWA works closely with the government. Naturally, the EU would want to partner with an industry that is generating the level of trade volume, export income, and job creation such as the SWA. These partnerships are often lacking by poorer country producers, but could be fashioned. It's important to remember, the close partnerships were not always present, but created over centuries.

In sum, Scotch whisky, one of the largest exports of the UK, and generating nearly $7 billion in annual revenue had humble beginnings. It is a story of struggling producers, once forced underground as their product was illegal. It is a story of an incredibly successful support and enforcement agency, the SWA that has achieved prominence and power just since World War II. In less than 75 years, this enforcement agency has gone from a small, nascent group to a most powerful enforcement agency. Though it is not a large body, it brings hundreds of cases per year against any infringement, near infringement or any country teasing with its protected brand. That is formidable IP control by those most interested in protecting a unique brand. The details of the SWA are included here to demonstrate what a small, but powerful watchdog group can achieve, one that is intent on enforcing its Intellectual Property and protect a lucrative brand.

Can poor countries replicate this model? The African IP Trust as an advocacy and enforcement association intends to advocate and enforce on an expanded basis. If the Scotch whisky producers can achieve protection for a product that may be currently highly reputed, but also holds a serious downside as an alcoholic product, and copious levels of competition, we believe that African producers of distinctive products can also replicate IP enforcement for their products and better control over their unique brands. The advantage of learning from these models is that examples such as Scotch whisky demonstrate a history of struggle for several hundred years to achieve current levels of successful enforcement. Learning from their success, and pathways forged in Intellectual Property protection, can provide a model, one with a much faster trajectory for African and LDC farmers and producers.

The case of Roquefort cheese

If the cases of French champagne and Scotch whisky seem to hold unfair advantages, such as the historically constructed popularity of the beverage, long years of acquiring the processing and unique, distinctive branding, alongside a well-developed and powerful country government partnership, consider the very common agricultural product – cheese. This export is interesting by contrast, as only about 4,500 cheese producers made Roquefort cheese. This case demonstrates the value of a distinctive product and how a stakeholder group can achieve serious control over its brand, even with relatively few producers.

Roquefort cheese dates back to 79 AD, when it was first mentioned in literature.[18] Cheese making in France dates back to Roman times and archeologists have confirmed that people have long been producing cheese there, with discoveries of colanders and cheese making materials dating back more than 700 years.

Centuries before modern systems of Intellectual Property were established, in 1411, Charles VI granted a monopoly for the people of the region, known as Roquefort-sur-Soulzon to ripen their cheese and exclusively use the name. According to the King's ruling, anyone else using the name Roquefort could be punished.

The French have a well-established history of cheese making, producing over 400 varieties. While we think of cheese in the modern day as being mass-produced, it is worth noting that factory-made cheese only became commonplace after World War II and for centuries prior, cheese making was considered artisanal. The deep historical basis coupled with specialized and verified knowledge and skill resident in a community served to establish the special case for Roquefort cheese.

To the legal environment, French Roquefort cheese was also the recipient of France's very first Appellation D'Origine contrôlée (or Appelation of Origin) in 1925. When imitations and copycat Roquefort were springing up, even within France, French authorities in 1961 ruled that only the cheese that was ripened in the caves of the Roquefort region could carry the name of the region.

Though the French moved to protect the regional IP, some aspects of Roquefort cheese can be duplicated, as would seem logical. Sheep graze on fine land emergent from limestone or of limestone origin in many places across the rich landscape of France. Unpasteurized ewes' milk is also readily duplicated. The specialized mold, associated with only the distinctive caves for which Roquefort established its initial claim to fame, has been duplicated in laboratories. Thus, from a pure "terroir" point of view, the notion that Roquefort requires a unique combination of aspects of grazing land plus cool, humid, limestone caves could be questioned as a bit spurious since the mold can be duplicated and the sheep's milk is plentiful from other regions outside of France. Thus to make a cheese that tastes like Roquefort cheese does not require the unique land, area, and process as claimed (and controlled)!

However, the French Roquefort cheese holds a prime reputation and place in history which even laboratory-copied processes could be said to model. The trademark designates respect to 600–1,000 years of unique origin and local, well-honed knowledge. It is clear that the policy environment with 90 years of legal protection established by being the first appellation of origin, coupled with legal precedent from 1925, through the 1961 case, has aided the success. Starting with a royal monopoly in the fifteenth century, French law and protection have served to protect the cheese as a national product, disallowing other regions, even within France, to copy or name cheese Roquefort.

The French are the third largest in the world in cheese production, so are strongly incentivized to protect the Intellectual Property of their specialty cheeses.[19] With only 2,000 farms and 4,500 people involved, the scarcity of the product with the brand works well for this cheese, as it helps to create a sense of value, reputation, and higher price.

There are relatively a very small number of producers, a fraction of the number involved in other products, such as, for example, 2 million Ceylon tea growers and nearly 1 million Sarawak pepper farmers. Yet, despite small numbers, the Roquefort cheese producers have been successful at creating a sense of scarcity and thus value, albeit with some mythology included.

Retail price

Roquefort cheese retails at about $10.00–13.00/7.5 ounces or roughly $20.00/lb (2015 data). It is generally presented in small quantities, as per its distinctiveness, and sharply pungent characteristics.[20] Online retailers distribute in similarly small quantities. At $20.00–$25.00/lb, Roquefort cheese compares to non-specialty commodity cheeses such as cheddar, Swiss provolone retailing at roughly $5.00/lb.

Roquefort cheese has been considered a specialty, unique, and distinctive product with intangible value, dating back to 1411. The story of origin has been protected to various degrees beginning with Charles VI, and though some aspects of the origin and required uniqueness border on mythology, the combination of IP protection, advocacy, and enforcement for a specialty product has been a success story. To tease out how much of this success correlates with the actual GI or the mythology, marketing, and positioning is challenging. What is clear in the historical record is that the power position of the Roquefort community is formidable. The product was created as the original product to hold the appellation d'origine and thus carries French government support.

Lessons learned for African and LDC producers

Producers in developing countries mostly sell to commodity markets, but will fare much better if they are assisted to develop a niche in gourmet or specialty markets where retail prices are high relative to production cost. The much higher share of retail price shown in this chapter is a result of excellent Positioning. Having income set as a share of retail prices, which are very stable, creates a benefit of great importance to poor producers – price and income stability.

- Niche or specialty markets, such as Roquefort cheese, carry the advantage of branding. Producers in developing countries can and should develop brands that resonate with consumers who buy branded products.
- Producers can benefit from examples like Scotch whisky and French Roquefort cheese in owning their Intellectual Property, and developing associations to protect and enforce the Intellectual Property of their specialty products.
- Despite massive competition in the cheese sector, Roquefort cheese stands out as distinctive and commands higher prices due to correct positioning in

marketing and branding, IP ownership, supply chain control, and IP protection with enforcement.

- If the Roquefort cheese producers can protect a product, wherein only about 4,500 producers are involved, farmers and producers of distinctive African products can, too.

The three cases, French champagne, Scotch whisky, and Roquefort cheese demonstrate IP business positioning success for sustainable, high income affecting millions of producers. The next two cases demonstrate the power of a more recent agricultural IP strategy.

Let's look at how Sunkist oranges has used Intellectual Property Business tools, collaboration, brand positioning, ownership, and enforcement. Sunkist transformed from a small cooperative of very poor California orange growers in the late 1800s to a powerful brand with its name on over 600 products in 45 countries, all owned, controlled, and producing revenue for Sunkist.

Looking back: In 1893, Sunkist Growers, Inc. was a cooperative created by independent farmers who banded together to consider how to earn more profit from their product. At the time, an orange was a commodity, grown very plentifully in many places in the world, prolifically in the US in California and Florida.

Also, oranges had not yet taken "their place" as the go to fruit for breakfast juices. The orange growers were out-numbered in competition, out powered in markets and grew a commodity product that was relatively fragile, lasting a mere few weeks after harvest in cool conditions, not particularly robust for shipping long distances.

Sunkist evolved into a corporation formed by orange farmers' cooperatives and orange producing businesses. Ownership of the Sunkist trademark was acquired in 1926. Sunkist then opened distribution companies in many countries around the world, very far from their California roots. Opening and owning distribution companies enabled Sunkist to control the profits their brand was earning in 45 countries.

Consider Sunkist merchandise licensing. When the brand name, Sunkist, is licensed to outside companies for use on orange-related products, such as orange liquor, for example, the standard market rate for licensing would be 5 percent of retail price. By the mid-1980s, Sunkist had developed such a profitable licensing strategy that the merchandise licensing royalties were earning more income than that of the oranges. Sunkist revenues went from $13 million to nearly $1.2 billion in a 10-year period, with licensing revenue contributing substantially. Another advantage of merchandise licensing is there are no production costs on the side of Sunkist to achieve licensing revenue. The licensing revenue thus contributes more directly to profits.

Sunkist positioned the corporation well, through the acquisition of trademarks, and merchandise licensing, alongside strict brand control to create a successful IP story – an IP business success story that is at once amazing *and* replicable!

Contrast with failing IP strategies

In these cases involving cumulatively about 12 million producers, we found the IP tool was not the pivotal factor determining success or failure for the producers. There are, for example, examples of trademarks that failed to produce increased income, and geographical indications (GIs) that did not serve the farmer or producers well, defined by increased income or increased share of retail value. In some cases, the focus on the IP tool without control or enforcement, and in some cases, without positioning the product and the business correctly led to grave disappointment.

As one case in particular, Ceylon tea from Sri Lanka is an example wherein the IP strategy has not proven effective with unfortunate implications. Consider that Ceylon tea is arguably a distinctive tea and is in demand across many countries. Since it involves around 2 million tea farmers, it is a nucleus of the Sri Lankan economy. The tea farmers and exporters of Sri Lankan Ceylon tea face a difficult problem. Counterfeit tea labeled Ceylon tea that is not from Sri Lanka has flooded the world. By some estimates, about three-fourths of the "Ceylon Tea" sold globally is not grown in or exported by Sri Lanka, despite the country holding a geographical indication (GI).[21] The case of Ceylon tea contrasts with the historical success cases highlighted in this chapter.

The pivotal factors differentiating success over a historical time period that enables us to look back and truly assess differences are the combination of:

- A distinctive product.
- Intangible value and price differential from that of commodity markets.
- Positioning of the product with marketing, branding, and retail market focus.
- Import company ownership.
- Effective stakeholder organizations, owned and operated by the producers.
- The appropriate IP tool, as GIs are not enforced in all countries, and Trademarks alone do not produce income, but trademarks with licensing are more effective.
- Effective support, training, and effective enforcement to protect the brand.

Summary

IP business is demonstrable in the historical record with success cases involving hundreds of years of low-income farmer and producer work to develop unique processes, and protect their specialized knowledge. The IP business positioning method has current, transformational cases involving about 20 million producers and their families. We have also demonstrated that IP business positioning is not mysterious or foreign, gimmicky, faddish, or rhetorical empowerment without results. It is a tried and true and replicable method. The question then begging for attention is why IP business is not being implemented more widely by international aid and development with multi-billion dollar expenditures in Africa and LDCs?

The following chapter provides a perspective on this question, with a brief history of the largest aid and international development countries. It outlines their historical trajectory as well as new trends toward sustainable business. The chapter intends not to critique, but to show the historical and political construct, the evolution toward business and why an advanced model is needed for developing IP businesses in developing countries.

Notes

1 A.J. Koinm, "Christopher Merret's use of experiment notes," Rec. R. Soc. Lond. 54 (1), 2000, pp. 23–32.
2 An example of this is the invention of the "riddling rack" by Madame Clicquot (the widow of Clicquot). This rack boosted the production and sales of champagne throughout France.
3 In the United States, the Bureau of Alcohol, Tobacco, and Firearms acts as the enforcement entity as stated in the Lanham Act. This enables US winemakers to label sparkling wine products as champagne as long as they display the designation of origin on the bottle. However, the US wine industry does not use the label for US sparkling wine.
4 There are many documents written by Napoleon that affirm this statement after his defeat at Waterloo, and are cited by other leaders such as Winston Churchill. There are entire marketing campaigns by famous champagne brands such as Mouet centered on this statement.
5 Bulletin of the Comité Champagne, 2014.
6 T. Stevenson, ed., *The Sotheby's Wine Encyclopedia* (4th ed.). New York: Dorling Kindersley, 2005, pp. 169–178.
7 Export volume and pricing taken at low average, with some bottles of French champagne exported at over $100.00/bottle.
8 M. Brindle and R. Layton, "Geographical indications: 10 cases of success and failure," prepared for the USPTO, January 5, 2016.
9 M. Jackson, *Whisky: The definitive world guide*, New York: Dorling Kindersley, 2005, p. 88.
10 The Scotch Whisky Association website (www.scotch-whisky.org.uk/understanding-scotch/faqs), accessed November, 2015.
11 Ibid.
12 J. Henley, "How the world fell in love with whisky," *The Guardian*, April 15, 2011, London.
13 The Scotch Whisky Association website (www.scotch-whisky.org.uk/understanding-scotch/history-of-scotch), accessed May 2016.
14 A. Park, "Marketing and protecting geographical indications around the world – The view from the Scotch Whisky Association," Worldwide Symposium on Geographical Indications, WIPO, Geneva, 2013.
15 Ibid.
16 L. Low, The Scotch Whisky Association Report, pp. 12–15, 2014.
17 SWA Legal report, Lindesay Low, SWA website publication, Legal Report, 2014, pp. 12–15.
18 M. Kazuko and Y. Tomoko, *French cheeses*. London: Dorling Kindersley, 1996, p. 178.
19 Overall, the US leads in cheese production, followed by Germany, and France is the third in cheese production (1,941,750 metric tons), compared to the US at over 5 million metric tons.
20 Data from the Gourmet Store, 508 Delaware Avenue, West Pittston, PA 18643.
21 Data from the United States Patent and Trademark Office (USPTO), Alexandria, VA, 2015.

10

THE POWER OF INTERNATIONAL DEVELOPMENT

Historical trends and challenges

We have shown how business positioning strategies can help to overcome weak negotiating power and trade isolation. The problems of trade isolation and distance from more lucrative retail markets and relative paucity of sufficient transport infrastructure in many countries have compounded the challenges in trading with more powerful importing companies. Millions of rural farmers and producers of distinctive products are separated by long distances from export ports. The challenges cannot be overcome by traditional agri-business methods as the prices paid to farmers and producers are altogether too low to overcome the costs of getting goods to export.

The preceding chapters have demonstrated that for distinctive products, by being positioned correctly and utilizing the tools of business ownership, dramatic income increases are possible, and the method can overcome the challenges of distance to market and low returns. We have also shown that the scale of opportunity affords a viable route for millions of Africans and LDC farmers, producers, and artisans to forge a pathway out of poverty and low incomes.

One final piece of the puzzle remains, as summarized by the following questions:

- If this method of creating sustainable business practices by positioning African distinctive products and producing businesses is a powerful solution why hasn't it been done more widely?
- Moreover, and most pointedly, why have international development agencies and traditional aid failed to enable remote Africa to move out of deep poverty, though aid agency workers are highly motivated and many billions have been spent?
- While aid and development have accomplished many valiant things, why hasn't business methodology been in sharper focus?

- Can a portion of the cumulative billions of dollars of aid now be pivoted for more sustainable, effective outcomes for LDCs?

In this chapter, and to address these questions, we will briefly describe the history of International Development, focused mainly on the two countries that provide the largest amounts of international aid to Africa – the United States Agency for International Development (USAID) and the UK Department for International Development (DFID). These two agencies are far from being the only development agencies,; however, we focus on them as their policies and practices have the longest historical time frame and provide the largest amount of aid. Also, DFID often takes the lead in trying innovative examples for other European, Canadian, and Asian agencies and their practices and policies are thus modeled. The intention here is to summarize patterns, and touch on the areas where aid for trade is "stuck." There is momentum to pivot the mindset that has kept international aid locked in past mental models. That which keeps international aid and development stuck, keeps Africa stuck.

One hypothesis is that the current model in aid and development largely addresses symptoms of poverty rather than root causes of trade inequity. Changing a model that addresses symptoms rather than root causes is hard, expensive, and challenging, but it is doable, and ultimately less costly than indefinitely continuing to treat the symptoms of poverty.

In this chapter, we will explore:

- The roughly 50-year history of the world's two largest aid donors: USAID as the largest and DFID as a leader that is followed by the world.
- Why international development is focused on symptoms of poverty, rather than root causes of poverty, despite billions of dollars of input alongside a sincere, well-educated army of African and foreign aid and development workers.
- How aid dollars are filtered through large agencies with institutional agendas.
- The development context into which a new method must fit.
- Why the establishment of more powerful African and LDC country business has *not* been a focus of major aid donors.
- What are the new trends in international development that point to more business investment and are laying foundations for a new business model?
- And, how can we change the mindset to bring development strategies for Africa and LDCs into the twenty-first century more effectively, more quickly, given the resources, the will, and the capacity to do so?

The history of USAID

International development had a start. It has a history. Some aspects of aid have worked; some have worked less well, and some have failed. We are defining "aid" for our discussion in this chapter as major aid and development from the west and Australia and Japan, also major aid donors – the US, the UK, DFID, the German, French, Swedish, Canadian, South Korean, Japanese, Australian, New Zealand, and Dutch aid programs. These agencies have some variance in their approach. But, to understand how we got to a situation of relative powerlessness in Africa, it is important to understand the historical landscape and mindset of international aid. It is beyond the scope of this book to provide an exhaustive comparative history of aid. Here, we summarize several important aspects of international aid, to highlight why aid has not been primarily focused on business creation, and why the time has come for a business model for the twenty-first century.

1 Aid and international development is a relatively young field

It is important to remember that the field of international development is relatively young and is tasked with a very large set of problems and challenging issues. International development began as a program spearheaded by the United States, post-World War II as the Marshall Plan. President John F. Kennedy turned the program into an international movement. The idea to seriously assist poor countries began with USAID (The United States Agency for International Development) officially in 1961. International development is still at a young stage – the overall global movement to systematically assist developing countries outside of church supported work that we call International Development is only about 50 years old. The best may yet be ahead, and learning from and pivoting past failures to success is sensible.

The goal of USAID when it first began is characterized by this quote from John F. Kennedy:

> There is no escaping our obligations: our moral obligations as a wise leader and good neighbor in the interdependent community of free nations – our economic obligations as the wealthiest people in a world of largely poor people, as a nation no longer dependent upon the loans from abroad that once helped us develop our own economy – and our political obligations as the single largest counter to the adversaries of freedom.[1]

When JFK inaugurated USAID, it was built on the principles and assumptions of the post-World War II Marshall Plan. This was to rebuild infrastructure in Europe alongside rebuilding economies largely to prevent the spread of communism, and to enable stable economies, and markets for US exports. Though simple enough in its aspirations, this philosophy characterized USAID policy for its formative decade. When USAID was created, there had never been a single agency charged with foreign economic development. On November 3, 1961, USAID was born and with it a spirit of progress and innovation. In the early decades, the agency focused its programming almost entirely on these basics: Food security; food and nutrition; population planning; health; education; and human resource development.

The institution's history is important to understand as policies are shaped by and often reside in history. These do not disappear or readily fade with the passage of time. One mindset dominated aid to Africa: using engineering programs for building infrastructure. USAID had two goals – the first was to reduce poverty by increasing production in poor countries, and the second was to diminish threats of communism by helping countries to prosper under capitalism.

By the 1970s, USAID stressed a "basic human needs" approach, a focus on food, population planning, health, education, and human resource development. In the 1980s, USAID shifted its priorities to include an acknowledgment that developing free markets would be advantageous. While still keeping its commitment to broad-based economic growth, emphasizing employment and income through agricultural revitalization, it also worked to expand domestic markets in developing countries.

A critical point that affects the present distribution of aid is this: Between 1980 and 1990, development activities were increasingly channeled through private voluntary organizations (PVOs), and aid shifted from individual projects to large programs.[2] In the 1980s, a term entered the language of USAID that has continued into the twenty-first century. "Sustainable development" became a goal, defined as:

> Sustainable development is development that meets the needs of the present, without compromising the ability of future generations to meet their own needs.[3]

As USAID entered the twenty-first century, there were two major wars ongoing, in Afghanistan and Iraq. Government officials were once again calling for reform of how the agency conducts business and USAID was called on to help those two countries rebuild government, infrastructure, civil society, and basic services such as health care and education. The Agency began an expansive campaign to reach out to new partner organizations – including the private sector and foundations – to extend the reach of foreign assistance.[4] Herein, trade and assistance to build agri-businesses became additional foci for USAID. However, the basic concept was that infusion into what Africa and LDCs were themselves farming and exporting was the best way to help – supporting rather than innovating. What we can see from the first 50 years of USAID is that basic human needs and infrastructure, rather than business, have been the priority.

Currently, USAID staff work in more than 100 countries around the world with the same overarching goals that President Kennedy outlined 50 years ago – furthering America's foreign policy interests in expanding democracy and free markets while also extending a helping hand to people struggling to make a better life, recover from a disaster or striving to live in a free and democratic country. Part of this effort is supporting health, with an emphasis on maternal and child health.

USAID, and UK Aid (DFID) as the second largest aid agency, are followed by Canadian Aid (CIDA) and French (AFD) and German, Norwegian, and other EU countries, Japan and South Korea. Many donor countries, including the US, have first and foremost government-funded agencies with government agendas. While the billions of dollars in aid and sustainable development have accomplished a great deal against the challenges of poverty, designing businesses is not the foremost priority of international aid agencies. Rather, meeting basic human needs, building infrastructure, and increasing production have dominated the institution's first 50 years.

FIGURE 10.1 President John F. Kennedy speaks to USAID directors and deputy directors on the White House lawn, June 8, 1962
Source: R. Knudsen photo, USAID website, as viewed July 2015.

2 Aid has become institutionalized inside of bureaucratic structures

Aid is run by government agencies – large, bureaucratic organizations. Though a simple and obvious concept, the implications have far reaching consequence. For one, aid agencies are not run by leaders with business training for the most part. Amongst aid agencies, USAID has the largest aid budget, followed by the UK's Department of International Development (DFID). International development began by governments in institutions, and has grown up along bureaucratic lines. Not atypically, agencies have an institutionalized life of their own. And, as development has grown to have multi-billion dollar budgets, staff and systems, and educational institutions feeding new employees into its ranks, US development assistance has become like many large institutions and bureaucracies. Institutionalization and power structures, established programs, and ways of doing things within bureaucracies are not easy to change. In addition, the largest aid donor in the world, USAID contracts out its work to large firms such as Chemonics and DAI, which are also large institutions with bureaucracies and thousands of employees each.

International aid institutions in countries such as the US and the UK want to be effective in the delivery of aid dollars, and indeed focus on outcome measures, by spending appreciable resources on monitoring and evaluation. However, large government institutions are not known for being flexible to new and entrepreneurial ways of doing things, while reporting to a public. Pet programs, divisions, authority structures, incentives to repeat the known, and evaluation systems – all of these aspects of organized bureaucracies do not generally applaud innovation. Finally, career success is often the product of success or failed projects and programs, thus incentivizing aid to keep up with known and more predictable projects over strongly entrepreneurial ones.

3 Aid is managed by external contractors with institutionalized structures

Consider, for example, the 2014 budgeting of USAID dollars.[5] In July, 2015, the USAID reported its top 15 vendors as:

1. WORLD BANK GROUP:
2. WORLD FOOD PROGRAM: $1.5 billion
3. CHEMONICS: $502 million
4. PFSCM: $400 million
5. FHI 360: $351 million
6. UNITED NATIONS CHILDREN'S FUND: $300 million
7. JOHN SNOW, INCORPORATED: $285 million
8. DAI WASHINGTON: $263 million
9. MANAGEMENT SCIENCES FOR HEALTH, INC.: $245 million

10. JHPIEGO CORPORATION: $219 million
11. ABT ASSOCIATES INC.: $217 million
12. RTI INTERNATIONAL: $207 million
13. CRS.ORG: Catholic Relief Services: $206 million
14. MERCY CORPS: $197 million
15. GAVI ALLIANCE: $175 million

While the World Bank received over $2 billion dollars, as the highest alloca-
tion, and the World Food Program, $1.5 billion, note also that the independent
company, DAI received over $262 million and Chemonics, over $500 million.

As USAID subcontracts its work, organizations such as Chemonics and DAI
occupy large buildings in Washington, DC and its surrounds with all of the
institutional mechanisms of large organizations with infrastructure to support
3,000 staff and subcontractors. Career specialists at government aid organizations
move amongst the institutions, working at USAID HQ and between and among
various subcontracting agencies, further solidifying some institutional challenges
to decision making.

As one example, Chemonics, to which $502 million was allocated from the
USAID budget, was founded in 1975 and hosts over 3,000 employees in
Washington, DC.[6] Although Chemonics was highly criticized after the Haiti
earthquakes, after receiving almost $200 million in predominantly no-bid con-
tracts, their revenue stream has grown. Chemonics does effective poverty alleviation projects and engages in significant monitoring and evaluation of its
projects. However, when we consider who is in charge of decision making for
poor people and who decides what is working and what is not working, the
analysis is complex, as subcontractors with incentives for project growth influence
decision making.

Another large consulting firm, based across town from USAID, is Development Alternatives, INC (DAI). This employee-owned firm opened in 1970, and
reports almost 2,500 employees. Unlike Chemonics, with non-competitiveness
for a large volume of its USAID grants, DAI reports that it enables vendors "to
compete for all of its contracts" believing this provides an important measure of
objectivity. They also have 60,000 consultants in their database.

An NGO, TechnoServe, provides business solutions in 30 countries, having
started about the same time as Chemonics and DAI. TechnoServe began in 1968,
and reports to have benefitted 1.6 million people in 2015. One challenge of the
larger institutions is that when a project fails or has serious challenges, such as in
the TechnoServe Mozambique cashew project, the agencies seem to engage in
numerous additional rounds of funding. For example, in the first phase of a project to increase income from Mozambique cashews for over 1 million cashew
farmers, the project restarted old processing plants and branded cashews with an
export brand "Zambique." However, the processed cashews were still sold to
importers, one of whom famously discarded the branded packaging. Due to low

incomes and low quality of work in resurrected processing plants, a second round of funding was provided by USAID. We note that TechnoServe had then several rounds of funding to work on the challenges. While not inherently wrong, the large, institutionalized aid machine enables patterns of re-funding without re-examining the business models and fundamental decisions of USAID.

Lest we begin to sound like the cynical author of the *Lords of Poverty*,[7] the critical point is that if we want to understand what is being done and why change in the international development sphere is hard, it is important to recognize entrenched mechanisms that are hard to change. Decisions, directions, and implementation of USAID projects are managed by what has grown to be an empire of consultants and bureaucracies. The institutions' missions may be focused on eradicating poverty, but are arguably equally copacetic with maintaining the growth, reputation, and ongoing capacity of the contractor to acquire future contracts.

To this, drawing on organizational literature, we know that change often comes from the periphery. New ideas and new models are often harder to bring to institutionalized bureaucracies which often find it more difficult to adapt and adopt new ideas. This has been true in the computer industry with Apple originating from the periphery and in numerous industries. Social change also often comes from the periphery.[8] We are witnessing this in the waves of innovation from social entrepreneurs in developing countries.

4 Aid has not been focused on business creation

The majority of staff at the largest aid organizations and their subcontractors hold degrees and experience in government, politics, international relations, development, and a host of other excellent subjects, but most typically, not in business. TechnoServe and other large contractors claim business skills, but work within the contracting framework of USAID policies on where to put business resources.

While business trained subcontractors are routinely brought in to assist USAID, business people do not generally set program policy or priorities. If thousands of employees who administer international aid are not themselves trained in business, it is reasonable to assume that implementing twenty-first-century business development is not a priority, even if it is global business best practice. USAID have policies that are based on nineteenth- and early twentieth-century growth patterns that ignore the overwhelming dominance of intangible value in global consumption.

5. A prevailing mindset in USAID to Africa is that Africa and LDCs can benefit from efforts aimed at low wage production, but are unable to manage western business models

As one leader in the Office of the US Trade Representative reflected on low wage production, "It is Africa's turn to do low-cost manufacturing." The sincerity behind the comment was that African countries need to employ large numbers of people in factories, no matter if the wage is below a living wage – it is the way to begin to "catch up."

A recent report from TechnoServe on Mozambique cashews asserts across the top: "The place for the factory is by the side of the farm" (citing a management article of 1913).[9] This early twentieth-century thinking may have been good for manufacturing in 1913, as America copied the industrial revolution tone. A vital assumption to processing investment is that there are profit margins to be made in such forms of "value added." Processing is a low margin business due to intense competition and over-supply of global processing capability. When the first round of applying a faulty assumption failed, regrettably it was repeated.

When one considers what a corporation would do in this situation, this strategy applied is startling. African business can own processing factories, but there are foreign competitors who have built high quality control and low-cost processing of cashews, notably in India.

What would a corporation do? A corporation would first position the product in final consumer retail markets that reward distinctive quality with consumer prices generating retail income. A corporation would simultaneously position the producing sector it owns in control of the retail brand that is presented to consumers. A corporation would be well versed in the value of its brand and promote this brand via smart marketing in ways that resonate with consumers. A corporation would, of course, employ enforcement to then protect its brand and property, just as a watchman would be hired to protect a factory. The brand is more valuable than the products of a factory, and must be protected.

Finally, and not least, a corporation would further assure quality by controlling the supply chain, as much as possible, certainly using the highest quality processing in the world to advance the reputation of the brand with consumers. Processing in Mozambique could have been best developed later, financed by the enhanced cash flow from the increased export income and targeted at the precise quality standards that built the retail market. New Mozambique processing factories, in the field or anywhere else, would flourish so much better given time and internal funding to meet consumers' standards. Jobs in the processing sector would have been much more secure. Higher value captured would have paid for processing.

These tactics are within reach of African and LDC producers. We can help them to get there, or we can repeat failures by using a twentieth-century sequence of development for opportunities that don't exist anymore. African development is generally not well served with early twentieth-century industrial production business models.

The bottom billion

Consider Sir Paul Collier's point of view. Collier, professor of economics and public policy at Oxford University, penned a popular book called, *The Bottom*

Billion.[10] Herein, he outlines four causative reasons or "poverty traps" why the bottom billion remain in poverty, despite appreciable efforts to help them:

1. The "Conflict trap" with civil wars destroying gains and costing an average of $64 billion per civil war.
2. The "natural resource trap": This refers to economies dominated with natural resources such as oil, diamonds, gold or minerals that beget corruption, lack of taxation, and accountability with great income disparity.
3. "Landlocked with bad neighbors trap": This refers to the numerous countries in Africa, in particular that are far from borders, but who also have conflict in neighboring countries. Collier argues that the resultant effect is to spill millions of refugees into relatively stable countries who themselves lack sufficient resources to care for their own citizenry.
4. Bad governance.

We appreciate Paul Collier's tome on international development, sometimes called the best book on development as it is clear and highlights four areas where poverty seems intractable. We appreciate that Collier is trying to explain the massive issue of poverty with compassion and succinctness and to focus on the big challenge of the people who will be the last to come out of extreme poverty.

However, we agree with some criticism by William Easterly[11] who believes Collier has confused causation with symptoms, such as conflict being a symptom rather than cause. These four areas may indeed contribute to poverty. However, the core reasons Africa has some of the poorest people in the world are chronically low income, very weak negotiating power, no power over foreign supply chains to final markets, extreme trade isolation, and what amounts to almost wholesale theft of the retail value of their fine, distinctive products. This poverty-level income does contribute to other aspects of poverty such as conflict. Landlocked countries are indeed problematic with millions who are trade isolated, but there are also millions of people in countries with ports but who are too remote, with poor infrastructure, and are hard pressed to live with the incomes from commodity markets. Only a strategy that secures revenue from non-physical elements (intangible value) can build economic activity in regions of extreme trade isolation.

It is important to keep perspective. There are those who argue that Africa will *always* be poor because, well, that is the way it is, or there is corruption in government, or the poor will always be with us. This perspective must not win because it is not true. Receiving 3–5 percent returns from distinctive retail products is costing billions of dollars because it reduces income, and creates ongoing need for aid. It must and can be changed.

Africans are quite capable of creating world-class businesses with world-class incomes and need not be aid-dependent indefinitely. However, a new model is needed that first, is based on this premise; and second, is willing to focus development efforts and invest resources toward effective business solutions, not merely the overwhelming symptoms. The last billion people in extreme poverty include many who produce high quality distinctive export products that generate hundreds of millions of dollars in wealthy retail markets globally. To remove the obstacles to these producers overcoming extreme poverty involves changing the business positioning of export sectors including the producers. Through rural multipliers, the direct impact of increased income for producers will spread to raise the economy of whole regions, such as northern Uganda.

6 Africa became poor through centuries of western colonialism and not from laziness, shifty governments, or inability to conduct business

African countries are commemorating only 50–60 years at best being free from colonial rule with all the related issues that centuries of colonial rule entails. Every country in Africa, except one – Ethiopia – was once colonized. The most damaging aspect of colonial rule was the destruction of complex economies (particularly Ghana and Zimbabwe) in order to convert colonies to combined producers of primary inputs to industrial production and also markets for industrial goods from the colonizing country. After decolonization wars and the energy of the Third World movement, many Africans moved past anger and expected a better life after independence.

The factor that was not expected was the continued dominance of exporting sectors in African countries by European importers that became the multinational corporations of the modern world. Globalization of commodities was and is harsh on poor producers who face instability in pricing and hence income. The global move to rapid expansion since 2000 in specialized retail stores offering fine teas, spices, oils, as well as fine coffees will not benefit the producers of these products significantly until the export price and supply chain is broken out of the commodity pricing framework. If the retail price is 20 times the export price, it is clear that a large opportunity exists for a more just outcome. The solution is to simply ask "what would a corporation do?" (if in the same position as the African producing business making a highly valued product).

7 International development aid has made progress against deep poverty

The focus has been on the Millennium Development Goals (MDGs) to:

- Halve the number of people living in extreme poverty and hunger
- Ensure that all children receive primary education
- Promote sexual equality and give women a stronger voice
- Reduce child death rates
- Improve the health of mothers
- Combat HIV & AIDS, malaria, and other diseases
- Make sure the environment is protected

While great advances have been made, we note that IP business positioning has not been a goal. As evidence of progress, USAID reported some noteworthy advances in 2015:

- Mortality rates among children under five years of age fell globally by 41 percent between 1990 and 2011.[12]
- Primary school enrollment has increased from 59 percent to 77 percent in sub-Saharan Africa over the past decade.[13]
- Malaria deaths fell over 20 percent worldwide in the last decade.[14]
- And, 89 percent of the world's 6.1 billion people had access to improved drinking water sources.[15]

In order to better assess the progress of international aid, it is vital to look to the underlying, root causes of poverty. Otherwise, aid will remain stuck as it addresses and continues to address the symptoms of poverty, rather than root causes.

What the US government has done to employ IP business positioning for African development

The USPTO and the Office of the US Trade Representative have both shown their understanding that twenty-first-century business models are centered on Intellectual Property.[16] Given the depth of knowledge of IP at the USPTO and width of examples of IP Business Positioning being used by corporations in developed countries, it is to be hoped that USAID will take a renewed look at the opportunity for poverty alleviation.

Intraregional trade in Africa

USAID has supported work on building trade within the countries of the East African Community and other regional trade structures in Africa and elsewhere. There has been some disappointment at the growth of intraregional trade, partly due to neighbors growing similar products. The authors simply state that IP business growth will be an expanding part of the future of twenty-first-century Africa, so an additional case for building African skills in IP Business Positioning can be made with long-term forecasts of the value of brand-intensive consumption over the next four decades.

Root causes of poverty

Africa is poor largely because it has been colonized for centuries; its people enslaved; its resources stripped and stolen. Even today, modern day corporations operate under the assumption that LDC export sectors earning a 2–3 percent share of retail value is acceptable. As the authors have experienced, when presenting to importers that some African exporters of distinctive products are receiving export prices that are only 1 percent of retail prices. "Well, that is okay. At least they are getting 1% and they are used to this."

That is not the voice of a mere bullish corporate, but an uninformed western consumer, and reflects a mindset that has done great, ongoing harm. It also reflects an understandable, but unfortunate human tendency to view things as okay if they are carried on long enough.

Long history of colonial rule

As noted, of the 54 countries in Africa, all but one was once under colonial rule. Colonial rule by the French, British, Belgians, Dutch, Germans, Portuguese, and Turkish controlled virtually all of Africa for the nineteenth century and the first half of the twentieth century. Many African countries achieved independence merely about 50 years ago such as Kenya in 1963. Countries only 50 years, or less, out of colonization have challenges. If we consider South Sudan, the world's youngest nation, it holds only about 100 miles of paved roads in a country the size of France.

The US, for example, at 50 years after its independence (the 1820s) was hardly a picture of equality and prosperity. When America first gained independence, America was a tattered place. More than one-third of Americans were enslaved and tragically, remained so for another century; fully 50 percent of the population were women who were not allowed to vote, own property, or attend institutions of higher learning at one of the nation's few colleges. Aside from an elite class, most of the population was poor, and a century later, remained largely so until the industrial revolution ushered in greater prosperity, but concurrently, great wage gaps. By and large, the overall population scraped by as farmers either on their own land, or on the land of larger landowners, or they were craftsmen, and in service. The population was comprised of more non-literates than literates, and the country had large problems such as a need for infrastructure, clean water, and sewerage.

Jumping ahead just 20 years, the US engaged in a very bloody and divisive Civil War on behalf of a large segment of its enslaved population. And, even after its famed industrial revolution, the population of the US quadrupled between the 1870s and 1920s with large groups of immigrants, and urban squalor, low-paying wage jobs, and entire cities with slum populations.

The sharp point of this brief historical summary is that America, too, had humble beginnings 50 years out of colonialism, and 100 years further. But, it did not remain poor. There are those in international development who take the perspective that African nations, too, will take this long and laborious trajectory from colonization to relative stability and eventual middle-income status. Should African and other poor nations need to wade through the same trajectory – from raw manufacturing; pennies on the dollar returns for commodity goods; and build up their methods, technology, education, and eventually earn more? After all, many countries have propelled large percentages of their populations forward out of poverty into developed nation status, including Poland and South Korea in recent history.

There are development strategies suitable to each decade, each age. Industrial progress from the lowest quality goods upwards is basically a lost method that had its time to propel a number of countries to development. Intense competition and the virtually unlimited supply of industrial workers in China alone took all the profit margin out of this strategy at least a decade ago. Africans will find the twenty-first-century strategies and use them, leaving the nineteenth- and twentieth-century concepts far behind.

There is a better way of reducing income inequality that is not based on the same long stages of production but on higher wages through IP business. There is also a strong macro-economic argument. Low-wage production-based systems were nineteenth- and twentieth-century phenomena, but if African countries take the route of low-wage production, they are unlikely to ever catch up in income levels. That is because other nations such as China and India and other Asian countries have cut the costs of production so dramatically, that products emergent from China will tend to undercut prices, leaving the pathway of following an "industrial revolution" model of advancing production, enhancing quality, and increasing exports at low prices a failing strategy for the twenty-first century.

In sum, the traps that keep Africa in poverty are historical, and structural, and oftentimes, inadvertently reinforced by the very agencies intending to assist. The premises above form a mindset that is diverting Africa from more modern strategies. Limiting Africans to the same slow trajectory of increased production and processing is unlikely to reverse the poverty trap.

How is aid spent?

Where aid dollars are spent also provides insight into poverty and development traps. In 2013, the total aid dollars provided, defined as ODA (Official Development Assistance), was $134.8 billion. This represents a little over 6 percent increase since falling in 2011 and 2012. According to the OECD, the $134.8 billion was an all-time high.[17] The countries that gave the largest amount were the US, UK, Germany, Japan, and France in that order. While $134.8 billion is an impressive amount of money, it is important to note that the total provided by western countries toward international aid is less than 1 percent of the total GNI (Gross National Income) of those countries, with the exception of Denmark, Luxembourg, Norway, and Sweden whose international aid budgets are slightly higher than 1 percent of GNI.

The G7 countries provided 70 percent of total net ODA in 2013, and the EU countries alone a little over half at 52 percent. The US remained the largest donor by value with net ODA of $31.5 billion, an increase of 1.3 percent in real terms from 2012. Most of the increase was due to humanitarian aid and support for fighting HIV/AIDS.[18]

The total aid to Sub-Saharan Africa in 2015 was $8.7 billion. While we can all agree that is a large sum of money, for perspective, the US spent $1.2 billion on fireworks for the 4th of July celebrations across the nation in 2015, creating displays of roughly 30 minutes on average to celebrate the nation's birthday and entertain the public.[19]

If a portion, even 10 percent of the USAID budget for Africa were pivoted to create IP businesses, the return would exceed expectations and create sustainable businesses based on distinctive products that are already there.

In our opinion, US expenditure on intangible values is now so great that many exporting countries could live entirely on distinctive exports to the US.

Trend toward aid for trade

More recently, the US and other countries have been seeking ways to improve trade, the concept of Aid for Trade deriving from the Doha summit in 2001. The Obama Administration, for example, initiated the "Trade over Aid" program. USAID provided $133.9 million to support key commitments and investments in Africa, including Power Africa ($76.7 million) to increase access to reliable, cleaner power for economic growth, as part of the Administration's expanded $300 million annual commitment. Trade Investment Capacity Building, including Trade Africa and Investment Hubs ($47.2 million), of which $30 million is part of the Administration's $75 million commitment to align, focus, and expand current USG bilateral and regional trade programs in sub-Saharan Africa; and Young African Leaders Initiative ($10 million). There are also smaller amounts ($190 million) to improve technology and innovations.

Another area where African trade has been supported is in the policy of AGOA (African Growth and Opportunity Act). In its initial phase, Trade Africa focused on the Partner States of the East African Community (EAC) – Burundi, Kenya, Rwanda, Tanzania, and Uganda. Within this region, Trade Africa sought to double intraregional trade in the EAC and increase EAC exports to the United States by 40 percent.

There are also a number of trade facilitation goals, including reducing by 15 percent the average time needed to import or export a container from the ports of Mombasa or Dar es Salaam to the land-locked interior, and decreasing by 30 percent the average time a truck takes to transit selected borders.

The duty free markets under AGOA resulted in a doubling of exports from the continent and $2 billion or a 24 percent increase in exported goods from Africa to the US between 2013 and 2014. However, while increased exports and duty free markets are a good outcome, if increased production does not equate to increased prices, it is limiting.[20]

Intraregional trade in Africa

USAID and other donors have supported work on building trade within the countries of the East African Community and other regional trade structures in Africa and elsewhere. There has been some disappointment at the growth of intraregional trade, partly due to neighbors growing similar products.

At a UK parliamentary inquiry in April 2016, Ali Mufuruki, chairman of Trademark East Africa, asked if it is possible to trade distinctive products across Africa. We replied that indeed a number of distinctive products have become part of brand-intensive consumption in Africa, particularly apparent among wealthy consumers in Nigeria, Kenya, and in capital cities across the continent.

Estimating the future rate at which people emerging from poverty will become brand-intensive consumers is not the purpose of this book. The authors simply state that growth in the use of Intellectual Property methods will be an expanding part of the future of twenty-first-century Africa. The African IP Trust at its formation meeting in Addis Ababa in 2011, declared a priority on building African skills in IP business positioning.

The symptoms of poverty

While there have been advances toward supporting trade over aid under the Obama administration, the great majority of aid continues to go toward the symptoms of poverty. For example, over $3 billion in USAID was toward managed humanitarian assistance for emergency food supplies and the underlying causes of food insecurity, assistance to internally displaced persons, and victims of conflict and natural disaster. And $2.8 billion was spent on maternal/childhood disease prevention and care. There are also USAID and State Dept. initiatives to stabilize governments. As we can see, the majority of USAID directed to Africa goes largely toward humanitarian assistance, conflict, and maternal and childhood prevention and care, comprising about $6 billion of the $8 billion or three-fourths of USAID. While $8 billion dollars of aid and assistance is generous, the creation of businesses using the most modern strategies has not been a demonstrable USAID priority.

It is our opinion that USAID Trade Africa expenditures could be better applied to the 97 percent of retail value generated by distinctive products that does not reach Africa than only working on the 3 percent of retail value that does reach Africa.

The UK aid program

DFID (Department for International Development) is the second largest bilateral provider of international aid to East Africa and complements the four biggest donors: the World Bank, the USA, the European Union, and the African Development Bank. It was founded in 1964 under a Labour Government.

In 2015–2016, UK total ODA (Overseas Development Assistance) was planned to be $8.6 billion official, sustaining the government commitment to 0.7 percent of GNI (Gross National Income), a higher percentage than the US. The largest region of assistance from DFID was Africa.[21] The total ODA by the UK has continued to increase. The total UK ODA has increased by 30.2 percent (£2,660 million) between 2012 and 2013, up from £8,802 million to £11,462 million – the largest increase since the ODA definition was first introduced. The generosity of the UK aid program (DFID) and the overall social consciousness found among the British people toward poverty and supporting programs such as Fair Trade is formidable.

The Rt. Hon. Justine Greening, Secretary of State for International Development, reported, "There has been good progress towards the Millennium Development Goals (MDGs), with a decline in the proportion of people living in poverty from 31% to 24.5%, and particularly towards MDGs on hunger, gender equality, HIV/AIDS treatment and access to safe water."[22] And, while DFID, like USAID, focuses on MDGs and humanitarian care, they also promote trade-related efforts with roughly 10 percent of their budget aimed at private sector development in 2014.

Secretary Greening, who holds an MBA, is also focused on private sector development and job creation:

> In Kenya, DFID's focus is on the private sector; job creation and market development; financial access and trade development to create 250,000 new jobs; food security; health and basic services such as reducing deaths from malaria. While meeting Millennium Development Goals (MDGs) is particularly focused, we believe that focusing on the symptoms of poverty, such as deaths from malaria and HIV/AIDS is important, crucial work, the continual focus on symptoms will never eradicate poverty unless the underlying causation is addressed.[23]

The top 10 organizations funded by DFID aid money are listed below. Thirteen of the 20 firms on the list have at least one of their offices in the United Kingdom; though of the top 10, four list headquarters outside of the UK and only one of them is based in a developing country. These firms are:

1. Crown Agents (£191.6 million)
2. PWC – Price Waterhouse Coopers (£122 million)
3. Adam Smith International (£88.4 million)
4. DAI (£58.3 million)
5. GRM Futures (£50.5 million)
6. Mott McDonald (£39.4 million)
7. Oxford Policy Management (£26.7 million)
8. Coffey (£23.7 million)

9. AbT International (£21 million)
10. Maxwell Stump (£19.9 million)[24]

Delivering aid through organizations is normative, but when assessing international aid, such as in the US or in Britain, aid is filtered through organizational realities. Organizations have agendas, and motives to maintain and advance operating budgets. For example, an enterprise known as Coffey International performs monitoring and evaluation for DFID and other UK charity organizations. As an enterprise, it has an infrastructure of its own, with concerns about profits, losses, net revenues, falling or growing "book orders," and maintaining and growing its business, as it has to answer to its private and public stakeholders. This type of filter to aid distribution matters because aid has become a business, itself. And, despite well-motivated individuals who enter aid for lofty reasons, decisions to advance the aid business are not always advances to Africa's poorest.

For example, Coffey's 2015 annual report claims $315.4 million in revenue from international development, comprising 57 percent of its total revenues of nearly $600 million. Coffey employs 2,000 people in the international development sector. Their principal role is monitoring and evaluation, attesting to value for money in projects, a good idea. According to Coffey's annual report of 2015, "International Development continued to deliver consistent returns throughout the year."[25]

For example, a grant of roughly 800,000 GBP to an NGO would carry a roughly 20,000 GBP monitoring and evaluation segment. Coffey could be contracted to perform the monitoring and evaluation, as objective outsiders attesting to value for money. This system is sensible. However, it would not be in Coffey's interest to support innovative projects that are different from current DFID priorities, and it would be in their ongoing interest to support less ambitious projects and provide assessments in tune with the interests more aligned with DFID. Their future business does not and will not emerge from grantees, but from DFID and other international development agencies.

This quote from an executive of Coffey International in the Coffey annual report reflects the complex point of view:

> International Development is now 57% of our continuing business (55% of total revenue), providing consistent and stable margins on longer-term projects. This is providing a strong and sustainable base …[26]

This example is not meant to criticize Coffey, but does underscore the politics resident in aid, tasked to deliver explicit and rather quick outcomes, and how more difficult innovative projects may be less satisfying to important gatekeepers fixed on the normative three-year period to show return on investment (ROI). In short, new business ideas carry risk, whereas tried and true areas such as schools and building health clinics are less risky, diminishing the likelihood one more notch that entrepreneurial business will be adequately supported via traditional aid routes. Despite the entrenched practices and attitudes, there is also growing awareness that yesterday's methods are not solving poverty and are spawning a movement toward private sector development.

DFID: private sector development

This summary highlights DFID's more recent focus on the value of private sector development for poverty reduction.[27]

> Businesses can have an impact on the poorest people in developing countries in a number of ways. They can act as employers of the poor or purchase the goods the poor produce. They can also supply basic goods and services that meet the needs of the poor. There may be spillover effects, both positive (such as through the dissemination of knowledge and technology) or negative (including through environmental degradation or competitive pressures on enterprises owned by the poor). Many larger firms have corporate social responsibility (CSR) programmes which aim to help the poor.

DFID has placed increasing emphasis in recent years on the importance of PSD (private sector development) for human, economic, and environmental development and humanitarian assistance. In 2008, partly in response to a report issued by the International Development Committee of the House of Commons, DFID published its strategy for PSD, *Prosperity for All: Making Markets Work*.[28]

DFID also focuses on investment opportunities:

> We know that there are investment opportunities in the poorest countries and that there are returns to be made. Driving up investment opportunities in the poorest countries is a crucial part of delivering poverty reduction. By catalyzing more private investment and deepening private sector links into communities we can multiply the reach of the private sector and increase opportunities for poor people.[29]

In her 2013 speech, Justine Greening further emphasized the connection between sustainable public and private sectors:

> But I believe you can't build a sustainable public sector without helping to build a private sector. Sustainable public services need a funding stream of tax receipts and that means a thriving private sector. A strategy to do one without the other risks a short term improvement for people in poverty without a long term plan to make sure those gains are locked in.[30]

Another stream is private sector investment, such as Unilever. "By 2020, Unilever expects developing markets to account for 70% of total sales – that's huge."[31]

It is important to note that countries such as Sweden, Canada, Japan, Germany, France, and the Netherlands have important and generous aid programs. Germany, for example, has given the third largest amount of bilateral aid. The Swedes are forward thinking and support African-owned business development. While it is beyond the scope of this book to assess each country's aid program, we have focused on USAID and also on DFID, as these larger agencies tend to set the pace, policy, and tone in development.[32]

The role of NGOs

Aside from government-based aid, non-governmental organizations are an important structure to consider in international development. The common factor uniting this group, apart from the fact that they were neither government agencies nor businesses in the traditional sense, is that they would have an avowed mission to work for a social good – whether it was as torchbearers for human rights, the environment or just "development."

Today, 30 new NGO or nonprofits are formed every day in Britain; and there are 1.5 million in the US alone. Fully 90 percent of currently existing NGOs have been launched since 1975. Though these numbers of NGOs are domestically as well as internationally based, aid to developing nations began to be distributed via NGOs more dramatically in the 1970s. Between 1975 and 1985, the amount of aid taking this NGO route shot up by 1,400 percent.

It is challenging to categorize or effectively comment on the effectiveness of NGOs, since their origins, form, missions, methods, and effectiveness vary greatly. An NGO can involve two individuals engaged in micro-credit in Bangladesh, or a hospital or enterprise to engage 5,000 people. A challenge of existing NGOs is that while countless NGOs do effective, dedicated, and efficient poverty alleviation work, the variance makes it difficult to analyze effectiveness. In addition, monitoring and evaluation of NGOs is carefully documented when NGOs contract with larger donors, but evaluating effectiveness is more difficult due to the wide distribution, variance of projects, and uncoordinated evaluation mechanisms.

Social entrepreneurs

Formal international development has been dramatically complemented by the rapid expansion of organized social entrepreneurship. If country programs in aid are governmental, often bureaucratic, and administered by large organizations, African and global social entrepreneurs are on the other end of this spectrum. The design and execution of far reaching projects is in the hands of individual social entrepreneurs, courageous, often bold and intuitive individuals believing in, and executing, world-changing ideas.

As defined by Bill Drayton, founder of Ashoka, "Social entrepreneurs are individuals with innovative solutions to society's most pressing social problems.

They are ambitious and persistent, tackling major social issues and offering new ideas for wide-scale change."[33] Rather than leaving societal needs to the government or business sectors, social entrepreneurs find what is not working and solve the problem by changing the system, spreading the solution, and persuading entire societies to take new leaps.

Bill Drayton is considered the father of social entrepreneurship, and Ashoka has a rigorous selection process for supporting social entrepreneurs. Rather than support random good ideas, the Ashoka team reviews, vets, and admits to the Ashoka support network those whose ideas are truly unique, considered system changing, rather than add-ons, and whose personal characteristics of compassion, drive, entrepreneurial skills, and knowledge warrant acceptance into the Ashoka organization.

The organization now has about 3,000 social entrepreneurs, most of whom are supported with stipends for the first three years after being elected as Ashoka fellows. As of the close of fiscal year 2013, Ashoka reported over $34,000,000 in contributions or over $41,000,000 in support and revenue.[34] There are currently 350 African Ashoka fellows, working across the African continent.

Ashoka entrepreneurs, acting with purpose and resolve, nimbly and flexibly have accomplished formidable system change in most countries in the world. Since books have been written about the Ashoka model, it is not our intention to provide an exhaustive commentary here. A sharp point is Ashoka is worth noting for the widespread vision, incredible commitment, and follow through that is changing the face of Africa and on every continent.[35] Bill Drayton has committed his considerable personal drive to promoting social entrepreneurship among youth under the heading "Everyone a Changemaker."

The social entrepreneur model is being expanded in Africa with recently formed groups spanning the African continent and promoting change making. For example, in Uganda, the Unreasonable Institute and Watson Institute support changemakers, training, and education in entrepreneurship and are carrying through on the mission that entrepreneurs, particularly young entrepreneurs in East Africa will change their countries with system-changing businesses.

Summary

While many proclaim a modicum of success the Millennium Development Goals have been at least partially achieved, inside the goal of 2015, namely to:

- Halve the number of people living in extreme poverty and hunger
- Ensure that all children receive primary education
- Promote sexual equality and give women a stronger voice
- Reduce child death rates
- Improve the health of mothers
- Combat HIV & AIDS, malaria, and other diseases

- Make sure the environment is protected
- Build a global partnership for those working in development.

The reality may well be that while progress has been made, none of these goals will be fully achieved so long as the gap between the share of retail value reaching Africa and the share that stays in richer countries continues to widen.

International aid and development is to be applauded for the ongoing generosity of its intentions against deep poverty, and real, appreciable spend. Progress has been made. There has been progress against MDGs and against all of the traditional areas with which aid and international development have long been concerned and upon which they focus as described above. There are, to be sure, sentiments toward trade over aid amongst the US and UK and all of the major western donor countries. In the US, the Office of the US Trade Representative focuses on increasing exports, which have increased appreciably out of Africa. Others focus on improved production, quality, and infrastructure.

While these are good and important measures, we believe these will not solve poverty. That is largely because the returns to African farmers and producers from distinctive exports remain too low at 3–5 percent and will not improve with increased export volume. As in many policies, the problem is not with the concept, theory or intention of large institutions, but with a failure to appreciate dramatic changes in modern business. Today, Africa competes with other countries that have mastered low wage, high, quality production of exports, some of them emerging from developing country status such as India, China, Vietnam, Malaysia, and other Asian countries.

Concerning DFID, the emergent thinking of the last decade is to advance aid to trade thinking. This often means advancing UK trade and opening doors for trade, as DFID's Director is first and foremost a government servant of the UK and must answer to the UK people. Thus, shoring up governments and eradicating extreme poverty is not only good for Africa, it is good for western trade. While that may sound cynical, it is important to note the origins of the two largest development programs in the world (USAID, and British Aid or DFID) began with these fundamental mandates.

Overall, despite international development's appreciable advances against deep poverty, the creation of sustainable business, entrepreneurship and new models such as Intellectual Property Business Positioning have not been well understood.

In this book, we have shown that a new model, which is global best practice, involves supporting African entrepreneurs, first and foremost, and enables the creation of farmer-, producer-, and artisan-owned business with greatly increased income and impact. This involves entrepreneurs, and it involves social impact investors, advocacy, training, and education. It will also require advocacy, support, and enforcement initially from organizations like the African IP Trust.

While there are, to be sure, many initiatives under way in Africa and LDCs, we have provided here a methodology backed by case study, proof of concept, and a clear way forward. Over 15 years of analysis and work has shown that there are four to five opportunities per country in Africa alone, whereby farmers, producers, and artisans and owners with distinctive products can earn $100 m more income per year. These opportunities are present and prolific. At present, the nineteenth- and twentieth-century models of development need to be augmented by models such as IP business positioning.

Notes

1 "Marking 50 years of progress," USAID website, accessed May 2016 (www.usaid.gov/news-information/videos/marking-50-years-progress).
2 "Marking 50 years of progress," USAID website (www.usaid.gov/news-information/videos/marking-50-years-progress) July 2015.
3 The Sustainable Development Commission (www.sd-commission.org.uk/pages/what-is-sustainable-development.html), accessed May 2016.
4 "Marking 50 years of progress," USAID website.
5 USAID report of top 40 vendors, USAID website, last updated March, 2015 (www.usaid.gov/results-and-data/budget-spending/top-40-vendors).
6 Washington Technology lists Chemonics' 2008 revenue as $340 million. The USAID record shows Chemonics allocation has increased by an additional $150 million, as recorded in 2015. FPDS-NG, USASpending, Houlihan Lokey and Washington Technology, washingtontechnology.com/toplists/top-100-lists/2015/chemonics.aspx.
7 G. Hancock, *Lords of poverty*, New York: Atlantic Monthly Press, 1994.
8 J. Pfeffer and G.R. Salancik, *The external control of organizations: A resource dependence perspective*, Harper & Row, New York, 1978.
9 B. Paul, *Factories in the field: Rural transformation and the organization of work in Mozambique's cashew triangle,* TechnoServe, July 2008 (www.technoserve.org/files/downloads/factoriesinthefield.pdf), accessed January 2016.
10 P. Collier, *The bottom billion: Why the poorest countries are failing and what can be done about it,* Oxford: Oxford University Press, 2007.
11 W. Easterly, *The white man's burden: Why the West's efforts to aid the rest have done so much ill and so little good*, London: Penguin, 2006.
12 Unicef Report, 2012 (www.unicef.org/ethiopia/apr_progress_report_2012_final).
13 www.brookings.edu/blogs/education-plus-development/posts/2013/05/28-quality-education-sub-saharan-africa-mwabu-ackerman.
14 "Malaria deaths fall over 20% in last decade," BBC, October 2011, http://www.bbc.com/news/health-15346624.
15 Millennium Development Goals, http://www.who.int/mediacentre/news/releases/2012/drinking_water_20120306/en.
16 USPTO understood that Africa had a negative view on IP in the 2000–2010 period, and provided funding demonstrating the wider application of the business method behind the Ethiopian Fine Coffee success would contribute to renewed interest in IP. The USPTO has funded Light Years with $1.25 m to create training materials in Intellectual Property business.
17 OECD website, 2014, http://www.oecd.org/development/aid-to-developing-countries-rebounds-in-2013-to-reach-an-all-time-high.htm.
18 "Development at a glance: Statistics by region, Africa, 2015 edition, OECD website (www.oecd.org/dac/stats/documentupload/2%20Africa%20-%20Development%20Aid%20at%20a%20Glance%202015.pdf).
19 In Boston, for example, the cost of 4th of July fireworks was $2.5 million, average cost for comparable sized cities.

20 USAID Trade Africa website, http://www.usaid.gov/tradeafrica, accessed February 2016.

21 Revised UNDP figures, 2014 (www.gov.uk/government/uploads/system/uploads/atta chment_data/file/403381/SID-2014-revised-UNDP-figure-feb15.pdf), accessed January 2016.

22 DFID website, 2010.

23 J. Greening, Speech at the London Stock Exchange, March 11, 2013, London, UK (www.gov.uk/government/speeches/investing-in-growth-how-dfid-works-in-new-an d-emerging-markets), accessed January 2016.

24 L. Piccio, "DfID's top private sector partners for 2014," April 2015 (www.gov.uk/gov ernment/speeches/investing-in-growth-how-dfid-works-in-new-and-emerging-markets).

25 J. Mulcahy, Coffey's Annual Report, 2015, p. 3. Coffey International Limited website (www.coffey.com/assets/Uploads/Coffey-Annual-Report-2015.pdf).

26 G. Simpson Group, Executive International Development, Coffey Annual Review, 2015, p. 16.

27 Business in Development, Independent Commission on International Aid (ACIA report), London, July 2014 p. 2 (icai.independent.gov.uk/wp-content/uploads/2014/ 07/Business-in-Development-TORs-final.pdf).

28 DFID's Private Sector Development Work, ICAI, May 2014, http://icai.independent. gov.uk/wp-content/uploads/2014/05/ICAI-PSD-report-FINAL.pdf. 2 Private Sector Development Strategy: Prosperity for all: making markets work, DFID, 2008, http:// www.enterprise.

29 J. Greening, "UK boosts support for businesses to create jobs in the world's poorest places," London, July 2015, www.gov.uk/government/news/uk-boosts-support-for-businesses-to-create-jobs-in-the-worlds-poorest-places, accessed April 2016.

30 J. Greening, "Investing in growth: How DFID works in new and emerging markets," September 2013. London. Justine Greening's speech at the London Stock exchange.

31 Ibid.

32 Over 2005–2011, DFID funded 14 scoping studies, 11 feasibility studies, 20,000 copies of a Light Years IP publication "Distinctive Values in African Exports," with work-shops across East Africa, West Africa, and Southern Africa.

33 B. Drayton, Pictet Perspectives, Washington, DC, April 2012.

34 Cleveland and Gotliffe, Certified Public Accountants, Ashoka Annual Report, August 31, 2013 and April,2014.

35 David Bornstein, *How to change the world: Social entrepreneurs and the power of new ideas*, Oxford, New York, 2007.

CONCLUSION

Positioning as a development strategy

Most twenty-first-century producing businesses achieve a gross income of 30–40 percent of retail value by using excellent positioning strategies. There is variance across product and sector lines, with some achieving higher percentages and some lower. Examples are abundant, from Champagne (50% of retail) to Burberry and Louis Vuitton luxury lines, to Coca-Cola and automobiles. It is no accident that luxury lines are positioned on high streets. While there is some variance in the income achieved from 30–40 percent averages, there is one common factor: These businesses own retail brands and control their product at all points in the entire supply chain.

By contrast, African and LDC export sectors are very badly positioned, earning an average 3 percent of the retail value of their distinctive products. The comparison is startling, but more damaging still is that the low percentage (3 percent) is taken for granted. Most strategies designed to assist African and LDC producers continue to assume low returns, even if quality is advanced, or employment numbers improved. This book has presented the argument that it is imperative to change this assumption, mentality, and entrenched way of doing things. Moreover, we have demonstrated a method to dramatically and sustainably improve income. This method is Intellectual Property positioning.

Why IP positioning?

Improving the positioning of African and LDC export sectors can generate incomes that are 10 times higher than current incomes. Earning only commodity prices for distinctive products is an injustice that threatens the future of Africa's most valuable exports. At a time in history when distinctive products are valued more highly by consumers than ever before, re-positioning is vital. Applying IP positioning is important and imperative because business best practice has large impact unlike any other strategy.

Growing like a corporation

- African distinctive export producers and sectors can leap forward to more prosperous exporting with self-funding investments in quality and volume. The leap forward will be self-funding if some key positioning is done first to increase the share of retail value.
- African export sectors need higher income now to boost their growth in the future. Reducing the cost of border controls has some value but not much because it is working within the 3 percent of retail value that reaches Africa, not the 97 percent that doesn't. Positioning captures higher shares of the 97 percent of retail value.
- There are many successful examples of correct positioning for African exporting sectors provided in this book, such as Ethiopian Fine Coffee wherein export income increased by $101 million in 2008.
- Divine Chocolate was designed with excellent positioning in 1998 to benefit the Kuapa Kokoo cocoa farmers of Ghana.
- 200 positioning opportunities will lift millions of people out of entrenched poverty. Re-positioning 200 or more African distinctive product export sectors will build revenue-empowerment for future levels of growth.
- It will also transform extremely remote regions, raising the level of producers and the many local suppliers of agricultural input.
- Rural multipliers carry the whole region upwards. We believe it to be one of the ways to draw the last 500 million out of extreme poverty. The WONS business is the clearest example of such regional impacts of positioning strategies with regional impact.

Gender business in South Sudan and northern Uganda

Women's Owned Nilotica Shea (WONS) is a fully developed positioning opportunity for at least 10,000 women, many former child soldiers in South Sudan and northern Uganda, as presented in Chapter 8.

To be correctly positioned, WONS and WONS UK will:

- Own the retail brand which the product will be sold under in consumer markets.
- Own the shea butter when it leaves the Ugandan processing plant.
- Control the product throughout the supply chain.
- Own the professional formula of the cosmetic product.
- Control the further processing of the final retail product by a high quality fulfillment company in Europe.

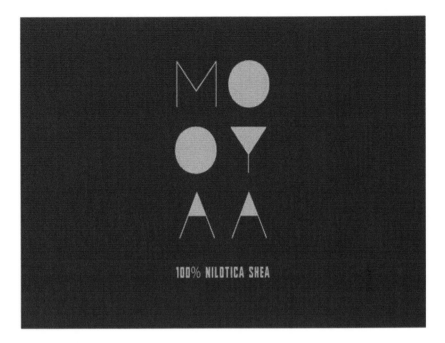

FIGURE 11.1 WONS packaging, second version
Source: Light Years IP.

- Own the distribution company marketing to higher end retail stores and online.
- Create packaging consistent with the higher end market. (The commercial brand for the product is shown in Figure 11.1, combining the Acholi name Moo'Ya, with classy champagne glasses).

WONS is designed as a revenue-powered business that can invest in volume and quality for decades, further building the brand value and income levels of some of the poorest people in the world and have impact on rural development in West Equatoria, one of the most remote parts of Africa, or 1,600 miles of unsealed roads from Mombasa, the nearest export port.

Positioning with vertical integration: Ethiopian fine leather supply chain

The Ethiopian fine leather export sector is a clear example of foreign companies vertically integrating while capturing a high share of retail value. Ethiopian tanneries, however, mostly struggle to meet government demands of more advanced processing. This example illustrates a massively important contrast between such export sectors and the business behavior of their import partners.

FIGURE 11.2 Ethiopian Fine Leather - prices at six steps in the supply chain, with potential for vertical integration
Source: Light Years IP.

Figure 11.2 shows the six roles in the supply chain. As shown in the graphic, there are 40 million Ethiopian herders who receive about $0.50 for half a skin, the amount needed to produce a pair of gloves. The collector sells these skins to tanneries, that produce the finished leather, selling the leather to the factory for about $2.40. The factory makes the leather gloves, sometimes inside Ethiopia and sometimes in foreign countries. The importer/distributor pays the factory about $10.00/pair that then sell at retail for $150.00.[1]

Pittards, a UK company, purchased one Ethiopian tannery in 2008. Pittards applied vertical integration – buying the tannery and setting up a factory in Ethiopia, effectively vertically integrating four steps of the supply chain. The Ethiopian stakeholders can also vertically integrate. Clearly, the foreign supply chain captures greater margins than the Ethiopian part of the supply chain. Owning an importer/distributor can increase income to Ethiopia by 10 times or more.

In just two examples, Ugandan and South Sudanese shea butter, and Ethiopian fine leather, the positioning method improves income dramatically, positively affecting 40 million herders in Ethiopia and over 10,000 women in northern Uganda.

A campaign to raise awareness of positioning

In this book, we have argued that it is time for IP Positioning to be enabled on a more systematic basis. The distinctive products are present; the farmers, producers, herders, and artisans are ready and deserving of higher than 3 percent returns for their hard work; and the method is tried and proven.

Business schools teach:

1. The final retail product must be positioned well in the retail market. Ethiopian fine coffee was indeed well positioned in the retail market, but WONS shea products are not.
2. The producing business gains most by owning the retail brand on the final retail product.
3. The business gains by controlling exclusive wholesale supply of the branded product to retail stores in foreign markets.
4. Exclusivity at the import/wholesale level creates the ability to control the entire supply chain.
5. The process can then be managed to capture a growing share of retail value up to the share of retail value achieved by the most sophisticated competitor.

Investment in Positioning and Growing the Pie

Existing supply chains take 97% of the value flowing into retail stores in developed countries for the sale of African distinctive products. The retailer bears the high fixed costs of renting a store in London and paying London wages, but the importing/distribution company is frequently a highly profitable business with modest costs. Operating such a business in the 21st century is to invite investors with disruptive business models to move into your sector – Uber and Airbnb are two examples of this process.

In 2016, Position Limited, a social impact company, invited impact investors to help poor producers disrupt the supply chains for African distinctive export products. Investors with social impact principles do not seek to own the IP of poor people, but to undertake an investment that yields transformational increases in income to the producers and a return of around 8% per annum to the investors.

Consider the "gate" that only allowed an annual $100 million to flow to the Ethiopian Fine Coffee sector out of total retail flow of about $2,000 million paid by fine coffee consumers annually to retail stores for the three most famous Ethiopian Fine Coffees. It took only $2m to use brand-owners power to open the gate enough that an extra $101 million flowed to Ethiopia in financial year 2008. Changing negotiating power costs something but not proportionate to the benefits. It is clear that the opportunities for re-positioning can and will be financed.

Growing the total retail sales enhances the benefits to all, especially licensed distributors. Ethiopia, with assistance from a number of partners, including diaspora and Light Years IP, launched a major promotion at the 2009 Specialty Coffee Association of America annual conference in Minneapolis, U.S.A. The license agreement with distributors was designed to coordinate such promotions.

How is positioning different

Positioning is different from Making Markets Work. This strategy continues to focus on the 3 percent of retail price that does reach Africa, and not the 97 percent that does not. Making Markets Work strategies should continue for less distinctive products.

Positioning is also different from private sector development driven by corporations that are importers or brand owners seeking to put African products under their brands. It is important to note that major companies have standard formulas to test whether to handle a particular product. If the profit margin does not reach that formulaic standard, the company will move out of the product.

However, donors achieve more through collaboration among aid providers, which allows the social mission to be pursued.

One of the authors worked for a period in Niue, a small Pacific island state extremely isolated in trade terms. He was also hired to examine the production and trading constraints facing people living on atolls in the Pacific and Indian Oceans – economies facing extreme remoteness and unreliable transport, similar to remote parts of Africa. These states and islands face the hard reality that intangible value capture through IP is more viable than physical product exporting.

However, Niue has earned export income from philatelic (collectors') postage stamp licensing for decades and other forms of IP, including Internet suffixes, support many small island states. The broad conclusion that intangibles and IP can contribute to overcoming remoteness led to IP business positioning theory and practice. From the sole application of IP as a strategy to overcome isolation and trade challenges, to the IP found resident in over 250 African distinctive products, has been a 40-year journey. The research and more importantly, the methodology have been refined. Hundreds of thousands of miles across continents; in the field; in desk analyses; market research; and integrating the business best practices have resulted in the theory and IP business positioning method presented here. The IP positioning method is now understood. It is not mysterious. The success stories can be replicated at scale and lead to transforming livelihoods for tens of millions.

Note

1 R. Layton, M. Garad, et al., "Ethiopian Fine Leather Feasibility study," DFID, 2009.

INDEX